Chemistry
of the
Environment

DAVID E. NEWTON

Facts On File
An imprint of Infobase Publishing

One Last Time . . .
for John McArdle, Lee Nolet, Richard Olson,
David Parr, David Rowand, Jeff Williams, and John D'Emilio
Thanks for the memories!

Chemistry of the Environment

Facts On File, Inc.
An imprint of Infobase Publishing
132 West 31st Street
New York NY 10001

ISBN-10: 0-8160-5273-5
ISBN-13: 978-0-8160-5273-8

Library of Congress Cataloging-in-Publication Data
Newton, David E.
    Chemistry of the environment / David E. Newton.
        p. cm.—(The new chemistry)
    Includes bibliographical references and index.
    ISBN 0-8160-5273-5 (acid-free paper)
    1. Environmental chemistry. I. Title.
    TD193.N49 2007
    628.5—dc22   2006029995

Facts On File books are available at special discounts when purchased in bulk quantities for businesses, associations, institutions, or sales promotions. Please call our Special Sales Department in New York at (212) 967-8800 or (800) 322-8755.

You can find Facts On File on the World Wide Web at
http://www.factsonfile.com

Text design by James Scotto-Lavino
Illustrations by Bob Cronan/Lucidity Information Design, LLC
Project editing by Dorothy Cummings

Printed in the United States of America

MP CGI 10 9 8 7 6 5 4 3 2 1

This book is printed on acid-free paper.

CONTENTS

Preface   vii

Introduction   ix

1   THE ROAD TO EARTH DAY   **1**

Pollution Issues in Human History   2

The Birth of Pollution Laws and Regulations   6

Earth Day 1970   8

Rachel Carson (1907–1964)   *10*

Gaylord Nelson (1916–2005)   *13*

Denis Hayes (1944–   )   *14*

2   CHEMISTRY OF THE AIR: POLLUTANTS   **18**

Carbon Monoxide   18

Oxides of Nitrogen   24

Eugene Houdry (1892–1962)   *30*

Sulfur Dioxide   33

Particulate Matter   38

Volatile Organic Compounds   42

Ozone   46

Lead   48

Air Quality Standards   51

3   CHEMISTRY OF THE ATMOSPHERE:

**   CHANGES IN THE ATMOSPHERE**   **55**

Properties of the Atmosphere   56

Acid Rain   57

Depletion of the Ozone Layer   67
   Thomas Midgley, Jr. (1889–1944)   *70*
Global Climate Change   79
   Veerabhadran Ramanathan (1944–   )   *88*

4   CHEMISTRY OF WATER POLLUTION   **95**
Common Pollutants and Sources   96
   John Cairns, Jr. (1923–   )   *100*
Oxygen-depleting Substances   100
Nutrients   105
Sedimentation and Siltation   108
Pathogens   111
   Ruth Patrick (1907–   )   *112*
Toxic Organic Chemicals   115
Heavy Metals   119
Acidity   124
Heat   126

5   CHEMISTRY OF SOLID WASTE DISPOSAL   **132**
An Overview of Solid Wastes   133
Municipal Solid Wastes   135
Municipal Solid Waste Disposal: Landfills   138
Municipal Solid Waste Disposal: Incineration   144
Reducing Municipal Solid Wastes: Recycling   146
   Vance Packard (1914–1996)   *150*
Industrial Wastes   155
   Robert Bullard (1946–   )   *156*
Nuclear Wastes   166

6   GREEN CHEMISTRY   **174**
The Problem: Releasing Hazardous Chemicals
  into the Environment   175
A Solution: Green Chemistry   178
The Structure of Green Chemistry in the United States   180
   Joe Breen (1942–1999)   *182*
   Paul Anastas (1962–   )   *185*

Atom Economy   186
Alternative Raw Materials   191
Catalysis   199
Solvents   203

CONCLUSION   **208**

Glossary   211
Further Reading   218
Index   221

PREFACE

The subject matter covered in introductory chemistry classes at the middle and high school levels tends to be fairly traditional and relatively consistent from school to school. Topics that are typically covered in such classes include atomic theory, chemical periodicity, ionic and covalent compounds, equation writing, stoichiometry, and solutions. While these topics are essential for students planning to continue their studies in chemistry or the other sciences and teachers are correct in emphasizing their importance, they usually provide only a limited introduction to the rich and exciting character of research currently being conducted in the field of chemistry. Many students not planning to continue their studies in chemistry or the other sciences may benefit from information about areas of chemistry with immediate impact on their daily lives or of general intellectual interest. Indeed, science majors themselves may also benefit from the study of such subjects.

The New Chemistry is a set of six books intended to provide an overview of some areas of research not typically included in the beginning middle or high school curriculum in chemistry. The six books in the set—*Chemistry of Drugs, Chemistry of New Materials, Forensic Chemistry, Chemistry of the Environment, Food Chemistry,* and *Chemistry of Space*—are designed to provide a broad, general introduction to some fields of chemistry that are less commonly mentioned in standard introductory chemistry courses. They cover topics ranging from the most fundamental fields of chemistry, such as the origins of matter and of the universe, to those with important applications to everyday life, such as the composition of foods and drugs. The set title The New Chemistry has been selected to emphasize the extensive review of recent research and advances in each of the fields of chemistry covered in the set. The books in The New Chemistry set are written for middle school and high school readers. They assume some basic understanding of the principles of chemistry that are generally gained in an introductory middle or high school course in the subject. Every book contains a large amount of material that should be accessible to the interested reader with no more than an introductory understanding of chemistry and a smaller amount of material that may require a more advanced understanding of the subject.

The six books that make up the set are independent of each other. That is, readers may approach all of the books in any sequence whatsoever. To assist the reader in extending his or her understanding of each subject, each book in the set includes a glossary and a list of additional reading sources from both print and Internet sources. Short bibliographic sketches of important figures from each of the six fields are also included in the books.

INTRODUCTION

◆

Chemistry of the Environment focuses on the role of chemistry in environmental issues, including air and water pollution, solid wastes, and the relatively new field of *green chemistry.* The term *pollution* refers to the release of harmful or objectionable substances into the environment, most commonly as the result of human activities. Some of the most obvious examples of pollution are smoke produced by industrial operations, carbon dioxide and other gases released into the atmosphere as a by-product of burning fuels, silt and sediment washed off land by rainwater, and garbage dumped on land.

People have had to deal with issues of pollution for thousands of years, probably from the first time that a cave dweller's home filled with smoke from a campfire. But for most of human history, pollution was simply accepted as an ongoing problem that individuals and society simply had to live with. Residents of large urban areas may not have liked having raw sewage flow down the streets in front of their homes, but there was little they could do about it. And, for the most part, rulers and governments cared little about such problems or did not know how to solve them.

Pollution issues became significantly more important, however, with the Industrial Revolution the early 18th century. At that time, the by-products of industrial operations were released into the surrounding environment, with little or no attempt to determine or control their effect on plants, animals, and human life. One can hardly think of Great Britain at the height of its imperial powers without remembering the huge clouds of smoke and fumes that continuously hung over the nation's urban areas. Problems of air and water pollution that had existed for centuries were now multiplied many times over as industrial progress brought wealth and/or employment to many and a foul environment to nearly everyone.

It was only in the second half of the 20th century that scientists, governments, and the general public began to focus on the effects of industrial by-products on the health of living organisms and to pass laws controlling many forms of pollution. An important factor in the new awareness of environmental problems was the contribution of chemical science to an understanding of the causes of pollution, the properties of pollutants, and the methods available for controlling pollution. Probably for the first time in human history, there was a confluence of the will to solve pollution problems and the technical knowledge needed to achieve that objective. A primary objective of this book is to summarize the information that chemists have developed that allows modern societies to understand and deal with pollution problems.

Chemistry of the Environment begins with a historical review of pollution in human societies, describing the kinds of pollution problems with which people have had to deal and the way in which progress and pollution are inextricably interwoven. It then discusses the growth of the modern environmental movement, a movement characterized not only by an appreciation of the pollution problems facing modern society, but also by an understanding of the ways in which science in general and chemistry in particular can be used to solve those problems.

Many historians trace the birth of this movement to April 22, 1970, the first Earth Day celebrated in the United States. In this event, large groups of people made it clear that they would no longer sit quietly by and watch the destruction of their natural environment. They demanded that their governments take more purposeful actions to understand the nature of environmental destruction and to limit or prevent such destruction of land, water, and air resources.

The progress made on environmental issues over the past 35 years is truly remarkable. Problems that most societies once simply had to live with are now thoroughly studied, well understood, and often capable of resolution. A good deal of this progress can be explained by the rise of a new specialty within the area of chemistry: environmental chemistry. An environmental chemist studies substances the are responsible for pollution of air, land, and water; the sources of those substances; the changes they undergo in nature; the effects they have on human health and the environment; and methods for alleviating those effects.

Chemistry of the Environment attempts to provide a general introduction to the chemical nature of air, water, and solid waste pollution; the biological, chemical, and physical effects of pollutants; and the methods available for the control of each type of pollution. In addition to purely scientific information, the book presents some historical background and a brief introduction to some social, political, economic, legal, and other issues related to environmental issues. Developments in any field of science, including environmental chemistry, do not occur in a historical, social, or political vacuum. They typically have a historical context and often arise in response to social problems. And in most cases progress in the field of chemistry (and other sciences), in turn, creates new challenges and questions for society as a whole. This book recognizes that reality by placing advances in environmental chemistry in a broader social context, wherever that approach is necessary or useful.

The field of environmental chemistry has now become so extensive that little more than a basic introduction can be provided to this fascinating discipline. For those wishing to pursue the subject in greater detail, a number of useful references are provided in the Further Reading section at the end of the book.

1

THE ROAD TO EARTH DAY

"The river is on fire!"

This most unlikely of alarms was sounded as residents of Cleveland, Ohio, prepared to sit down to Sunday dinner on June 22, 1969. Over a 20-minute period, the fire raged across the top of Cleveland's major waterway, the Cuyahoga River, just southeast of the city's downtown area. Although it was extinguished rapidly by a combination of three land-based fire battalions and the city's *Anthony J. Celebrezze* fireboat, the fire badly damaged the Norfolk & Western Railway bridge and caused lesser harm to the Newburgh & South Shore Railroad bridge. The total damage of about $50,000 was not as serious as was the public image produced by photographs of a major urban river on fire in the next day's newspapers. The fire was later blamed on extensive amounts of volatile petroleum wastes that polluted the river.

Strangely enough, the 1969 fire was not the first to have struck the Cuyahoga. Previous such events had occurred as far back as 1936, when one fire caused more than $1 million in damage to bridges and riverside facilities. The difference in 1969 was that governmental officials and ordinary citizens had become more aware of environmental problems that had become part of their everyday lives. Indeed, the city of Cleveland was already in the midst of a $100 million effort to clean up the river and its water treatment facilities when the Cuyahoga fire broke out.

As the rest of this chapter shows, the Cuyahoga fire of 1969 was, in some ways, an old story. Although a burning river was unusual, people throughout the ages had become familiar with skies filled with smoke, rivers running with carcasses of dead animals, gutters overflowing with human waste, and many other forms of pollution. The difference was that Americans in the 1960s were no longer willing to accept these conditions as something about which nothing could be done. They had begun to demand action to protect their health and the natural environment against the kinds of air, water, and land pollution with which their ancestors had lived for centuries. How did the world get from a point where pollution was an acceptable fact of everyday life to one that demanded action by government and individuals?

Pollution Issues in Human History

Pollution problems are hardly a new phenomenon, unique to the current century. Indeed, the history of every human culture appears to contain stories of the cavalier way we have treated our waste products. Until quite recently, people simply dumped wastes into the nearest river or lake, open pits, or the surrounding air, without thinking about the possible effects of those products on plants, animals, or their own lives.

When there were few people on large expanses of land, such practices did little harm. The solid, liquid, and gaseous wastes of the residents of a small village in rural medieval France, for example, were unlikely to cause serious, long-term problems for the surrounding environment. A common folk saying in rural America even as late as the mid-20th century was that "running water purifies itself every 10 feet" (or "every 100 yards," or "every mile," or the like). But as urban areas grew and people lived more closely together, the cumulative effects of such practices became more serious. One could no longer depend on running water or any other part of nature's being able to purify itself.

One of the earliest records of complaints about pollution—air pollution specifically—dates to about 900 B.C.E., when the Egyptian pharaoh Tukulti wrote about his visit to Babylon. He described the terrible smells emanating from an asphalt mine near the town of Hit, saying the pollution that covered the area was like "the voice of the gods" issuing from the earth. The gases Tukulti was complaining about were primarily hydrogen sulfide and sulfur dioxide, with the characteristic odor of rotten eggs and burning matches, released during the extraction of asphalt from the ground.

Notwithstanding Tukulti's experience, the primary cause of air pollution for most of history has been wood or coal fires, especially in crowded urban communities. The streets of Rome, for example, were notorious for their terrible, smoky character, caused by thousands of wood and coal fires. In 61 C.E. the Roman philosopher Seneca described how this foul air affected his mood: "As soon as I had gotten out of the heavy air of Rome and from the stink of the smokey chimneys thereof," he once wrote, ". . . I felt an alteration of my disposition."

Many surviving reports of later air pollution episodes are from Great Britain. In 1157, for example, King Henry II's wife, Eleanor, demanded permission to move out of Tudbury Castle in Nottingham because air pollution from wood burning in the area had become unendurable. Great Britain also adopted some of the earliest laws attempting to reduce air pollution by limiting or banning the burning of wood and coal. In 1306, for example, King Edward I prohibited the use of coal for fires, declaring, "Whosoever shall be found guilty of burning coal shall suffer the loss of his head." Later kings attempted to enforce this ban in somewhat more humane ways, usually by instituting a tax on any home or facility that chose to burn coal.

Throughout the next six centuries, English writers continued to describe the murky, oppressive air that hovered over London and other large British cities. By the 17th century, scientists, physicians, and other concerned citizens were studying the causes and effects of air pollution and recommending steps to improve conditions. In 1661, for example, a minor government official named John Evelyn (1620–1706) wrote a tract about the foul air of London, entitled *Fumifugium,* which he directed to the attention of King Charles II. Evelyn explained that the purpose of his tract was to show "how this pernicious Nuisance [air pollution] may be reformed; and [to] offer at another also, by which the Aer may not only be freed from the present Inconveniency; but (that remov'd) to render not only Your Majesties Palace, but the whole City likewise, one of the sweetest, and most delicious Habitations in the World." Evelyn went on to recommend the use of coke, rather than coal, for heating; the creation of a protected greenbelt area around the city and the banishment of all industrial operations to areas outside the greenbelt; and the construction of taller chimneys to carry smoke higher into the air.

Other developed nations wrestled with the same problems, but there is little evidence to show that any of the proclamations, laws, or recommendations (such as those of Evelyn) had any long-term effect on the chronic air pollution problems experienced by London and other large cities. Instead, air pollution became even more severe than in previous centuries, largely as a consequence of the Industrial Revolution, a period of rapid industrial growth beginning in the late 18th century.

The Industrial Revolution was a huge transformation in the system of production, a change from one based on human labor located in individual homes and farms to one based on mass production that took place in large factories. The operation of these factories was based on the combustion of fossil fuels, primarily coal. Industrial methods of production generated very large amounts of waste, but methods of disposal were unchanged: Waste products were still dumped directly into rivers and lakes or released directly into the atmosphere. As a result, by the early 19th century people living in urban and industrialized areas were accustomed to breathing heavily polluted air and drinking highly contaminated water.

People did notice the problem, and a few recognized the dangers posed by pollution. For example, the English lawyer Edwin Chadwick (1800–90) published a report in 1842 entitled "Sanitary Conditions of the Labouring Population of Great Britain," asking for legislation providing more sanitary living conditions for England's working classes. It included the observation that

> various forms of epidemic, endemic, and other disease caused, or
> aggravated, or propagated chiefly amongst the labouring classes
> by atmospheric impurities produced by decomposing animal and
> vegetable substances, by damp and filth, and close and overcrowd-

ed dwellings prevail amongst the population in every part of the kingdom, whether dwelling in separate houses, in rural villages, in small towns, in the larger towns—as they have been found to prevail in the lowest districts of the metropolis.

Chadwick's report contained 17 conclusions about environmental conditions in Great Britain with 15 recommendations for ways of improving these conditions.

Action, however, was a long time coming. The British government, for example, created a number of special committees to deal with problems of air and water pollution, the first in 1819, but no legislation resulted until 1848. In that year, the first Public Health Act was adopted, establishing a Health Agency, whose responsibility it was to control the release of smoke and ash in English cities. It took another 24 years before the first person specifically responsible for air pollution control, Robert Angus Smith (1817–84), was appointed.

Additionally, not all pollution was equally well understood. Concerns about water pollution were less focused than those about air pollution, essentially because clouds of smoke blowing through a city are difficult to ignore. One can see and smell the offensive effusions of factories without having any special training in the detection of pollutants. But recognizing water pollution can be more difficult. A bottle of water that looks safe to drink may very well harbor disease-causing microorganisms that have no color, taste, or odor. Besides, until the germ theory of disease was first enunciated in the 1860s, no one really understood the mechanism by which polluted water can be responsible for the spread of diseases such as cholera, plague, typhus, and typhoid. In fact, it was not until the middle of the 20th century that scientists knew very much about the chemistry of water pollution, including what pollutants might be present in water; how they get there; what effects they have on humans, other animals, and the environment; and how they can be controlled.

Some progress was made, however, in understanding the biological pollutants present in water. In fact, by the mid-19th century the connection between polluted water and disease was becoming clearer. One breakthrough occurred in 1853, a classic example of epidemiology, the study of the outbreak and spread of disease. In that year, a terrible cholera epidemic swept through London, with its worst effects focused on and around Broad Street. A physician by the name of John Snow (1813–58) determined that most of the cholera victims used a public well located on the street. He hypothesized that the pump was delivering contaminated water that transmitted cholera to everyone who used it. Snow announced his solution to the problem in a now-famous warning: "Remove the pump handle." Although government officials were dubious about the effects of such a simple action, they did so—and the epidemic quickly came to an end. Later studies showed that the water from this pump had been contaminated by sewage from a tenement in which the first cholera victim had lived.

Despite being recognized since at least the 10th century B.C.E., the problem of pollution was still largely unsolved as of the mid-19th century C.E.

The Birth of Pollution Laws and Regulations

At first glance, it might be difficult to understand how such terrible environmental conditions could persist for hundreds of years in sup-posedly advanced societies. Great Britain during the 19th century was a sophisticated, prosperous nation, the largest and most pow-erful empire of its time. And yet, the vast majority of its citizens were daily exposed to toxic levels of air and water pollution that Americans in the 21st century can barely imagine. Why did people tolerate such conditions?

Fundamentally this level of environmental degradation was ac-cepted as a sign of success. Severe pollution was an indication of a prosperous economy. The more successful industrial operations were, the higher the standard of living for at least some of the nation's population—certainly the upper class, who owned the factories, and often the new and growing middle class. If successful factories also released excessive amounts of *hazardous waste* products into rivers and lakes and the air, that was perhaps unfortunate, especially for members of the working class, but it seemed to be an unpreventable by-product of a nation's overall economic success.

By this logic, it is hardly surprising that successful pollution-control legislation was largely unknown in most developed nations until well into the 20th century. The British government, for example, adopted amendments to the Public Health Act of 1848 in 1875 and 1891, but no new legislation of consequence was introduced again until the 1926 Public Health (Smoke Abatement) Act.

Even such laws failed to control pollution, as was demonstrated repeatedly, not only in Great Britain, but also in other European nations and the United States. The most dramatic signs of failure were catastrophic events of air pollution in which hundreds or thousands of people lost their lives. Many of these events occurred in London, where industrial pollution and unfavorable weather conditions combined to form a smothering cloud of polluted air known as *smog* (*smoke* + *fog*). In February 1880, for example, the city was blanketed with an unusually heavy layer of smog, resulting in the death of more than 1,000 individuals. Similar cases of smog epidemics later occurred in Meuse, Belgium, in December 1930 (63 deaths); Donora, Pennsylvania in October 1948 (20 deaths); Poca Rica, Mexico, in November 1950 (22 deaths); and London in December 1952, causing 4,000 deaths, perhaps the worst such event in modern history. Events such as these convinced government officials to consider even stronger laws and regulations to control the release of pollutants into rivers, lakes, and the air.

In the United States, the first environmental legislation of almost any kind was the Rivers and Harbors Act of 1899 (also known as the Refuse Act of 1899). This act was designed to deal with problems of navigation, disease, and oil discharges in navigable waters. Portions of the act were later superseded by newer water pollution control legislation. But sections dealing with the construction of dams, bridges, dikes, causeways, wharfs, piers, and other structures were so broadly drafted that they are still being used today to deal with certain kinds of modern water issues.

The next significant piece of U.S. water pollution legislation was not passed until 1948 with the adoption of the Water Pollution Control Act, also known as the Clean Water Act. This legislation provided funding for states to construct water treatment plants, identify polluted bodies of water, and locate individuals and corporations responsible for pollution. But it did not deal with pollution problems or prevention on a national scale and did not propose the development of water quality standards, as later legislation did. Responsibility for carrying out provisions of the 1948 act was given, strangely enough, to the Surgeon General's Office, with assistance from the Water Pollution Control Advisory Board. The act was largely ineffective in resolving the water pollution problems faced by the nation.

The first national legislation dealing with polluted air was not adopted until nearly a decade later. In 1955, the U.S. Congress passed the Air Pollution Control Act, which provided $5 million annually to support research on air pollution by the Public Health Service. As had its counterpart, the Clean Water Act, the Air Pollution Control Act had no discernable effect on the nation's air pollution problems. It did, however, inspire some government officials to think more seriously about the threats posed by air pollution to public health, agriculture, livestock, and physical property. In addition, a handful of books about environmental issues that encouraged the American public to think more deeply about problems of air and water pollution appeared. One of the most influential of those books was *Silent Spring,* published in 1962 by Rachel Carson, whose life is described in the accompanying sidebar on page 10.

By the middle of the 20th century, then, the first legislation designed to protect human health and the natural environment had been passed in the United States and other developed nations. Some effort to protect the quality of air, water, and other natural resources was being made.

Earth Day 1970

The 1960s was a decade of quite remarkable change with respect to environmental awareness in the United States. People had become accustomed to hearing about all manner of risks present in the environment as a result of industrial activity. Swimmers and anglers commonly found signs prohibiting the use of lakes and rivers because of high levels of pollution. Newspapers reported on areas discovered to be so badly contaminated with industrial chemical wastes that they were not safe for habitation. In some cases, whole towns were vacated and families forced to move away from such sites. Governmental agencies regularly released notices warning the elderly, the very young, and the ill not to go out of doors because of unusually high levels of pollution. The deterioration of the quality of the nation's land, air, and water resources had become general knowledge among the general public.

Yet, the federal government moved slowly in dealing with these problems. The Water Pollution Control Act was amended in 1961, 1966, and 1970, but people concerned about environmental issues frequently criticized this legislation for doing too little too late. Similar charges were leveled at a series of acts passed during the 1960s dealing with air pollution. The first of these acts was the Clean Air Act of 1963. That act set emission standards for pollutants released by stationary sources, such as power plants and steel mills. The law also provided grants to individual states to assist them in carrying out whatever air quality programs of their own might have been established. The law did not, however, deal with the most important single source of *air pollutants* at the time: emissions from motor vehicles (such as cars and trucks), trains, and airplanes.

Congress attempted to correct that deficiency and other air pollution problems in a series of amendments to the 1963 act passed in 1965, 1966, 1967, and 1969. The 1965 amendments, for example, authorized the secretary of health, education and welfare to establish nationwide standards for automobile exhaust emissions. This legislation and later amendments also authorized the surgeon general to study the effects of air pollutants on human health, expanded local air quality programs, set compliance deadlines for meeting new air quality standards, established air quality control regions (AQCRs), and authorized research on low emission fuels and more fuel-efficient automobiles.

Unfortunately, the original act and its amendments had one serious flaw: They left enforcement of the acts largely to the states and, in some cases, the financial support needed to meet the acts' goals was insufficient. As a result, little improvement in the nation's air quality was seen by the end of the decade.

◁ RACHEL CARSON (1907–1964) ▷

The United States in the 1940s was fascinated by chemicals. In the preceding decades, chemical research had begun to unleash a number of exciting new compounds that promised to alter the way we grew our crops radically and to protect us from disease and infection. One of the most important of these chemicals was dichlorodiphenyltrichloroethane, more commonly known as DDT. During World War II, DDT had shown its potential for killing insects and microorganisms that caused a number of terrible diseases. After the war, manufacturers of the compound pushed for its widespread use by farmers as a way of controlling the pests with which humans compete for agricultural crops. Only a handful of individuals seemed very concerned about the potential risks of using DDT on such a broad scale. Among these individuals was the biologist and writer Rachel Carson.

Born in Springdale, Pennsylvania, on May 27, 1907, Rachel Carson became interested in writing at an early age, and one of her stories, "A Battle in the Clouds," was accepted by *St. Nicholas* magazine when she was only 10. In 1925, Carson entered the Pennsylvania College for Women (now Chatham College), planning to become a professional writer. Her plans changed, however, after her exposure to a first-year biology class. She found that she was fascinated by the subject and decided to combine her two major interests—writing and biology—in a career of science writing. She eventually earned her bachelor's degree in zoology in 1928.

After graduation, Carson spent a summer at the Marine Biology Laboratory at Woods Hole, Massachusetts (now the Woods Hole Oceanographic Institute). She then enrolled at Johns Hopkins University, from which she received her master's degree in 1932, during the Great Depression. She was able to find part-time teaching assignments at the University of Maryland and Johns Hopkins but was just barely able to survive financially. Her problems were made more difficult in 1935 when her father died, leaving her responsible for her mother, who was also in poor health.

At this point in her life, Carson was fortunate enough to find a more lucrative position, as a science writer at the U.S. Bureau of Fisheries. Her job there was to prepare radio scripts and to edit a variety of government publications dealing with fisheries. She was also able to do some freelance writing on the side and, in 1937, published her first major article, "Undersea," in the *Atlantic Monthly* magazine.

The article attracted the attention of an editor at Simon & Schuster, a major book publisher, who encouraged Carson to write a book on the topic of her *Atlantic Monthly* article. Carson did so, and the book, *Under the Sea Wind,* appeared in 1941. Unfortunately, the book was published just as World War II was beginning, and it was never a commercial success. In 1945, Carson wrote to the popular magazine *Reader's Digest* proposing an article about the possible risks posed by DDT. The magazine rejected her idea, but she never completely forgot about the problem.

Carson remained at her job with the Bureau of Fisheries (later renamed the Fish and Wildlife Service), where she eventually became chief editor of the agency. Her experience with *Under the Sea Wind,* however, had convinced her to try her luck with another book on the topic of marine science. That book, *The Sea around Us,* was published in 1951 and achieved much greater success. It was chosen as an alternative selection by the Book of the Month Club and remained on the *New York Times* best-seller list for 86 weeks. The book also won Carson a National Book Award and honorary doctoral degrees from Chatham College and Oberlin College. Perhaps most important, the financial success of *The Sea around Us* allowed Carson to retire from government service and write full-time.

Carson's next book, *The Edge of the Sea* (1955), was also a great critical and financial success. In addition, she devoted her time to a variety of other projects, including a script for the *Omnibus* television series entitled "Something about the Sky."

In 1958, Carson was once more forced to think about DDT. A friend from Massachusetts wrote to tell her of the large number of birds dying on Cape Cod, apparently as the result of DDT sprayings. Carson decided to attack the issue of DDT in a book, which came out in 1962 under the title *Silent Spring.* The title is from a scenario posed by Carson: If the uncontrolled use of DDT were to continue, a season would occur in which birds and other wildlife had been killed off by the poison, leaving behind only a "silent spring." Many people argue that Carson's book was as responsible for the growth of the modern environmental movement as any other single piece of literature. Carson remained active in the environmental movement until her death of heart failure on April 14, 1964, at the age of 56.

Throughout the 1960s, the general public grew increasingly frustrated with the slow pace at which the U.S. Congress and successive presidents were dealing with environmental issues. As the decade drew to a close, the political effects of the public's frustration were just beginning to become obvious. For example, the nation's single most important piece of environmental action, the National Environmental Policy Act of 1970, was signed into law on January 1. Among its many provisions, the act established the Environmental Protection Agency (EPA), now the nation's single most important agency for dealing with environmental policies and practices.

What was in some ways the most influential single event to occur in the nation's recent environmental history took place on April 22, 1970, with the nationwide observance of Earth Day. The idea for Earth Day was first announced in September 1969 by the U.S. senator Gaylord Nelson, profiled in the adjoining sidebar. Nelson was later to write that his primary objective in suggesting Earth Day was to "show the political leadership of the Nation that there was broad and deep support for the environmental movement." He wanted to "shake up the political establishment and force this issue into the national agenda." He called for a program of demonstrations, teach-ins, lectures, discussions, trash cleanups, tree planting, and other expressions of support for action by the government on environmental problems.

Nelson admitted to having doubts about the Earth Day concept. "It was a gamble," he said. But, in the end, it was a successful gamble. A major contributor to the success of Nelson's idea was Denis Hayes, whose life and work are summarized in the sidebar on page 14. On April 22, more than 20 million Americans participated in one Earth Day activity or another, ranging from public speeches to parades to teach-ins to public protest demonstrations. Many of these activities were conducted on the campuses of over 2,000 participating colleges and universities and 10,000 high schools and grade schools. The U.S. Congress even decided to adjourn for the day to allow members to speak at events in their home districts.

Earth Day has continued to be celebrated annually since its 1970 inception. Each year, the event grows larger and more comprehensive. In 2002, for example, Earth Day was celebrated (as usual, on

◁ GAYLORD NELSON (1916–2005) ▷

During his 18-year career in the U.S. Senate, Gaylord Nelson introduced a number of bills dealing with environmental issues. Among these were legislation to ban the use of two potentially dangerous chemicals, DDT and 2,4,5-T (also known as Agent Orange); to mandate fuel efficiency standards in automobiles; to create the St. Croix Wild and Scenic Riverway and the Apostle Islands National Lakeshore (both in Wisconsin); to control strip mining practices; and to preserve the 2,000-mile Appalachian Trail in the eastern United States. He was also sponsor of legislation that led to the Clean Air Act, the Federal Environmental Pesticide Control Act, the Water Quality Act, and the National Lakes Preservation Act. He is undoubtedly best known, however, as the "father" of the first Earth Day in 1970.

Nelson was born in Clear Lake, Wisconsin, on June 4, 1916. After graduating from Clear Lake High School, he attended San Jose State College, from which he received his bachelor of arts degree in 1939. He then enrolled at the University of Wisconsin Law School, from which he received his L.L.B. degree in 1942. He then served four years in the U.S. Army during World War II.

In his first try at political office, Nelson was defeated as a Republican candidate for the Wisconsin legislature in 1946. He then changed his registration to the Democratic Party and was elected to the state senate in 1948, where he served for 10 years before being elected governor in 1958. After serving two terms in that post, he was elected to the U.S. Senate from Wisconsin, a post he held for three terms.

After leaving the Senate in 1981, Nelson became counselor of the Wilderness Society, where he remained for the next 14 years. After retiring from that position in 1995, Nelson remained active in environmental organizations and programs, serving in 1995 as chairman of Earth Day XXV. In that year, Nelson gave 34 speeches in a three-month period to celebrate that occasion. In the same year, he was awarded the Medal of Freedom by President Bill Clinton.

Nelson has also been given two awards from the United Nations, the Environmental Leadership Award in 1982 and the "Only One Earth" award in 1992. His native state has honored him by establishing the Gaylord Nelson State Park in Madison. Nelson has written two books about the environment, *America's Last Chance* (1970) and *Children's Letters to Senator Gaylord Nelson about the Environment* (1971). He died at his home in Kensington, Maryland, on July 3, 2005.

◁ DENIS HAYES (1944–   ) ▷

Credit for the idea of Earth Day 1970 goes to Senator Gaylord Nelson of Wisconsin. But having an important idea of this kind and seeing that it is actually carried out are two different matters. In the case of Earth Day 1970, much of the day-to-day work that made this event possible was coordinated by Denis Hayes.

Denis Hayes was born in Wisconsin Rapids, Wisconsin, on August 29, 1944. He earned his A.B. degree from Stanford University in 1969. At the time that Nelson made his first speech about Earth Day, Hayes was enrolled at Harvard University's Kennedy School of Government. Called upon by Nelson and other Earth Day organizers, however, Hayes left Harvard and became national coordinator of Earth Day. Because of his intimate involvement with the environmental movement, it was another 15 years before Hayes was able to complete his graduate studies. In 1985, he was also awarded his degree in environmental law from Stanford. Between 1983 and 1988, Hayes was adjunct professor of engineering at Stanford.

After having earned his law degree, Hayes practiced law in Silicon Valley. He later held jobs as director of the Illinois State Energy Office and head of the federal Solar Energy Research Institute (now the National Renewable Energy Laboratory) during the administration of President Jimmy Carter. He also served as senior fellow at the Worldwatch Institute and as visiting scholar at the Smithsonian Institution. Hayes is now president of the Bullitt Foundation, an environmental foundation located in Seattle.

Hayes has received a number of honors and awards, including the Charles Greeley Abbot Award of the American Solar Energy Society and the World Bank's Global Environmental Leadership Award. He has been selected by *Time* magazine for one of its "Heroes of the Planet" awards.

April 22) in 184 countries around the world, in cooperation with more than 5,000 national and international environmental groups. Participants took part in a very large variety of activities, many of them associated with other environmental programs, such as the Community Health Assessment Program, the Ecological Footprint

More than three decades after the first Earth Day, people still gather in April to celebrate that event, as shown by this beach cleanup in a regional park in Berkeley, California. (Lawrence Migdale/Photo Researchers, Inc.)

Campaign, the World Summit on Sustainable Development, the Car Free Day, and Global Releaf (a tree-planting program).

Historians tend to agree that Earth Day had a profound effect on the environmental consciousness of public officials and ordinary citizens. The 1970s saw the adoption of a series of environmental programs at both federal and state levels. Two major acts passed during this period were the Clean Air Act of 1970 and the Federal Water Pollution Act of 1972.

The Clean Air Act of 1970 established National Ambient Air Quality Standards (NAAQSs) and set New Source Performance Standards (NSPSs) that regulated the amount of emissions to be permitted from a new source in an area. The act also required individual states to create their own state implementation plans (SIPs), and set stiff fines for violation of clean air regulations and established a clear and specific schedule for compliance with the new legislation. A 1977 amendment to the act dealt primarily with motor vehicle emission standards.

The Federal Water Pollution Control Act of 1972 (later renamed the Clean Water Act) established a permit system for the discharge of pollutants into waterways, which was intended to reduce and eliminate such discharges; fines of $25,000 were established for violators of the act. Second, the act allowed individuals and public interest groups to seek action against polluters if the federal government did not do so. Third, the act authorized the Environmental Protection Agency to establish standards limiting the kind and amount of pollutants discharged from any given facility. Finally, it provided financial, administrative, technical, and other types of support for states and local municipalities that design and introduce new methods of water pollution control.

Congress also adopted a host of other acts dealing with environmental issues during this period. Some of the most important of these were the following:

➤   The Federal Insecticide, Fungicide, and Rodenticide Act of 1972 required the EPA to study the consequences of pesticide use and to require users (such as farmers) to register when purchasing pesticides.

➤   The Endangered Species Act of 1973 authorized the U.S. Fish and Wildlife Service to create and maintain a list of endangered plant and animal species and to take action to protect those species, within certain limits.

➤   The Safe Drinking Water Act of 1974 instructed the EPA to set national standards for drinking water that would protect the general public against both naturally occurring and human-made contaminants that might be found in drinking water.

➤   The Toxic Substances Control Act of 1976 gave the EPA authority to screen and monitor the use of more than 75,000 industrial chemicals produced, used in, or imported into the United States.

➤   The Resource Conservation and Recovery Act of 1977 established programs to regulate the use and disposal of hazardous and nonhazardous wastes.

➤   The Comprehensive Environmental Response, Compensation, and Liability Act of 1980 created a program known as *Superfund,* designed to clean up hazardous waste sites as well as accidents, spills, and other releases of pollutants into the environment.

In sum, the 1970s saw a flurry of legislative action on environmental issues that was to set the framework of the nation's policies for dealing with the pollution of air, water, and land resources. Almost all of this legislation has been modified, but the guiding principles represented by the laws continue to influence the nation's environmental policies today.

The flurry of legislative activity on environmental issues in the 1970s established a solid federal policy and legal basis for protection of the nation's environment. But it accomplished a great deal more than that. It created a social and political environment in which concerns about the purity and safety of the nation's water, air, and other natural resources were to have an important federal and state focus. It would never again be possible for any public official to say with impunity that environmental quality was not a topic of concern to him or her. Today, virtually every elected official and bureaucrat is likely to be on board the "environmental bandwagon" created in the 1960s and 1970s.

2
Chemistry of the Air
Pollutants

Throughout human history, air pollution has been one of the most physically apparent forms of environmental contamination. As mentioned in chapter 1, writers have long commented on the fumes produced by mining, the smoke released by fires used for home heating, and the suffocating smog that results from fuel burning in industrial operations. Differences of opinion exist as to the precise meaning of the term *air pollutant.* Some environmental chemists use the term to describe any material released into the atmosphere, either directly or indirectly, at a level that poses risk to humans, other animals, plants, or the physical environment. Other authorities prefer to omit the latter portion of this definition and define a pollutant as a solid, liquid, or gas that is released into the atmosphere, whether it has the potential to cause harm to the living and nonliving environment or not.

Among the chemicals regarded as air pollutants under the definition are carbon monoxide, oxides of nitrogen, sulfur dioxide, *particulate* matter, *volatile organic compounds* (VOCs), *ozone,* and lead.

Carbon Monoxide

Carbon monoxide is a colorless, almost odorless, tasteless gas with the chemical formula CO. It is produced naturally by a wide variety of processes, perhaps the best known of which is the incomplete combustion of carbonaceous (carbon-containing) fuels (trees, grass, brush, and so on). When such fuels burn in the absence of sufficient oxygen to oxidize all the carbon present in the fuel (which is almost always the case in the real world), some of the carbon is converted to carbon monoxide.

$$C_xH \text{ (from fuel)} + O_2 \rightarrow CO + CO_2 + H_2O$$

Carbon monoxide is also produced by living green plants that are exposed to sunlight, from dead and decaying plant matter, from the soil and wetlands, from rice paddies, and from bacteria, algae, jellyfish, and other organisms that live in the oceans. The gas is also produced indirectly in a complex sequence of reactions that begins when methane in the atmosphere reacts with hydroxyl radicals (chemical structures consisting of a single oxygen atom bonded to a single hydrogen atom with a single unpaired electron and having the chemical formula $OH^{\bullet}$), forming formaldehyde (HCHO) and then carbon monoxide:

$$CH_4 + OH^{\bullet} \rightarrow CH_3{}^{\bullet} \rightarrow CH_3O_2{}^{\bullet} \rightarrow HCHO \rightarrow HCO^{\bullet} \rightarrow CO$$

The total amount of carbon monoxide in the atmosphere has been estimated at about 3.06 million short tons (2.78 million metric tons). Of this, about half (1.438 million metric tons) is produced naturally and about half (1.350 million metric tons) through anthropogenic (human-made) sources. Naturally occurring carbon monoxide is not generally regarded as an environmental problem because it is so widely spread at very low concentrations (about 0.1 ppmv [parts per million by volume]) throughout the atmosphere.

If anthropogenic carbon monoxide were also distributed equally throughout the atmosphere, it would contribute little to any natural health risks posed by the gas. The problem is that the carbon monoxide from anthropogenic sources tends to accumulate at dangerously high concentrations in certain geographic locations, such as urban centers. In such cases, the level of carbon monoxide to which humans and other organisms are exposed may be sufficiently great to pose a significant health hazard.

The most important single source of anthropogenic carbon monoxide in the United States is motor vehicles. Cars and trucks account

Emissions from various types of industrial operations, such as this paper pulp processing mill, are a major source of air pollution throughout the world. (Ken Biggs/ Photo Researchers, Inc.)

for about 60 percent of all the carbon monoxide produced nation-wide, but they produce up to 95 percent of all the carbon monoxide emitted in some urban areas with extensive vehicular traffic. Other types of internal combustion engines, such as those used in boats and construction equipment, account for about 20 percent of all carbon monoxide emissions nationwide. Other sources of the gas are industrial processes (such as metal production and chemical manufacturing), fireplaces and woodstoves, aircraft, and electrical power generating plants. Carbon monoxide concentrations tend to fluctuate throughout the year, with higher concentrations observed in the winter. One reason for this trend is the greater use of fuels for heating. A second reason is the greater likelihood of nighttime inversions, in which warm layers of air above the Earth's surface tend to trap carbon monoxide (and other pollutants) near the ground.

The U.S. Environmental Protection Agency (EPA) has been monitoring the emission of air pollutants and measuring air quality since the 1970s. For a number of reasons, emission and air quality data are not always comparable. For example, stations that measure air quality are usually located in urban settings. Data obtained at those settings (where problems are usually more severe) may differ from nationwide emission data. Also, local weather conditions may affect the data obtained at monitoring stations that are not reflected in nationwide trends in weather conditions.

Carbon monoxide emissions and air quality, however, have both shown an improvement for more than 20 years. The amount of carbon monoxide emitted by all sources in the United States dropped from about 121 million short tons (110 million metric tons) in 1982 to about 99 million short tons (90 million metric tons) in 2001, the last year for which data are available. The improvement in air quality was more dramatic, with a 62 percent decrease in carbon monoxide concentration between 1982 and 2001, from about 8 ppmv in 1982 to about 3 ppmv in 2001.

The health effects of carbon monoxide are among the most thoroughly studied and best understood of any air pollutant. The risks posed by the gas (as for all pollutants) vary on the basis of two factors: the concentration to which one is exposed and the length of time the exposure lasts. That is, the most dangerous conditions are those in which a person is exposed to large concentrations of carbon monoxide for long periods. A lesser risk is involved when the exposure is to lower concentrations of the gas for shorter periods.

The earliest symptoms of exposure to low concentrations of carbon monoxide include headaches, fatigue, nausea, dizziness, confusion, and irritability. Higher concentrations or longer periods of exposure may result in vomiting, loss of consciousness, brain damage, heart irregularity, breathing difficulties, muscle weakness, coma, and even death.

These symptoms are caused by carbon monoxide's chemical properties, specifically its tendency to bond to hemoglobin in the blood. Hemoglobin is a protein found in red blood cells that transports oxygen from the lungs to cells. It contains an iron atom located at the center of the molecule to which oxygen bonds to form the complex known as oxyhemoglobin:

$$Hb \text{ (hemoglobin)} + O_2 \rightarrow HbO_2 \text{ (oxyhemoglobin)}$$

The bond between the iron atom in hemoglobin and oxygen in oxy-hemoglobin is only moderately strong, as it must be if the compound is to release oxygen readily when it reaches a cell.

Carbon monoxide also bonds to hemoglobin to form a compound known as carboxyhemoglobin:

$$Hb + CO \rightarrow HbCO \text{ (carboxyhemoglobin)}$$

The bond between iron and carbon monoxide, however, is at least 300 times stronger than that between iron and oxygen. When carbon monoxide is present in the lungs, therefore, it displaces oxygen from oxyhemoglobin, forming carboxyhemoglobin instead:

$$HbO_2 + CO \rightarrow HbCO + O_2$$

When this happens, cells are deprived of the oxygen they need to function normally, they begin to die, and the symptoms of carbon monoxide poisoning appear.

Under normal conditions, carbon monoxide is bonded to iron in about 1 percent of the hemoglobin molecules present in blood. That concentration is about twice as high among smokers because of the carbon monoxide inhaled in cigarette smoke. The first observable symptoms of carbon monoxide poisoning begin to appear when the concentration of carbon monoxide reaches about 100 ppm, at which point carbon monoxide has bonded to iron in about 15 percent of the hemoglobin molecules present in blood. Clearly there is a strong health incentive against adding carbon monoxide to the air where people live.

The control of carbon monoxide emissions is based on the principle that less of the gas is produced when the efficiency of combustion is improved. One device to achieve this objective is the catalytic converter, now required on all motor vehicles sold in the United States. A catalytic converter provides a second stage of combustion in motor vehicles, allowing carbon monoxide and other unburned components of a fuel to be oxidized before release into the atmosphere. (The operation of a catalytic converter is described later in this chapter.)

Another way of reducing the amount of carbon monoxide released during combustion is to add something to the fuel that will increase the amount of oxygen available to support combustion and, there-fore, to increase the efficiency of combustion. Fuels that contain such additives are known as *oxygenated gasoline.* Oxygenated gaso-line is one form of *reformulated gasoline,* a term that applies to any type of gasoline that has been specifically designed to burn more efficiently and produce less carbon monoxide and other pollutants.

The additives used in oxygenated gasoline are alcohols and ethers, the most common of which are ethanol (ethyl alcohol; grain alcohol) and methyl *t*-butyl ether (MTBE). Two less commonly used additives are ethyl *t*-butyl ether (ETBE) and *t*-amyl methyl ether (TAME). The chemical structures of these four additives are shown in the dia-gram on page 24.

In their effort to reduce carbon monoxide emissions, regula-tors embraced the use of oxygenated gasoline. The Clean Air Act Amendments of 1990 required petroleum companies to sell only oxygenated gasoline at times of the year when carbon monoxide emissions were greatest and in regions of the nation where pollu-tion problems were most severe. That program went into effect in 1995 and was revised in 2000 to include a larger number of affected regions.

By that time, however, some observers were raising a number of questions about the safety of using oxygenated gasoline. Most of those questions centered on the use of MTBE, which, by 2001, had become one of the top 10 chemicals produced in the United States and was used in 85 percent of all oxygenated gasoline sold in the country. Evidence indicated that the additive had begun to leak from storage tanks into the ground, where it entered the water table. Since the EPA has MTBE listed as a potential human carcino-gen, environmentalists were concerned about the long-term health risks posed by continued use of the additive. Some states revised regulations controlling the sale of oxygenated gasoline that contains MTBE, and the petroleum industry began to look for alternatives to its use in reformulated gasoline.

One possible solution is to increase the use of ethanol as an oxygen additive to gasoline. Some experts had long recommended a gasoline-alcohol mixture known as *gasohol* as an inexpensive, efficient fuel for use in motor vehicles that would reduce the emission of carbon

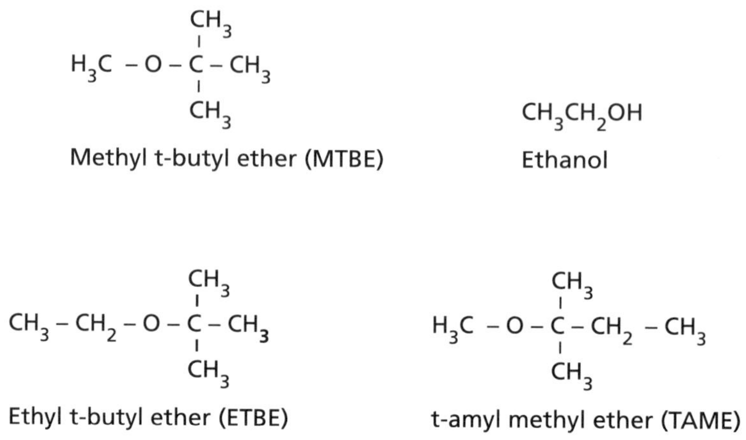

$$CH_3$$
$$H_3C - O - C - CH_3$$
$$CH_3$$

Methyl t-butyl ether (MTBE)

$$CH_3CH_2OH$$

Ethanol

$$CH_3$$
$$CH_3 - CH_2 - O - C - CH_3$$
$$CH_3$$

Ethyl t-butyl ether (ETBE)

$$CH_3$$
$$H_3C - O - C - CH_2 - CH_3$$
$$CH_3$$

t-amyl methyl ether (TAME)

© Infobase Publishing

Structures of four gasoline additives.

monoxide and other pollutants. The problem is that gasohol is relatively expensive to produce, releases other harmful pollutants, and may damage some parts of an internal combustion engine. The product is, therefore, little used in the United States, although in other nations (notably Brazil) gasohol has become a very popular fuel for motor vehicles.

Oxides of Nitrogen

Nitrogen reacts with oxygen to form five oxides, as shown in the table on the adjoining page. The two most important with regard to air pollution are NO and NO_2, which are sometimes referred to together as NO_x. In some circumstances, the formula may also include other oxides of nitrogen.

Nitrogen and oxygen coexist in the atmosphere without reacting to any significant extent. At room temperature, for example, air normally consists of no more than about 0.000,000,000, 1 (1×10^{-10}) ppm of NO, formed in the following reaction:

$$N_2 + O_2 \rightarrow 2NO$$

The reaction rate for this reaction accelerates rapidly, however, with increases in temperature. For example, at about 1,000°C, the concentration of NO reaches about 100 ppm and at about 1,500°C, it reaches nearly 1,000 ppm.

The most common source of nitrogen oxides, therefore, is high-temperature combustion processes, such as those that take place in automobiles and trucks, in electrical power generating plants, and in industrial processes. Residential sources, such as gas stoves and home heaters, are also responsible for the release of significant amounts of NO_x into the atmosphere. At the end of the 20th century, the EPA reported that motor vehicles were responsible for 49 percent of all NO_x released into the atmosphere in the United States;

◀ OXIDES OF NITROGEN ▷

FORMULA	NAME(S)
N_2O	dinitrogen oxide; nitrous oxide; "laughing gas"
NO	nitric oxide
N_2O_3	dinitrogen trioxide
NO_2	nitrogen dioxide; also occurs as N_2O_4, dinitrogen tetroxide
N_2O_5	dinitrogen pentoxide

utilities accounted for another 27 percent; industrial, commercial, and residential sources produced an additional 29 percent; and all other sources made up the remaining 5 percent.

Between 1982 and 2001, emissions of nitrogen oxides increased by about 9 percent, from roughly 22 million short tons annually to about 24 million short tons. The major reason for this increase was an increase in emissions from nonroad and diesel engines. During the same period, however, monitored levels of NO_x actually decreased, from a national average of about 0.025 ppm in 1982 to about 0.020 ppm in 2001. Again the difference in trends for emissions and monitored levels of nitrogen oxides reflects efforts to reduce the concentration of these gases in areas where pollution is most severe.

The primary health effect of nitric oxide results from its tendency to react with hemoglobin in red blood cells, in much the same way as carbon monoxide does. The concentration of nitric oxide is normally so low, however, that this effect is relatively minor, especially compared with the effects of carbon monoxide exposure.

By contrast, nitrogen dioxide is a highly toxic gas with potentially serious effects on the human respiratory system, depending on the degree of exposure. Exposures to low concentrations of the gas for short periods (less than three hours) typically produces relatively modest effects, including changes in airway responsiveness and lung function in individuals who have a history of respiratory disorder. Children under the age of 12 are more likely to experience respiratory disorders under such conditions. At higher concentrations, the effects are often more serious. Exposures to concentrations of 50–100 ppm for periods of six to eight weeks may cause inflammation of lung tissue. Exposure to greater concentrations (150–200 ppm) for shorter periods may result in a disease known as bronchiolitis fibrosa obliterans, which can be fatal within three to five weeks.

The concentration of nitrogen oxides found in the air is almost always much less than these levels, and the health effects described here rarely occur except in accidents or spills in which nitrogen dioxide is released to the air. Instead, the most serious health consequences related to NO_x exposure occur indirectly, when nitrogen dioxide reacts with other air pollutants to form *photochemical smog* and acid rain. (Smog is discussed later in this chapter; acid rain is described in chapter 3.)

Methods for controlling the release of nitrogen oxides to the atmosphere fall into three major categories: precombustion, combustion, and postcombustion systems. The goal of precombustion systems is to remove nitrogen from a fuel so that, once it is burned, it releases lower concentrations of nitrogen oxides to the atmosphere. One method for achieving this objective is *hydrodenitrogenation,* a process in which hydrogen gas is mixed with a liquid fuel and then heated gently over a *catalyst,* such as nickel-molybdenum or nickel-vanadium. (A catalyst is a substance that changes the rate of a reaction without undergoing permanent change itself.) These conditions encourage nitrogen compounds in the fuel to react with hydrogen to form ammonia, which can be removed and reused:

$$N_2 + 3H_2 \rightarrow 2NH_3$$

The fuel that remains contains less nitrogen and burns "more cleanly," that is, with the release of fewer nitrogen oxides.

Combustion systems aim to reduce the release of nitrogen oxides by lowering the combustion temperature. Because the rate at which nitrogen and oxygen react is very temperature sensitive, reducing the combustion temperature can also reduce the rate at which nitrogen oxides are produced.

The problem with this approach is that reducing combustion temperature also reduces the efficiency of fuel combustion. Therefore, the more effective the process for reducing nitrogen oxide emissions, the less efficient the combustion of fuel in a furnace or an automotive engine. The challenge to chemical engineers is to find some mechanism that achieves a reasonable compromise between these two goals, maintaining the efficiency of fuel combustion while reducing the emission of nitrogen oxides.

A number of systems have been devised to meet these two competing objectives. In one approach, water is mixed with oil before it is sprayed into a combustion chamber. The presence of water reduces combustion temperatures enough to reduce nitrogen oxide emissions by up to 15 percent without significantly reducing combustion efficiency. Another approach is to reduce combustion temperatures by using cool air in the combustion chamber, adding cool inert gases to the chamber, or recycling cool exhaust gases through the chamber.

One of the most effective methods for controlling NO_x production in combustion chambers is called *low-excess-air firing.* As the name suggests, this approach makes use of just enough air to allow combustion of the fuel, reducing to a bare minimum the amount of oxygen available for the conversion of nitrogen to NO_x.

The problem inherent in this approach is that fuel combustion may not be complete, resulting in the release of unburned carbon (soot) and unburned hydrocarbons and the formation of carbon monoxide. To deal with this problem, low-excess-air firing is usually conducted as a two-stage process. In stage one, combustion takes place at a high temperature that promotes complete combustion of the fuel, but in an atmosphere with just less than sufficient quantities of oxygen to burn all available fuel. In such conditions, very little NO_x is formed because of inadequate amounts of oxygen. In the second stage, fuel combustion is completed at a lower temperature in excess amounts of air. Under these conditions, NO_x does not form because of the low temperature, although combustion of the fuel can proceed efficiently enough to prevent release of soot, unburned hydrocarbons, and carbon monoxide.

Finally, the emission of NO_x can be reduced by treating exhaust gases that leave the combustion chamber. In automotive vehicles, the most common postcombustion system involves a *catalytic converter,* as shown in the diagram on page 29. The catalytic converter has evolved from a prototype first designed by Eugène Houdry, whose life and work are discussed in the sidebar on page 30. This device is sometimes called a *three-way catalytic converter* because it acts on three pollutant gases released from an internal combustion engine: NO_x, CO, and HC (unburned hydrocarbons).

The chemical reactions by which these pollutants are converted to harmless emissions take place as exhaust gases pass through two chambers. Each chamber contains a catalyst that has been deposited on large numbers of very small ceramic beads or on the surfaces of a honeycomb-shaped filter. In the first chamber, unburned hydrocarbons and water from exhaust gases react to form elemental hydrogen (H_2). The most common catalyst in this chamber of the converter is finely divided rhodium metal.

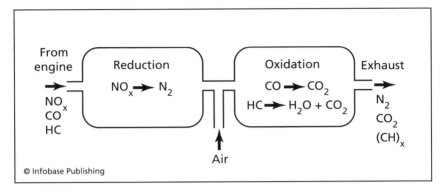

Three-way catalytic converter

$$HC + H_2O \rightarrow H_2 + CO$$

The hydrogen produced in this reaction then reacts with oxides of nitrogen in exhaust gases, reducing them to elemental nitrogen:

$$2NO + 2H_2 \rightarrow N_2 + 2H_2O$$

Carbon monoxide formed from the reduction of water to hydrogen is also available to reduce nitrogen oxides:

$$2NO + 2CO \rightarrow N_2 + 2CO_2$$
$$\text{and}$$
$$NO_2 + 2CO \rightarrow N_2 + 2CO_2$$

These gases then pass out of the first chamber of the converter and into the second chamber, which usually contains a platinum/palladium catalyst. Oxidation reactions take place in the second chamber. Carbon monoxide is converted to carbon dioxide and any remaining unburned hydrocarbons are converted to carbon dioxide and water:

$$2CO + O_2 \rightarrow 2CO_2$$
$$HC + O_2 \rightarrow CO_2 + H_2O$$

As already noted, even the use of catalytic converters has not produced an overall reduction in the amount of nitrogen oxides released in the United States (and many other parts of the world). Therefore, engineers are constantly working to devise new methods

◄ EUGENE HOUDRY (1892–1962) ►

Historians sometimes point to Earth Day 1970 as the beginning of the modern environmental movement. And in some important ways, they are correct. But many people were worried about the dangers posed by polluted air decades before that event. One such individual was the French-born American chemist Eugene Houdry. Houdry spent much of his professional career studying the nature of catalysis, the process by which the rate of a chemical reaction is changed by the addition of a nonreactive substance.

Eugene Houdry was born in Domont, France, near Paris, on April 18, 1892. His father owned a successful steel factory, and Eugene enrolled in mechanical engineering at the Ecole des Arts et Métiers in Paris to prepare to take over the family business. He graduated in 1911 with a gold medal for the best grades of any student in his class.

After graduation, Houdry began work at the family plant but was soon drafted into the French army to serve in World War I. He was seriously wounded at the battle of Juvincourt in 1917 while overseeing the repair of damaged tanks. For his service in the war, he was awarded the croix de guerre.

Houdry returned to the steel plant after the war. But he soon found a new subject that interested him even more than steel production: fuels research. In 1922, the French government approached Houdry with a request that he look for a new method for converting coal into liquid fuels. Houdry discovered such a method but found that it was too expensive to use commercially. Nonetheless, he found that he was fascinated by the subject of fuel research, and he spent much of the rest of his life pursuing that subject.

for improving the efficiency of the catalytic converter. One problem occurs with lean-burning engines, engines that use a low fuel-to-air ratio. With such engines, the relatively high concentration of oxygen in the exhaust makes it difficult for a traditional three-stage catalytic converter to reduce all of the NO_x that passes through it.

One solution that has been devised makes use of barium carbonate to trap the NO_x. The trap contains a finely divided platinum cata-

In 1930, Houdry was offered an opportunity to continue his research on fuels by the Vacuum Oil Company of the United States. He accepted that offer, moved to the United States, and formed his own company, Houdry Process Corporation, in partnership with Vacuum Oil. During World War II, he was a vocal opponent of the Vichy government in France, which repealed his French citizenship. Houdry became a U.S. citizen in 1942.

Shortly after the end of World War II, Americans were beginning to experience some of the side effects of the economic boom that began in the late 1940s and early 1950s. Suffocating photochemical smog had become an almost daily fact of life in many large cities, most notably Los Angeles. It had become clear to at least some people that something had to be done to prevent the surge of automotive traffic from turning large cities into huge death traps.

Houdry's solution to the problem was the first catalytic converter ever designed for an automotive vehicle. The catalytic converters found on almost all cars and trucks in use today are still strikingly similar to his invention. Exhaust gases passed into the converter and over a bed of platinum catalyst, then exited with a greatly reduced concentration of carbon monoxide, nitrogen oxides, and unburned hydrocarbons. Houdry obtained a patent for his device in 1956 and founded a company, Oxy-Catalyst, to manufacture and sell the new product.

Unfortunately for Houdry, the lead in gasoline used at the time fouled the catalyst. After operating for a short period, the catalyst lost its ability to filter out noxious gases. Houdry's company failed. Two decades later, however, after lead had been banned in gasoline, his idea was reinvented and became the basis of nearly all modern catalytic converters.

Houdry died in Upper Darby, Pennsylvania, on July 18, 1962.

lyst embedded in barium carbonate. The carbonate reacts readily with oxides of nitrogen, forming barium nitrate:

$$2BaCO_3 + 4NO + 3O_2 \rightarrow 2Ba(NO_3)_2 + 2CO_2$$

When the fuel-to-air mixture temporarily becomes richer (contains more fuel and less air), as during acceleration, larger amounts of carbon monoxide are produced for a short period. This carbon monoxide

Catalytic converters like the one shown here are highly efficient devices for the conversion of harmful exhaust by-products formed during the combustion of gasoline, diesel oil, and other fuels. (Sheila Terry/Photo Researchers, Inc.)

then reacts with the oxides of nitrogen "stored" in the barium nitrate, converting them to elemental nitrogen:

$$5CO + Ba(NO_3)_2 \rightarrow N_2 + BaCO_3 + 4CO_2$$

The postcombustion systems used at power generating plants and factories are somewhat different. These systems remove nitrogen oxides from the waste gases (*flue gases*) processes using classified as selective noncatalytic reduction (SNCR) and selective catalytic reduction (SCR). Oxides of nitrogen are also removed by some systems used to extract sulfur dioxide from flue gases (see "Sulfur Dioxide" on pages 33–38 for a description of these systems).

Selective noncatalytic reduction systems make use of the tendency of certain compounds, ammonia (NH_3) and urea ($CO[NH_2]_2$) in particular, to react with and reduce oxides of nitrogen:

$$4NH_3 + 6NO \rightarrow 5N_2 + 6H_2O$$

and

$$2CO(NH_2)_2 + 6NO \rightarrow 5N_2 + 4H_2O + 2CO_2$$

When either ammonia or urea is injected into flue gases at temperatures of about 870°C–1,100°C for ammonia and 900°C–1,150°C for urea, NO_x removal can reach as high as 50 percent.

Selective catalytic reduction operates on the same principle as SNCR, using ammonia or urea as the working gas along with a catalyst. A number of catalysts have been used, the most effective of which appear to be oxides of molybdenum, titanium, tungsten, and vanadium as well as zeolites, which are naturally occurring alumina silicates. In the presence of a catalyst, the reactions shown take place at a lower temperature, ranging from about 300°C to 425°C. In SCR systems, the removal of nitrogen oxides from flue gases may reach 90 percent or more.

Sulfur Dioxide

Sulfur dioxide is a colorless gas with a sharp, pungent odor, like that of a burning match. Most people are able to detect this highly characteristic odor at concentrations of about 0.5 ppm or greater. Its chemical formula is SO_2. Sulfur dioxide is readily soluble in water, forming the weak acid sulfurous acid (H_2SO_3). Sulfur dioxide is formed when sulfur or a sulfur-containing compound is burned:

$$S + O_2 \rightarrow SO_2$$

or, for example:

$$4FeS_2 + 11O_2 \rightarrow 8SO_2 + 2Fe_2O_3$$

Sulfur dioxide is an irritant to the eyes, the respiratory system, and, in some cases, the skin. One factor in producing this effect is the interaction of sulfur dioxide with water to form sulfuric acid, a strong biological irritant. At concentrations normally found in ambient air (the typical atmospheric environment surrounding us), these effects are annoying, but not particularly dangerous for most people. But for some individuals, such as those who have respiratory disorders, the young, or the elderly, even these low levels may pose a risk. Such individuals may experience more serious breathing problems that require medical attention. People who are constantly exposed to relatively high concentrations of sulfur dioxide (such as smelter workers) may experience more serious long-term health problems, such as asthma, chronic bronchitis, lung disease, or emphysema. In addition to its effects on human health, sulfur dioxide has some important consequences for the physical and biological environment caused by the gas's contribution to the formation of acid rain.

Sulfur dioxide is produced by both natural and anthropogenic sources. The most important of the natural sources are volcanic eruptions, which account for about 40 percent of all natural emissions of the gas. Since volcanic eruptions are episodic events, the amount of sulfur dioxide attributable to this source in any one year varies widely. Other natural sources of the gas are forest fires and other natural burns, biological decay, and certain metabolic processes carried out by living organisms, especially marine plankton and bacteria. Natural sources release about 27.5 million short tons (25 million metric tons) of sulfur dioxide per year.

The most important anthropogenic source of sulfur dioxide are power generating plants, which account for about 70 percent of all the gas produced in the United States. Another 25 percent of the sulfur dioxide emitted in the country is from a variety of industrial and manufacturing operations. Less than 5 percent of the gas is produced by motor vehicles and other forms of transportation.

Sulfur dioxide is released during these operations when either coal or oil is burned. Coal and oil both naturally contain compounds of sulfur that, when burned, produce sulfur dioxide. The sulfur content of both coal and oil ranges from less than 1 percent to more than 7 percent, although refined petroleum tends to have lower concentrations of sulfur than do most forms of coal. Natural gas, by contrast, tends to have very low sulfur concentrations, usually less than 0.001 percent.

The concentrations of sulfur dioxide both emitted into the air and measured at monitoring stations have decreased significantly over the past two decades. Emissions dropped from about 26.4 million short tons (24 million metric tons) annually in 1982 to about 17.6 million short tons (16 million metric tons) in 2001. The largest decrease during this period occurred between 1992 and 2001, when the amount of sulfur dioxide released annually dropped by about a quarter. The only area in which improvement did not occur was in emissions from transportation, which rose from about 770,000 tons (700,000 metric tons) in 1980 to about 2 million short tons (1.8 million metric tons) in 2000.

Sulfur dioxide concentrations are currently measured at 253 locations around the United States. The average sulfur dioxide concentration collected at monitoring stations dropped from just over 0.01 ppm in 1982 to under 0.005 ppm in 2001, a decrease of 51 percent. More than half of that decrease (35 percent) occurred between 1992 and 2001.

Control of sulfur dioxide emissions from stationary sources (such as power plants) usually takes one of three forms: fuel cleaning, also known as fuel *beneficiation;* removal of sulfur during combustion; or flue gas processing.

The goal of beneficiation is to remove as much sulfur from a fuel as possible before it is ever burned. When burned, fuel with lower sulfur content will produce less sulfur dioxide. Beneficiation is usually accomplished by a physical process that separates one form of sulfur, pyritic sulfur, from coal. Pyritic sulfur consists of sulfur minerals (primarily sulfides) that are not chemically bonded to coal in any way. The name is taken from the most common form of mineral sulfur usually found in coal, pyrite, or iron sulfide (FeS_2).

Mineral sulfides have significantly different densities from those of coal, so they can be removed from it by methods that take advantage of this difference, such as hydrocycloning, dry cycloning, and froth flotation. In hydrocycloning, for example, a slurry of coal and water is introduced into a centrifuge-type tank with a central cylinder. As the tank spins, the sulfides are thrown outward against the inner wall of the tank, while the coal is ejected upward and out of the tank through the central cylinder. The operation of a cyclone is similar to that of a hydrocyclone, except that dry coal rather than a coal slurry is injected into the device. Froth flotation is used to remove sulfide particles too small to be removed by means of centrifuging. The process is based on the principle that sulfide particles tend to stick to water, while coal does not. The first step in the process is to grind coal finely. Water and a flotation chemical are then added. The purpose of the flotation chemical is to produce a bubbly mixture, or froth. Some of the most popular frothing agents are alcohols and methyl isobutyl carbinol (MIC). The mixture is then allowed to separate and the watery portion, containing sulfides adhered to water bubbles, is removed through an outlet pipe, leaving the cleaned coal behind.

Beneficiation may be effective in removing up to half of all the pyritic sulfur found in coal. None of the methods just described is effective, however, in removing organic sulfur intimately bound to coal particles.

One of the most popular methods of removing sulfur from coal during the combustion process is called fluidized bed combustion. In this process, finely ground coal is mixed with limestone, suspended above a screen by jets of air blown upward through the screen, and then ignited. The abundance of air and very large surface area of coal result in highly efficient combustion. At the same time, any sulfur dioxide formed during combustion is trapped by and reacts with the limestone:

$$CaCO_3 + SO_2 \rightarrow CaSO_3 + CO_2$$

The combustion temperature is kept relatively low, in the range of 750°C–925°C, to prevent the formation of oxides of nitrogen. Fluidized bed combustion is generally able to remove up to 95 percent of the sulfur found in coal.

Most postcombustion cleaning systems make use of scrubbers to remove sulfur dioxide. Scrubbers are devices that contain some chemical that will react with sulfur dioxide in flue gases. Two kinds of scrubbers are used, wet and dry. As their names suggest, the two types differ in the extent to which water is mixed with the chemical used to remove sulfur dioxide. In wet scrubbers, the chemical is dissolved in or mixed with water and then sprayed into flue gases. In dry scrubbers, the chemical is pulverized and then sprayed into flue gases.

The most common chemical used in scrubbers today is limestone (calcium carbonate; $CaCO_3$) because it reacts with sulfur dioxide readily to form calcium sulfite ($CaSO_3$), which can be collected and sold as gypsum. In recent years, a new *scrubber* design that uses lime (calcium hydroxide; $Ca(OH)_2$) rather than limestone has been introduced in many plants:

$$Ca(OH)_2 + SO_2 \rightarrow CaSO_3 + H_2O$$

Lime is more chemically reactive than is limestone, so the amount needed to remove sulfur dioxide from flue gases is comparably less.

Most industrial operations today now have pollution control systems, like the one shown in this chemical plant, to reduce the levels of sulfur dioxide and oxides of nitrogen released to the atmosphere. (Maximilian Stock Ltd./Photo Researchers, Inc.)

Other basic compounds have been used in scrubbers for the removal of sulfur dioxide. Among the most promising are amines. An amine is an organic compound analogous to ammonia in which one or more of the ammonia hydrogens is replaced by an alkyl group ($R-NH_2$). Amines react readily with sulfur dioxide to form a salt. When the salt is treated with steam (a process known as steam stripping), the sulfur dioxide dissolves and is removed and the amine is regenerated. The amine can then be reused in another cycle of sulfur dioxide removal.

Particulate Matter

Particulate matter is the term used to describe solid particles and liquid droplets found in the atmosphere. Particulates are produced by a host of natural and anthropogenic sources. Mist and fog are both forms of natural particulates, as are windblown soil, dust, smoke from forest fires, and biological objects, such as bacteria, fungal spores, and pollen. The incomplete combustion of fossil fuels is one of the most important anthropogenic (human-made) sources of particulates. Such processes release unburned carbon particles, oxides of sulfur and nitrogen, and a host of organic compounds into the air.

The particles and droplets that make up particulate matter range widely in size. Some are large enough to be seen, such as the tiny particles of sand stirred up in a dust storm. Others are so small as to be invisible to the naked eye. In general, these particles and droplets are divided into two major categories, based on their size. Particles designated as $PM_{2.5}$ have diameters less than or equal to 2.5 µ (microns or micrometers) in diameter. Particles with diameters between 2.5 µ and 10 µ are designated as PM_{10} particulates. The terms fine and coarse are sometimes used to described $PM_{2.5}$ and PM_{10} particulates, respectively.

Particulates are also classified as to their mode of formation. Some, designated as primary particulates, are released directly to the atmosphere in the form of tiny particles or droplets. Droplets of salt and water blown off the surface of the ocean are examples of primary particulates. Other particulates are formed in the atmosphere as a result of chemical and/or physical reactions. For example, sulfur dioxide released from power generating plants reacts with oxygen and water in the air to form droplets of sulfuric acid, a primary component of acid rain. Chemically formed particulates such as these droplets of sulfuric acid are called *secondary particulates.*

The Environmental Protection Agency (EPA) and other federal agencies began monitoring air quality and emissions standards for some particulates as far back as 1987, although a complete program for both $PM_{2.5}$ and PM_{10} particulates has been in operation only since 1999. Data from 770 monitoring sites indicate that PM_{10} air quality has improved from a nationwide average concentration of just under 30 micrograms per cubic meter ($\mu g/m^3$) in 1992 to just under 25 $\mu g/m^3$ in 2001. Emissions of PM_{10} particulates have also decreased consistently over the past two decades, from about 4.2 million short tons (3.8 million metric tons) in 1985 to about 3.6 million short tons (3.3 million metric tons) in 2001.

EPA has collected data on the emission of $PM_{2.5}$ particulates since 1992 and on air quality for the pollutant since 1999. These data indicate that the direct emission of $PM_{2.5}$ particles has decreased about 10 percent over the monitoring period, from about 2.75 million short tons (2.5 million metric tons) in 1992 to about 2.4 million short tons (2.2 million metric tons) in 2001. Over the short span of monitoring, $PM_{2.5}$ concentration decreased by about 5 percent from about 14 $\mu g/m^3$ in 1999 to about 13.3 $\mu g/m^3$ in 2001.

One reason monitors created the $PM_{2.5}$ and PM_{10} designations is that the human respiratory system effectively blocks particles larger than these sizes from penetrating. They are either exhaled or trapped in the upper respiratory tract, from which they are expelled by coughing, spitting, sneezing, or the like. The human body removes about 99 percent of all inhaled particulates from the respiratory system by one or another of these mechanisms. A few particles make their way into the trachea (windpipe) and the lungs, where they are trapped in mucus and then expelled by one of the mechanisms described.

A relatively small amount of particulates with diameters of less than 10 μ are able to penetrate more deeply into the respiratory system, blocking the capillaries and alveoli of the lungs. When this happens, a number of health problems may result. The severity of those problems depends on a number of factors, one of which, of course, is the concentration of the particulates to which one is exposed and the length of exposure.

The people who are most at risk for health problems from particulate exposure are those who already have some form of respiratory disorder or heart disease, the elderly, and children. Such problems begin to appear when the ambient concentration of pollutants reaches about 40 $\mu g/m^3$ for $PM_{2.5}$ particulates and about 150 $\mu g/m^3$ for PM_{10} particulates. Such concentrations are observed during dust storms, along dusty unpaved roads, and in areas with high levels of motor vehicle traffic, for instance. Increasing concentrations of both $PM_{2.5}$ and PM_{10} particulates result in more serious health problems, including asthma, bronchitis, emphysema, and cardiac problems.

Individuals whose jobs expose them to unusually high particulate concentrations are especially susceptible to health problems from the pollutant. For example, men and women who work with the mineral asbestos are very prone to development of a serious and usually fatal condition known as asbestosis, in which fibers of the mineral become embedded in the interstices (the empty spaces within tissue) of the lung. Similar conditions are observed among coal workers who inhale coal dust (pneumoconiosis, or black lung disease); textile workers (byssinosis, or brown lung disease); those who work with clay, brick, silica, glass, and other ceramic materials (silicosis); and workers exposed to high levels of beryllium fumes (berylliosis).

Particulates are responsible for two environmental problems in addition to the health issues already described. One of these is *acid deposition,* in which secondary particulates are carried to the ground in the form of rain, snow, hail, or some other form of precipitation. These particulates then pose a threat to the living and nonliving materials on which they fall. (Acid deposition is discussed in chapter 3.) The other problem is impairment of visibility: The clearness of the air diminishes as the concentration of particulates in it increases. Particulates affect visibility in three ways: by scattering light away from the path of sight from an object to a viewer, by scattering surrounding light into a viewer's eyes, and by absorbing light transmitted from an object to a viewer's eyes. The sum total of these effects is to reduce visibility from clear in areas of low particulate concentration to hazy in areas of high particulate concentration.

One place this problem has become especially severe is the nation's national park system. Visitors to national parks have found their enjoyment of the natural scenery compromised by poor air quality that leaves famous and noteworthy features only barely visible. For this reason, one section of the 1977 Amendments to the Clean Air Act provided for a program of monitoring and pollution control in the nation's 156 national parks and wilderness areas. Poor visibility resulting from high particulate concentration has safety effects also. Automobile drivers and airline pilots may find that they are able to see shorter distances and less clearly, increasing the likelihood of accidents involving other vehicles and aircraft.

Control devices for particulate matter fall into five major types: gravity settling chambers, cyclones, wet scrubbers, electrostatic precipitators, and baghouses. Gravity settling chambers are large rooms through which flue gases pass; in them the largest and heaviest particulates fall out under the influence of gravity. Gravity settling chambers are effective in the removal of particles whose diameter is about 75 μ or more.

Cyclones are large centrifuges that put flue gases into a spinning motion. The larger and heavier particles in the gases are thrown outward against the inner walls of the cyclone, where they adhere and are later removed.

In wet scrubbers, upward-flowing flue gases have contact with a stream of water flowing down from the top of the scrubber chamber. The water absorbs particles in the flue gas and carries them to the bottom of the chamber, where they can be removed in the form of sludge.

The particles in a flue gas can pick up an electric charge when they move through an electrical field. The operation of an electrostatic precipitator makes use of this property. After passing the flue gas through the field, the device exposes the charged particles to plates carrying the opposite charge, which attract them. The particles stick to the plates and are periodically scraped off for disposal.

A baghouse can be thought of as a very large vacuum cleaner whose walls are lined with a semipermeable filter. Flue gases pass into the baghouse and are then forced outward through the filter. Particles carried along in the flue gas are trapped by the filter, from which they are scraped off and removed. The efficiency of most particulate removal devices is now quite high. Many are able to extract at least 99 percent of the particulates present in flue gases.

Volatile Organic Compounds

The term *volatile organic compounds* (VOCs) refers to carbon-containing compounds that exist as gases or that vaporize easily. Some examples of VOCs are benzene, formaldehyde, toluene, xylene, hexane, ethylbenzene, 1,3-butadiene, and a group of compounds known as polycyclic aromatic hydrocarbons (PAHs). The vast majority of VOCs are hydrocarbons, often represented by the chemical formula RH, where R may represent either an alkyl or an aryl group. An alkyl group is an alkane lacking one hydrogen, and an aryl group is an aromatic hydrocarbon lacking one hydrogen.

Volatile organic chemicals are released during a number of industrial and manufacturing operations. For example, 1,3-butadiene is an important raw material in the manufacture of synthetic rubber: During manufacture small amounts of the chemical escape into the air. Formaldehyde is a raw material used in the manufacture of a variety of building materials, such as phenol-formaldehyde and melamine resins. Many household products, such as cleaning products, varnishes, waxes, paints, and organic solvents, contain VOCs, which vaporize and escape easily into the atmosphere when they are used. For this reason, VOCs often build up indoors.

The Environmental Protection Agency and other federal agencies have been collecting data on VOC emissions since 1940. The EPA does not include VOCs among pollutants included in its monitoring programs, so comparable data on its contributions to air quality are not available. The pattern of VOC emissions shows an increase from about 16.5 million short tons (15 million metric tons) in 1940 to a maximum of about 30.8 million short tons (28 million metric tons) in 1970, followed by a reduction to 1940 levels in 1998. Emission levels have remained nearly constant since that time. About 40 percent of all VOCs released into the atmosphere are from on-road vehicles, an additional 32 percent from solvent use and evaporation, about 12 percent from combustion operations, and the remaining 17 percent from a variety of other sources.

Because they tend to build up indoors and to react with and damage living tissue, VOCs constitute an important element in the special problem of indoor air pollution. Exposure to low concentrations of VOCs produces a number of annoying but relatively benign symptoms, such as irritation of the eyes, nose, throat, and respiratory system; headache, fatigue, dizziness, and nausea; visual problems; impairment of memory and other thought processes; and skin reactions. Some VOCs, such as benzene, formaldehyde, perchloroethylene, and derivatives of xylene and toluene, pose more serious concerns in that they have been found to be carcinogenic. Long-term exposure to these compounds may, therefore, pose a serious health risk.

The most serious health and environmental problems associated with VOCs, however, relate to their role in the formation of photochemical smog. Photochemical smog is a form of air pollution that occurs when sunlight converts oxides of nitrogen and volatile organic compounds to noxious chemicals. The term *smog* itself is a contraction of the words *smoke* and *fog*. It was coined in 1905 by a public health physician Dr. H. A. des Voeux, who announced at the Public Health Congress in London that "it required no science to see that there was something produced in great cities which was not found in the country, and that was smoky fog, or what was known as 'smog.'"

Smog may result from a variety of environmental conditions; when solar energy is responsible for the development of such conditions, it is referred to as photochemical smog. The production and destruction of photochemical smog are very complex events that involve hundreds of different chemical reactions. A full discussion of those reactions is beyond the scope of this book, but a general outline of the changes that take place is possible as follows.

In the first step of photochemical smog production, sunlight (hv) acts on nitrogen dioxide to produce nitric oxide and free oxygen:

$$NO_2 + h\nu \rightarrow NO + O$$

Oxygen atoms formed in this reaction react readily with diatomic oxygen present in the atmosphere to form ozone (O_3). The symbol M in the following equation represents some third body that acts as a catalyst, removing energy from the O_2/O collision, making it thermodynamically feasible:

$$O + O_2 + M \rightarrow O_3 + M$$

Levels of ozone produced by this reaction are controlled to some extent by a "scavenging" reaction that takes place with nitric oxide:

$$O_3 + NO \rightarrow O_2 + NO_2$$

The reaction is referred to by this term because nitric oxide forages among ozone molecules, attacking them at random and converting them to oxygen molecules.

These three reactions constitute a cycle that begins with the production of nitrogen dioxide (usually from motor vehicle exhaust) and results in the production of large amounts of atomic oxygen and ozone. When concentrations of nitrogen dioxide decrease (as during evening hours, when traffic tends to decrease), the scavenging reaction tends to remove excess amounts of ozone from the atmosphere.

Oxygen atoms formed in this cycle of reactions initiate one of two important chain reactions. In the first, they react with water molecules to generate highly reactive (indicated by the asterisk) hydroxyl radicals:

$$O^* + H_2O \rightarrow 2OH^*$$

In the second, the oxygen atoms react with hydrocarbons (VOCs) present in automotive exhaust to produce *free radicals* (atoms or molecules with a free unpaired electron, indicated by the symbol $R^\bullet$ in the following equation) that may or may not contain oxygen:

$$O + RH \rightarrow R^\bullet$$

Reactive hydroxyl radicals and ozone may initiate similar changes:

$$OH^* + RH \rightarrow R^\bullet + H_2O$$
$$O_3 + RH \rightarrow R^\bullet$$

The free radical R• is especially important because it reacts very readily with oxygen to form the *peroxyl radical,* ROO•, which may itself initiate a series of important reactions:

$$R^• + O_2 \rightarrow ROO^•$$

One of the most important of these reactions occurs between a peroxyl radical and nitrogen dioxide to produce compounds known as peroxyalkyl and peroxyacyl nitrates:

$$ROO^• + NO_2 \rightarrow ROONO_2$$

One product commonly formed in this reaction is peroxyacetyl nitrate (PAN), an important and common component of photochemical smog. PAN, ozone, and many of the other compounds formed in the series of reactions just described are strong oxidants and are responsible for some of the initial and most aggravating features of smog, including nose, eye, and throat irritation.

The primary system for controlling VOC emissions from automotive vehicles is the catalytic converter, described earlier in this chapter (see "Oxides of Nitrogen" on pages 24–33). A number of different technologies have been developed for removing VOCs from flue gases of stationary sources. They include thermal and catalytic incineration, adsorption, absorption, and biofiltration.

Incineration systems are based on the principle that all volatile organic compounds are combustible and can, in principle, be eliminated simply by being burned. Combustion can be achieved without catalysts (thermal systems) or with catalysts (catalytic systems). In either case, flue gases are passed into a chamber where they are heated in an excess of air, resulting in the oxidation of VOCs. Thermal systems operate at temperatures of 750°C–1,000°C, while catalytic systems operate at temperatures of about 350°C–500°C.

Adsorption systems make use of the fact that VOCs are attracted to and will adsorb to (attach to the surface of) certain special materials, the most common of which is activated charcoal. Activated charcoal consists of finely divided particles of charcoal. Flue gases containing VOCs are passed through a chamber and over a bed of the adsorbent, where they collect on its surface. The system may be designed such that the VOCs can then be removed from the adsorbent, which can then be reused. Or the adsorbent with VOCs attached is simply discarded.

Absorption systems operate as scrubbers. Flue gases are directed into and upward through a large cylindrical tank, where they encounter a downward spray of some solvent, in which they dissolve. The solvent can then be removed, evaporated, and collected for future use. Or it can be incinerated or otherwise discarded, destroying the VOCs in the process.

In the past two decades, a number of novel systems for the control and removal of VOCs have been developed. One such technology is biofiltration. In this type of system, flue gases are passed through a large tank containing microorganisms that digest and degrade the organic chemicals in the gases. The waste products of this process are carbon dioxide and water, harmless compounds that can be released directly to the environment.

Ozone

Ozone is an allotrope of oxygen with the chemical formula O_3. (Allotropes are different forms of an element.) That is, ozone molecules contain three atoms per molecule in contrast to the two atoms per molecule found in the more abundant dioxygen (O_2). It is a bluish gas with a pungent odor that is chemically unstable.

Ozone is produced naturally when bolts of lightning or other sources of high energy cause molecules of dioxygen to react with each other and produce ozone:

$$3O_2 + energy \rightarrow 2O_3$$

The concentration of ozone near the Earth's surface is very low, typically in the range of 15–45 ppbv (parts per billion by volume). In contrast, ozone is more abundant in the Earth's stratosphere, where it is formed by the action of ultraviolet radiation on molecules of dioxygen. A distinction is sometimes made between stratospheric ozone ("good ozone") and tropospheric (low-level or surface ozone; "bad ozone"). This distinction arises from the fact that stratospheric ozone reduces the amount of ultraviolet radiation that reaches the Earth, reducing the rate of skin cancer and other medical problems (see "Depletion of the Ozone Layer" on pages 67–79). Tropospheric ozone, by contrast, is responsible for damage to the health of humans and other animals and to plants. In spite of this distinction, all forms of ozone, wherever they occur, are chemically identical.

As describer earlier in this chapter, ground-level ozone is formed when nitrogen dioxide released from the combustion of fossil fuels dissociates in the presence of solar energy, forming nitric oxide and atomic oxygen (see "Volatile Organic Compounds" on pages 42–46). The atomic oxygen formed in this reaction then reacts with dioxygen to form ozone:

$$NO_2 + h\nu \rightarrow NO + O$$
$$O + O_2 + M \rightarrow O_3 + M$$

The Environmental Protection Agency has collected data on ozone air quality from 379 sites since 1982. The EPA uses two standards for measuring air quality, one based on an eight-hour average of measurements, and one based on a one-hour average. Since 1982, the one-hour average has decreased from 0.127 ppm to 0.104 ppm in 2001. Over the same period, the 8-hour average has dropped from 0.092 ppm to 0.082 ppm. These trends differ quite substantially for various parts of the nation and for rural, suburban, and urban areas. For example, improvements in ozone air quality were greater in New England and along the West Coast over the 1982–2001 period than for the midwestern, southern, and mountain states. Also, suburban areas consistently show higher concentrations of ozone than rural or urban areas. This pattern can be explained by the fact that wind and other air movements tend to carry ozone out of the urban areas where it is produced and into surrounding suburban areas.

Health and environmental effects resulting from exposure to ozone are caused by the compound's very strong oxidizing properties. Ozone molecules decompose readily to form dioxygen and atomic oxygen, which is highly reactive.

$$O_3 \rightarrow O_2 + O$$

Atomic oxygen attacks and destroys enzymes and other protein molecules, deoxyribonucleic acid (DNA) and ribonucleic acid (RNA) molecules, and other essential biochemical molecules, interrupting essential biochemical functions and causing cell damage and death. These biochemical changes are reflected in a wide range of physical disorders, depending on the concentration of ozone and length of exposure. Clinical symptoms include irritation of the eyes, nose, and throat; coughing and chest pain; and increased susceptibility to respiratory disorders, such as asthma and bronchitis.

As with other pollutants, the types and severity of effects depend on an individual's age, level of activity, and general health. The elderly, young children, and those who have preexisting respiratory and cardiac disease experience more serious problems as a result of exposure to ozone. The table on page 49 summarizes health advisories for various levels of ozone exposure, as recommended by the EPA.

Ozone is produced in the atmosphere when oxides of nitrogen react with volatile organic compounds in the presence of sunlight. Control of ozone production is achieved, therefore, by use of systems designed to reduce the emissions of NO_x and VOCs, such as those described in the sections on these two pollutants.

Lead

A number of metals and their compounds have been found to pose health risks to humans, other animals, and plants. When they occur in air, these metals are sometimes regarded as pollutants. Title III of the 1990 Amendments to the Clean Air Act, for example, lists the following elements and their compounds as "hazardous air pollutants": antimony, arsenic, beryllium, cadmium, chromium, cobalt, lead, manganese, mercury, nickel, and selenium.

Of these chemicals, the EPA has traditionally focused its monitoring efforts on only one, lead. The reason is that lead (in the form of tetraethyl lead; $(C_2H_5)_4Pb$) was once used extensively as a fuel additive to reduce the problems of engine "knocking" in automotive vehicles. Because of the health problems posed by lead, however, tetraethyl lead was banned from use in automotive fuels in 1976.

In 1970, the total emission of lead into the atmosphere amounted to about 242,000 tons (220,000 metric tons). Of this amount, about 95 percent was from automotive vehicle exhausts, through the decom-

◄ HEALTH EFFECTS OF OZONE ►

8-HOUR OZONE CONCENTRATION	AIR QUALITY DESCRIPTION	HEALTH EFFECTS
0.0–0.064 ppm	Good	None
0.065–0.084 ppm	Moderate	Unusually sensitive people should limit prolonged outdoor exercise
0.085–0.104 ppm	Unhealthy for sensitive groups	Active children and adults and people who have respiratory problems should limit prolonged outdoor exercise
0.105–0.124 ppm	Unhealthy	Active children and adults and people who have respiratory problems should avoid prolonged outdoor exercise; everyone else should limit prolonged outdoor exercise

(continues)

◁ HEALTH EFFECTS OF OZONE *(continued)* ▷		
8-HOUR OZONE CONCENTRATION	**AIR QUALITY DESCRIPTION**	**HEALTH EFFECTS**
0.125 ppm and higher	Very unhealthy	Active children and adults and people who have respiratory problems should avoid all outdoor exercise; everyone else should limit outdoor exercise

position of tetraethyl lead. The remaining 5 percent of the emitted lead was produced by smelters, battery plants, and fuel use from stationary sources. By the end of the 20th century, total lead emissions had dropped to about 5,500 tons (5,000 metric tons), with virtually all of that reduction a result of the 1976 ban on the use of tetraethyl lead in gasoline. Today smelters and other metal-processing activities account for about half of all the lead emitted to the air, with stationary fuel sources and waste disposal accounting for most of the remaining lead. In 2001, the average concentration of lead measured at 39 EPA sites was less than 0.1 $\mu g/m^3$.

The health effects of lead have been studied extensively. One characteristic of special concern is the metal's tendency to accumulate in the blood, bones, and soft tissues, causing damage to the nervous system, kidneys, liver, and other organs. Thus, a person who ingests only a small amount of the metal, but over long periods, is at risk for serious long-term diseases and disorders. Such risks include neurological impairments, such as seizures, mental retardation, and behavioral disorders; vomiting, diarrhea, convulsions, and coma; high blood pressure and heart disease; and anemia, appetite loss, abdominal pain, constipation, fatigue, sleeplessness, irritability, and headache. In cases of massive and/or long-term exposure, lead poisoning can lead to death.

The toxic effects of lead on animals other than humans and on plants have been less extensively studied. One area of special concern, however, relates to animals that are hunted and killed for sport. Studies have shown, for example, that seven times more waterfowl die as a result of lead poisoning from lead in bullets than from gunshots by human hunters. For this reason, manufacturers of ammunition are finding substitutes for the lead that had previously been the primary component of most bullets.

The ban on the use of leaded gasoline in the 1970s produced one of the most successful episodes in the search for the control of air pollutants. As already noted, the concentration of lead in the air dropped dramatically and to very low levels within a matter of years after the ban was put into place. Currently, efforts to control lead emissions focus on improving the methods used to remove lead from air and water wastes of smelters, metal processing plants, and other such plants. The most common systems currently used are variations of traditional waste control techniques in which physical devices (such as baghouses) or chemical systems (such as precipitation reactions) are used to extract particles of lead from wastes.

Air Quality Standards

Under the terms of the Clean Air Act of 1970, as amended in 1990, the Environmental Protection Agency is required to establish National Ambient Air Quality Standards (NAAQS) for pollutants considered to be hazardous to public health and the environment. These standards are of two types: primary and secondary. Primary standards apply to "sensitive" members of the population, including the elderly, young children, and people who have respiratory disorders. Secondary standards apply to the general public and include risks to other parts of the environment, including visibility, animals, crops, vegetation, and buildings.

The NAAQS in effect as of June 2004 are summarized in the chart on pages 53–54. Note that only six air pollutants are included in this table: carbon monoxide, nitrogen dioxide, ozone, lead, particulate matter, and sulfur dioxide. These pollutants are called *criteria pollutants*.

The quality of the nation's air has clearly improved since Earth Day 1970. Air quality measurements for all six criteria pollutants have improved, in some cases quite dramatically. The battle to control pollution is hardly over, however. As this chapter has indicated, emissions of many pollutants continue to increase. The dialogue continues between those who wish to regulate air quality more rigorously and those who prefer to move more slowly and protect economic growth. There seems little doubt that that debate will continue well into the future.

◁ NATIONAL AMBIENT AIR QUALITY STANDARDS (NAAQS) ▷

POLLUTANT	PRIMARY STANDARDS	AVERAGING TIMES*	SECONDARY STANDARDS
Carbon monoxide	9 ppm (10 mg/m^3)	8-hour	None
	35 ppm (40 mg/m^3)	1-hour	None
Lead	1.5 µg/m^3	Quarterly average	Same as primary
Nitrogen dioxide	0.053 ppm (100 µg/m^3)	Annual (arithmetic mean)	Same as primary
Particulate matter (PM$_{10}$)	50 µg/m^3	Annual (arithmetic mean)	Same as primary
	150 ug/m^3	24-hour	

(continues)

◁ NATIONAL AMBIENT AIR QUALITY STANDARDS (NAAQS) *(continued)* ▷

POLLUTANT	PRIMARY STANDARDS	AVERAGING TIMES*	SECONDARY STANDARDS
Particulate matter (PM$_{2.5}$)	15 µg/m³	Annual (arithmetic mean)	Same as primary
	65 µg/m³	24-hour	
Ozone	0.08 ppm	8-hour	Same as primary
	0.12 ppm	1-hour	Same as primary
Sulfur oxides	0.03 ppm	Annual (arithmetic mean)	—
	0.14 ppm	24-hour	—
	0.5 ppm (1,300 µg/m³)	3-hour	—

Source: Environmental Protection Agency

*Averaging time is the period over which the stated exposure occurs.

3

CHEMISTRY OF THE ATMOSPHERE

CHANGES IN THE ATMOSPHERE

Over the past half-century, scientists have become increasingly aware that human activities may be having a profound effect on the composition of the Earth's atmosphere. First, a number of industrially important gases have begun to break down the *ozone layer*, a thin section of gas in the stratosphere that protects life on Earth from damaging ultraviolet radiation. Second, waste gases released into the air from industrial plants and power generating facilities are undergoing chemical reactions that result in the formation of precipitation acidic enough to threaten plant and animal life on the ground. Third, carbon dioxide released during the combustion of fossil fuels is accumulating in the atmosphere and, according to many experts, contributing to a rise in the atmosphere's average annual temperature.

All three of these examples illustrate a new kind of environmental problem, one that threatens to change the very composition of the atmosphere. The problem arises for two reasons, one demographic and one technological. In the first place, the ever-increasing number of humans on Earth is responsible for larger amounts of pollutants released into the atmosphere each year. In the second place, many technological developments release waste gases into the air, both combustion by-products and countless synthetic chemical compounds.

Properties of the Atmosphere

One might wonder how much of a threat people can really pose to the Earth's atmosphere. The air that surrounds our planet occupies an almost unimaginably large volume of about 7 billion cubic miles (30 billion cubic kilometers) and has an enormous mass of about 5.5 quintillion tons (5 quintillion metric tons). Even given the quantities of waste gases involved, can human-released gases really have any significant effect on the atmosphere's composition, temperature, or other properties? For example, suppose that scientists measure an increase in the concentration of just one gas (carbon dioxide) of 60 ppm (parts per million) over the past 50 years. Is it conceivable that such a small change could have serious long-term effects on the atmosphere or *climate?*

Questions like this one have long placed atmospheric issues in a somewhat different framework from problems of pollution like those discussed in chapter 2. It is not difficult to recognize the threats posed by smog, particulates, ozone, and other familiar pollutants. We can often see and smell and even taste polluted air around us. But it is more difficult for the average person to imagine that the ozone layer a few dozen miles high in the atmosphere is breaking apart or that such a change could have any real effect on his or her daily life. Besides, even in the absence of all human activity, the Earth's atmosphere is not a constant, unchanging entity. Natural processes are continually changing its composition, temperature, and other properties. For example, volcanic eruptions are sometimes powerful enough to eject very large quantities of solids, liquids, and gases that change the atmosphere's properties for months or years.

Probably the most dramatic such event in recorded history was the eruption of Mount Krakatoa, off the west coast of the island of Java, on August 26, 1883. Scientists estimate that that eruption released more than five cubic miles (more than 20 cubic kilometers) of material into the air, some of it reaching an altitude of more than 50 miles (80 kms). The volcanic dust from Krakatoa was dense enough to block out the Sun for more than two days before winds dispersed it around the planet. Even after dispersal, however, the dust was dense enough to reduce the amount of sunlight reaching the lower atmosphere, reducing the planet's annual temperature by more than 2°F (more than 1°C) over the next year. In fact, it was five years before annual average temperatures around the world returned to normal.

In spite of the occurrence of natural events such as the eruption of Krakatoa, scientists are now well aware that human activities can have serious long-term effects on the Earth's atmosphere. The first such effect to be noticed historically was the increase in *acid precipitation* resulting from the combustion of fossil fuels. Acid precipitation is also known as acid rain or acid deposition. The second, discovered in the mid-20th century, was the depletion of stratospheric ozone. More recently, atmospheric scientists established a link between so-called *greenhouse gases* and global *climate change.*

Acid Rain

The term *acid precipitation* refers to any form of precipitation, such as rain, snow, sleet, or hail, with a *pH* less than that typical of rain-water. You may recall that pH is a measure of the concentration of hydrogen ions in a solution, an indication as to how acidic the solution is. Plain water has a pH of 7.0, while acidic solutions have a pH less than 7 and basic solutions, a pH of greater than 7.

Rain and other forms of precipitation typically have a pH of less than 7 because they absorb carbon dioxide as they fall through the atmosphere. When carbon dioxide dissolves in water, it reacts with it to form the weak acid carbonic acid (H_2CO_3):

$$H_2O + CO_2 \rightarrow H_2CO_3$$

Because of this reaction, the pH of rainwater tends to be about 5.6.

The term *acid rain* was first coined in 1872 by the English chemist Robert Angus Smith (1817–84). Smith studied the composition of rain in the region around Manchester, England, and observed its effects on soil and plants in the area. Through his studies, he had identified three types of acid rain and recorded where each could typically be found: "carbonate of ammonia in the fields at a distance, . . . sulphate of ammonia in the suburbs, and . . . sulphuric acid, or acid sulphate, in the town." Smith first published his research in 1852 in a paper entitled "On the Air and Rain of Manchester" in the *Memoirs and Proceedings of the Manchester Literary and Philosophical Society.* He eventually became convinced that the acid rain he observed was caused by smoke produced from the many factories in the Manchester area and was successful in having laws passed that established certain "smokeless zones" around the city.

But Smith's research had relatively little impact on the scientific community over the next seven decades. During this time, acid deposition continued to be of some minor interest to scientists in parts of Europe. For example, the Swedish biologist J. R. Erichsen-Jones reported in the late 1930s that acid from rainwater dissolved aluminum in soil and that that dissolved aluminum was toxic to certain types of aquatic organisms.

The modern era of acid deposition research can probably be traced to the work of the English ecologist Eville Gorham (b. 1925). During the 1950s, Gorham wrote a series of papers on the acidity of rain and its effects on aquatic organisms. He showed that acid precipitation resulted in a loss of alkalinity in freshwater lakes and an increase in the acidity of bogs. He demonstrated that these effects were the result of compounds produced during the burning of fossil fuels, especially sulfuric acid, formed from sulfur dioxide in waste gases. Gorham used the destruction of vegetation, soils, and lake water in the vicinity of smelters to support his case.

The key turning point in the case against acid rain occurred with the work of the Swedish soil scientist Svante Odén (1924–86) in the 1960s. By that time, the natural environment in Scandinavian nations was suffering extraordinary damage as a result of acid rain produced by waste gases from industrial plants in other parts of Europe. Those gases were being blown eastward by prevailing winds from England and northward from industrialized areas of western Germany over the forests of Norway, Sweden, and Finland. Odén not only reported on his results in scientific journals but also wrote about his concerns in newspapers. He accused England, Germany, and other parts of Europe of launching an "insidious chemical war" on Scandinavia.

At the time, other scientists and the general public regarded Odén's conclusion with suspicion. It was difficult to imagine mechanisms by which waste gases released at one point on the globe could exert disastrous effects on the environment a thousand miles away. Yet, time and more research were to prove the Swedish scientist correct and earn him the title "the Father of Acid Rain."

The mechanisms by which acid rain forms and exerts its effects on the environment are now quite well understood. The primary culprit in this process is sulfur dioxide, produced when sulfur-containing coal is burned in power generating plants:

$$S + O_2 \rightarrow SO_2$$

Once sulfur dioxide has escaped into the atmosphere, it undergoes a series of reactions by which it is converted to sulfuric acid. Those reactions are somewhat complex and may follow at least three different courses. In the first of these reaction sequences, sulfur dioxide reacts with hydroxyl radicals in the atmosphere in the presence of some metallic catalyst (M) to form the bisulfite radical ($HSO_3^\bullet$):

$$SO_2 + OH^\bullet + M \rightarrow HSO_3^\bullet + M$$

The bisulfite radical then reacts with molecular oxygen to produce sulfur trioxide and the hydroperoxyl ($HO_2^\bullet$) radical:

$$HSO_3^\bullet + O_2 \rightarrow SO_3 + HO_2^\bullet$$

The sulfur trioxide formed in this reaction is very soluble in water and dissolves in water droplets to form sulfuric acid:

$$SO_3 + H_2O \rightarrow H_2SO_4$$

A second pathway to the formation of sulfuric acid depends on the presence of hydrogen peroxide (H_2O_2) in clouds, fog, rain, and other forms of water in the atmosphere. Hydrogen peroxide is now known to form in such locations when hydroperoxyl radicals react with each other:

$$2HO_2{}^\bullet \rightarrow H_2O_2 + O_2$$

The availability of hydrogen peroxide allows the direct oxidation of sulfur dioxide to sulfuric acid:

$$SO_2(aq) + H_2O_2(aq) \rightarrow H_2SO_4(aq)$$

The symbol (aq) indicates that the chemical species shown, H_2SO_4 in this case, exists in aqueous, or water, solution.

In the third pathway, sulfur dioxide first dissolves in water and then is oxidized to sulfuric acid by a variety of reactions:

First: $\qquad$ $SO_2 + H_2O \rightarrow H_2SO_3 \rightleftarrows H^+(aq) + HSO_3{}^-(aq)$

Followed by: $\qquad$ $HSO_3{}^-(aq) + H_2O_2(aq) \rightarrow HSO_4{}^-(aq) + H_2O$

and: $\qquad$ $HSO_4{}^-(aq) + H^+(aq) \rightarrow H_2SO_4(aq)$

or: $\qquad$ $HSO_3{}^-(aq) + \frac{1}{2}O_2 + M \rightarrow HSO_4{}^-(aq) + M$

and: $\qquad$ $HSO_4{}^-(aq) + H^+(aq) \rightarrow H_2SO_4(aq)$

where M in the reaction is iron and/or manganese.

Oxides of nitrogen also contribute to the formation of acid deposition. These oxides are formed whenever sufficient heat is generated in a power generating plant or industrial operation to allow the formation of nitric oxide from nitrogen and oxygen:

$$N_2 + O_2 \rightarrow 2NO$$

As is the case with sulfur dioxide, nitric oxide undergoes a complex variety of reactions by which it is converted to nitrogen dioxide. For example, it too reacts with hydroperoxyl radicals to form nitrogen dioxide:

$$2NO + HO_2{}^\bullet \rightarrow 2NO_2 + HO^\bullet$$

Nitric oxide also reacts with atomic oxygen to produce nitrogen dioxide:

$$NO + O \rightarrow NO_2$$

Finally, nitrogen dioxide is oxidized to nitric acid in a number of ways. For example, it may react with a hydroxyl radical, producing the acid:

$$NO_2 + HO^\bullet \rightarrow HNO_3$$

Nitric acid is very soluble in water, so it dissolves in rain and other forms of precipitation and is carried to Earth's surface in the form of acid deposition.

One reason that the term acid *deposition* is preferred to the term acid *rain* is that sulfuric and nitric acid formed by the processes described may return to Earth's surface in either a wet or a dry form. Wet deposition consists of acids dissolved in water, as occurs in acid rain or acid snow. Dry deposition occurs when acids or nonmetallic oxides remain in gaseous form or adhere to solid particles, on which they are carried to the ground. About half of the components of acid deposition fall back to Earth in each of these two forms, wet and dry.

Acid deposition is sometimes classified as a regional environmental problem in contrast to both smog, which is a local environmental problem, and global warming, which is a *global* environmental problem. The reason for this classification is that the sources of sulfur and nitrogen oxides tend to be far removed from the locations where those chemicals affect the environment. In the United States, for example, the major sources of sulfur oxides are power generating plants located in the midwestern states. Gases released from those plants remain in the atmosphere for about a week. Prevailing winds blowing from the west tend to carry those gases and the pollutants they contain eastward until they are washed out of the atmosphere by precipitation or settle out as dry deposition. By then, the pollutants have reached the northeastern states and the Atlantic provinces of Canada. The average pH of precipitation falling in these regions tends to be about 4.2 to 4.5 compared with more natural levels of 4.9 to 5.3 in the Plains states.

Elsewhere acid deposition tends to be more of a local problem. For example, in the western states, oxides of nitrogen produced by motor vehicles are a more important source of acid rain than is sulfur dioxide. Acid deposition in California, then, is more a consequence of extensive automobile traffic than of power generation.

The environmental effects of acid deposition that have been most thoroughly studied are probably those on lakes, ponds, and other bodies of fresh water. When acid and oxides of sulfur and nitrogen are added to such bodies of water, the pH of the lake or pond tends to decrease. Decreased pH (increased acidity) threatens the survival of aquatic organisms. For example, at a pH of about 6.0, snails and crustaceans begin to die. More sensitive species of fish, such as salmon, whitefish, and rainbow trout, begin to die off at a pH of 5.5. The hardiest aquatic organisms, such as brook trout and eel, are able to survive acidic conditions at pH levels down to 4.5, at which point they too begin to die.

Lakes respond differently to acid deposition, depending on their underlying rocks. Lakes that rest in a hollow of limestone, for example, are protected from acid deposition to some extent by the buffering capacity of the limestone, which is chemically basic:

$$CaCO_3 + 2H^+(aq) \rightarrow Ca^{2+}(aq) + CO_2(g) + H_2O(l)$$

(The symbols (g) and (l) in this equation indicate that the species shown, CO_2 and H_2O, exist as a gas and a liquid, respectively.) The removal of hydrogen ions by calcium carbonate tends to protect the lake from an increase in acidity. By contrast, lakes that are embedded in granite rock do not have this buffering capacity. They tend to become more acidic than do limestone lakes when exposed to the same level of acid deposition.

A combination of geographical, meteorological, geological, and topographic conditions means that some lakes and streams are at greater risk than are others for damage from acid deposition. For example, more than 90 percent of the streams in New Jersey's Pine Barrens area have pH levels low enough to pose a risk to aquatic organisms. About three-quarters of the lakes and half of the streams in the Adirondack Mountains are thought to be highly acidic because of acid deposition.

The components of acid deposition also pose serious threats to plant life. Both nitrogen oxides and sulfur dioxide are toxic to plants. At concentrations of less than 0.1 ppmv, for example, sulfur dioxide begins to inhibit plant growth. At higher concentrations, in the range of 0.1 to 1.0 ppmv, damage to plants is often visible after a few hours of exposure to the gas. Oxides of nitrogen produce similar effects, although they are somewhat more difficult to identify because nitrogen is also a plant *nutrient*. Reduced pH also appears to impair plant growth, both by damaging plant parts and by altering the pH of soil in which they grow.

The most prominent example of damage to plants by acid deposition is probably that to trees. Some environmentalists have blamed acid rain for widespread damage and destruction of forest areas in the northeastern United States, eastern Canada, and many parts of Europe, including the Black Forest of Germany. The observed pattern begins with the yellowing of leaves, a condition known as *chlorosis.* Leaves then begin to turn brown and die. In the absence of leaves to provide nutrients, the tree itself eventually dies. In one study of European forests, conducted in 1999, about a quarter of all trees studied were found to be dead or dying as a result of a combination of environmental factors, the most important of which was probably acid deposition.

The effect of acid deposition on forests remains a topic of some dispute among experts. While there is little doubt that sulfur dioxide and other forms of acid deposition do cause damage to trees, a number of other factors may also be responsible for the widespread die-off of trees observed in forests in Europe and North America over the past 50 years. For example, other elements of polluted air, such as ozone or heavy metals, may also contribute to at least some extent to these disasters.

Some of the most dramatic environmental effects of acid deposition have involved buildings, statues, monuments, and other structures made of metal and stone. The explanation of this kind of damage is obvious: Acids in acid deposition react with metals and with many of the compounds of which rock and other building material are made. For example, corrosion occurs when metals such as iron are exposed to hydrogen ions in the presence of oxygen:

$$2Fe(s) + O_2(g) + 4H^+ \rightarrow 2Fe^{2+}(aq) + 2H_2O(l)$$

As the acidity of the atmosphere increases, the rate at which corrosion occurs is also accelerated.

Similar effects occur with structures made of materials easily attacked by acids, the best example of which is limestone. When limestone (calcium carbonate) is exposed to an acid, the acid dissolves it:

$$CaCO_3 + 2H^+(aq) \rightarrow Ca^{2+}(aq) + CO_2(g) + H_2O(l)$$

Over long periods, the features of stone structures are gradually eroded in an acidic atmosphere, as shown in the photograph.

Oxides of sulfur and nitrogen have harmful effects on humans and other animals, as explained in chapter 2. For example, at concentrations of more than 6 ppm, sulfur dioxide begins to irritate people's lungs and throat, causing throat soreness, difficulty in breathing, coughing, headaches, and nausea. At higher concentrations and in conjunction with other pollutants in the air, it may induce more serious respiratory problems, such as bronchitis and chronic lung disease. Children, the elderly, and those who have respiratory disorders (such as asthma) are at elevated risk for such conditions.

The first major U.S. effort to deal with acid precipitation dates to 1980, when Congress created the National Acid Precipitation Assessment Program (NAPAP). NAPAP's mandate was to carry out

The erosion caused by acid rain is dramatically illustrated by the damage it causes to buildings and works of art, including pieces of sculpture, such as this bas relief in Venice, Italy. (Cristina Pedrazzini/Photo Researchers, Inc.)

A method sometimes used to counteract the effects of acid rain is the addition of a basic substance that will neutralize the water's acidity, lime in the example shown here, to a body of water. (Martin Bond/Photo Researchers, Inc.)

a comprehensive 10-year program of research, monitoring, and assessment on the causes, effects, and controls of acid precipitation. During its first decade, NAPAP produced 27 *State of Science and Technology Reports* on all aspects of acid deposition. In 1990, Congress renewed NAPAP's mandate under Title IV of the 1990 Clean Air Act Amendments, a section titled "Acidic Deposition Control Program." An important feature of that program was the creation of standards for emissions of sulfur and nitrogen oxides. Specifically, the legislation called for (1) a 40 percent reduction in sulfur dioxide emissions by 2010 from a 1980 base, with an eventual national cap of 15 million short tons (13.6 million metric tons), and (2) a reduction of nitrogen oxide emissions from stationary sources of 10 percent by the year 2000 (with no national cap).

These reductions were to be achieved by essentially the same mechanisms used to reduce sulfur dioxide and oxides of nitrogen described in chapter 2, including the use of precombustion cleansing of fuels, improvements in the efficiency of combustion systems, and various postcombustion systems for removing pollutants from flue gases, such as scrubbers and electrostatic precipitators.

Efforts to reduce acid deposition have had mixed results thus far. For example, measurements at five locations in Nova Scotia, New Brunswick, Newfoundland, and Labrador by Canadian researchers found that sulfate deposition dropped between 27 and 50 percent between 1980 and 1995. During the same time, however, there was a significant reduction in acid deposition at only one of the five monitoring sites.

In the northeastern United States, sulfate deposition has also been reduced substantially since the 1980s. The average annual wet deposition of sulfates dropped in three environmentally sensitive areas (the Adirondacks, Mid-Appalachian, and Southern Blue Ridge mountains) by 26, 23, and 9 percent, respectively, from the period 1983–94 to the period 1995–98. That trend is also reflected in data collected from monitoring stations throughout the eastern United States, which show a 26 percent decrease in sulfate deposition between the two monitoring periods, 1983–94 and 1995–98.

Data for wet deposition of nitrogen compounds, however, are not comparable to those for sulfates. Measurements at the same three locations reveal that nitrogen deposition decreased by only 5 and 4 percent, respectively, in the first two regions, and actually increased by 11 percent in the third. Overall trends throughout the eastern United States indicate a reduction in nitrogen wet deposition of only 2 percent.

Similar trends were detected in a more limited study conducted by the Adirondack Lakes Survey Commission during the 1990s. The commission found a reduction of 92 percent in sulfate deposition in a selected sample of lakes in the Adirondack Mountains between 1992 and 1999, but an increase of 48 percent in nitrogen deposition in the same lakes.

These data suggest that the federal government's efforts to reduce sulfur dioxide emissions were successful in reducing the amount of sulfates being deposited in the northeastern United States and Maritime Provinces of Canada. Comparable success for nitrogen deposition has not been observed, however, partly because nonstationary sources of nitrogen emissions—primarily motor vehicles—have continued to increase since 1985.

Depletion of the Ozone Layer

While efforts to solve the problem of acid deposition have met with mixed results, a rather amazing success story can be told for another global environmental problem: depletion of the ozone layer in the stratosphere.

The term *ozone layer* applies to a region of the Earth's atmosphere at a height of 10 to 50 kilometers, in the region known as the stratosphere. This region contains an unusually dense concentration of ozone, the allotrope of oxygen with three atoms per molecule (O_3). The density of ozone within this region is very low, about 8 ppmv, but is significantly greater than in any other region of the atmosphere (except near ground level, where concentrations may be unusually high as a result of human activities).

The existence of an ozone layer was first suggested in 1878 by the French physicist Alfred Cornu (1841–1902), who detected a reduction in the amount of sunlight reaching Earth's surface in the region of the electromagnetic spectrum between 240 and 310 nanometers (nm). Cornu hypothesized that the reduction in sunlight was caused by the presence of some chemical substance in the atmosphere that absorbed the radiation. His suspicions were confirmed two years later when the English chemist Walter Noel Hartley (1846–1913) measured the optical properties of ozone and was able to show that it satisfied the conditions of Cornu's absorber.

The earliest attempts to measure the concentration of ozone in the stratosphere were those of two French physicists, Charles Fabry (1867–1945) and Henri Buisson (1873–1944). In the 1920s, the English meteorologist George M. B. Dobson (1889–1976) expanded and improved upon Fabry and Buisson's work. Dobson devoted most of his professional life to the study of stratospheric ozone, collecting data on ozone concentrations from many locations around the world, at various times of the day and night, and during different seasons of the year. In recognition of his research, the unit now used to measure the concentration of ozone in the stratosphere is called the *dobson.* One dobson unit (DU) is defined as a layer of ozone 0.01 mm thick at standard temperature and pressure (STP: 0 °C and 1 atmosphere [atm]).

One of the positive results of World War II was the development of a host of new technological devices for studying the Earth's atmosphere. The availability of these technologies was one reason that 70 countries banded together to launch a massive program of research on the geological, physical, chemical, astronomical, and meteorological properties of the Earth, known as the International Geophysical Year (IGY). Despite the name, IGY activities actually extended over two calendar years, from 1957 through 1958. One focus of IGY research was a study of the ozone layer, and one of the most important centers for research on that topic was the Halley Research Center in the Antarctic, operated by the British Antarctic Survey (BAS). (BAS has now been collecting data on ozone levels above the South Pole for more than 40 years.) Beginning in the early 1970s, additional data on ozone concentrations over Antarctica were collected by U.S. satellites, particularly the *Nimbus-7* weather satellite.

Among the first BAS discoveries made at Halley Bay was that ozone concentrations above the South Pole fluctuated on a regular basis annually, with concentrations in late spring about 35 percent higher than in winter. "Spring," in this case, refers to austral, or Southern Hemisphere, spring, beginning after about September 15. Further studies conducted over the next two decades consistently confirmed this seasonal variation.

Then, in 1978, a new pattern showed up in the BAS data. Ozone concentrations began to fall off during October, a month during which they had previously reached their highest levels. Decreased ozone levels continued to show up each austral spring, on a regular basis, over the next decade. The new pattern was not a one-year irregularity, but part of a trend. Scientists around the world began to worry that the protective ozone layer was somehow being damaged. The general consensus was that that damage was being caused by some type of human activity.

A number of culprits were suggested. Some researchers hypothesized that the launch of space vehicles or the use of high-flying jet aircraft might be responsible for the destruction of ozone in the stratosphere. Other scientists suspected a group of chemicals known as chlorofluorocarbons (CFCs) as the possible cause for ozone depletion. In one of the landmark studies on ozone depletion, the U.S. scientists Mario Molina (1943–   ) and F. Sherwood Rowland (1927–   ) developed a theory that explained how CFCs released into the stratosphere would attack and destroy ozone molecules, reducing concentrations of the gas in the atmosphere. Molina and Rowland predicted a loss of 7–13 percent of stratospheric ozone over the next century as a result of CFC reactions.

The history of ozone depletion took a dramatic turn in 1985 when J. C. Farman at the BAS Halley Bay station announced that ozone levels over the Antarctic had decreased by more than 40 percent between 1977 and 1984. Farman explained that ozone levels had fallen so low that one could say that a "hole" had formed in the ozone layer above the South Pole. In 1984, that "hole" covered an area of more than 15 million square miles (40 million square kilometers), equal to the size of the continental United States. Clearly, ozone depletion was not a long-term problem about which scientists could debate for the next century or so. It was an issue that demanded quick attention and action.

By 1987, most authorities had become convinced that the primary cause of ozone depletion was the release of CFCs into the atmosphere. CFCs were one of the "wonder chemicals" developed by chemists in the mid-20th century. They were discovered by Thomas Midgley, Jr. (1889–1944), then an employee of the Ethyl Corporation, a company created to produce tetraethyl lead for automotive fuels. At the time of his discovery, Midgley was looking for a new material that could be used as a heat exchange agent (coolant) in refrigerators, freezers, and other cooling systems.

As it turned out, CFCs were ideal for the purpose. The members of this chemical family are nonflammable, noncorrosive, nontoxic, odorless, and very stable. Within a short period, they became widely popular for a variety of industrial applications. In addition to their applications in refrigeration systems, they became popular as aerosol propellants, cleansing agents for electrical and electronic components, and foaming agents in the manufacture

◄ THOMAS MIDGLEY, JR. (1889–1944) ►

Home refrigeration was one of the great inventions of the 20th century. The idea of using some kind of mechanical device for keeping food cold had been proposed and tested as early as 1805. But commercial machines suitable for the average home were not produced until 1914, when the Electro-Automatic Refrigerating Company (later known as the Kelvinator Company) began the manufacture of refrigerators. Such machines were far too expensive for the average family, however, and iceboxes were still the most popular devices for keeping food cold well into the 1930s. The work of Thomas Midgley changed all that, putting effective refrigeration in the home.

Thomas Midgley, Jr., was born in Beaver Falls, Pennsylvania, on May 18, 1889. In 1895 his family moved to Columbus, Ohio, where Midgley attended elementary and high school. In 1905, he enrolled at the Betts Academy in Stamford, Connecticut, to complete his secondary education. Two years later, he was accepted in the mechanical engineering program at Cornell University, from which he received his degree in 1911.

After graduation, Midgley returned to Ohio and took a job at the National Cash Register Company. After only a year in that position, he left to work at a small company founded by his father to make and sell automobile tires. When the company failed in 1916, Midgley went to work for Charles Kettering, one of the nation's greatest inventors and president of Delco Manufacturing (the Dayton Engineering Laboratories Company). One of the first projects that Kettering assigned to Midgley was to find a substance that would reduce the "knocking" that occurs when an internal combustion engine runs on gasoline. Although he was not a chemist, Midgley took on the challenge and, after a five-year search, discovered that tetraethyl lead met all the requirements set by Kettering. Had he made no other important discovery in his life, tetraethyl lead would have ensured Midgley's place in the history of technology. But he also solved the problem of household refrigeration.

of plastics. Production of the two most popular CFCs increased dramatically from the 1950s through the 1980s, peaking at 382,050 metric tons for CFC-11 and 424,726 metric tons for CFC-12 in 1987. By that time, an international effort was under way to reduce the

One of the major problems inherent in the manufacture and use of early refrigerators was that all of the heat exchange media on which they operated—ammonia, butane, sulfur dioxide, and methyl chloride, for example—were either toxic or flammable. Until this problem was overcome, selling consumers on the idea of home refrigeration units posed some serious challenges.

In 1928, Kettering challenged Midgley to solve the problem. "Find us a safe substance to use as a coolant in home refrigerators," Kettering said to Thomas Midgley. And Midgley responded. After combing through the periodic table to find combinations of elements that were likely to produce compounds that were both safe and capable of being used as heat exchange media, Midgley began to test a variety of compounds made of carbon, nitrogen, oxygen, hydrogen, fluorine, chlorine, and bromine. One of those compounds was dichlorodifluoromethane, later to be known as Freon-12. It proved to be the ideal substance for use in home refrigerators and other types of refrigeration systems, as well as having a variety of other valuable properties for many industrial applications—at least until their effect on the ozone layer in the stratosphere was discovered in the last quarter of the 20th century.

After Midgley announced the discovery of Freon-12 in 1930, General Motors and the Du Pont Chemical Company combined to form a new company, Kinetic Chemicals, Inc., for the purpose of making and selling the new product. Midgley was appointed vice president of the new company. Although he continued to hold that title for many more years, much of his later research was conducted in the laboratories at Ohio State University.

Midgley was stricken with polio at the age of 51, a remarkable event since the disease usually afflicts children. He eventually became crippled by the disease, but he invented a system of ropes and pulleys that allowed him to get into and out of bed. On November 2, 1944, he accidentally became entangled in the system and strangled to death. He died at his home in Worthington, Ohio, at the age of 55.

production of chlorofluorocarbons, as a way of preventing further damage to the ozone layer.

Chlorofluorocarbons are chemical compounds that contain carbon, chlorine, and fluorine. The chemical structures, names, and

◁ SOME COMMON CHLOROFLUOROCARBONS ▷

CHEMICAL NAME	FORMULA	COMMON NAME(S)	PHYSICAL STATE (AT ROOM TEMPERATURE)
trichlorofluoromethane	CCl_3F	CFC-11, Freon-11	liquid (boils at 23.7°C)
dichlorodifluoromethane	CCl_2F_2	CFC-12, Freon-12	gas
chlorotrifluoromethane	$CClF_3$	CFC-13, Freon-13	gas
1,2-difluoro-1,1,2,2-tetrachloroethane	CCl_2FCCl_2F	CFC-112, Freon-112	solid
1,1-difluoro-1,2,2,2-tetrachloroethane	$CClF_2CCl_3$	CFC-112a, Freon-112a	solid
1,1,2-trichloro-1,2,2-trifluoroethane	CCl_2FCClF_2	CFC-113, Freon-113	liquid
1,1,1-trichloro-2,2,2-trifluoroethane	CCl_3CF_3	CFC-113a, Freon-113a	liquid
1,2-dichloro-1,1,2,2-tetrafluoroethane	$CClF_2CClF_2$	CFC-114, Freon-114	gas
1,1-dichloro-1,2,2,2-tetrafluoroethane	CCl_2FCF_3	CFC-114a, Freon-114a	gas

physical state of some common CFCs are shown in the table on page 72. CFCs are sold commercially under the trade name *Freon*. Thus, CFC-11 is sold commercially under the name *Freon-11*.

Ozone in the Earth's atmosphere is formed when solar radiation with a wavelength of less than 242 nm causes the dissociation of an oxygen molecule into two oxygen atoms:

$$O_2 + hv \rightarrow O + O$$

Free oxygen atoms formed in this reaction are then available to combine with other oxygen molecules to form ozone:

$$O + O_2 \rightarrow O_3$$

Ozone molecules formed by this reaction are relatively unstable and, in the presence of solar radiation of wavelengths less than 325 nm, dissociate to form oxygen atoms and molecules:

$$O_3 \rightarrow O_2 + O$$

Eventually, an equilibrium is reached between the production and dissociation of ozone that results in the steady-state concentration currently observed in the stratosphere.

The role of CFCs in the destruction of ozone in the stratosphere was something of a surprise to some researchers because those compounds are normally quite stable. In fact, their stability is one of their most desirable properties for many industrial and commercial applications. But, when CFCs escape into the atmosphere and drift upward, they are exposed to ultraviolet radiation in sunlight and, as is oxygen itself, are dissociated by that radiation. In the case of Freon-12 (CCl_2F_2), photo-dissociation results in the formation of free chlorine atoms:

$$CCl_2F_2 + hv \rightarrow CClF_2{}^\bullet + Cl^\bullet$$

Note that the free chlorine atom is also a free radical, a very reactive chemical species that may react with other atoms, molecules, and free radicals with which it has contact. For example, free chlorine reacts with ozone molecules to produce diatomic oxygen and the chlorosyl radical ($ClO^\bullet$):

$$Cl^\bullet + O_3 \rightarrow ClO^\bullet + O_2$$

The chlorosyl radical produced in this reaction tends to react with atomic oxygen, as follows:

$$ClO^\bullet + O \rightarrow Cl^\bullet + O_2$$

The significant feature of this reaction is that it results in the regeneration of chlorine free radicals, which are then available to react with other ozone molecules. In fact, the net result of the preceding two reactions is the dissociation of ozone molecules into diatomic oxygen molecules:

$$O_3 + O \rightarrow 2O_2$$

CFCs are nearly ideal substances for attacking ozone molecules and damaging the ozone layer. On the one hand, they tend to be very stable, even in the stratosphere. Many CFCs have half-lives of 100 years or more; that means that once they have escaped into the upper atmosphere, they are likely to remain there for very long periods. On the other hand, some small number of CFC molecules do dissociate to form chlorine free radicals, with the ability to destroy ozone molecules. Although the number of CFC molecules that do dissociate is relatively small, the actual number is not important since chlorine free radicals that are generated in the process are used over and over again. That is, they are catalysts in the destruction of ozone and are not, themselves, used up in their reactions with ozone molecules.

CFCs are the most important, but by no means the only, chemicals capable of destroying ozone molecules. For many years, researchers have recognized that oxides of nitrogen have the capacity both to increase *and* to decrease the concentration of ozone in the stratosphere. They can increase ozone concentrations in the presence of ultraviolet (uv) radiation by undergoing uv-mediated reactions similar to those that occur in the lower troposphere. For example:

$$NO_2 + h\nu \rightarrow NO + O$$

followed by: $$O + O_2 + h\nu \rightarrow O_3$$

But oxides of nitrogen are more likely to undergo reactions, similar to those involving CFCs, in which ozone is destroyed. For example, nitric oxide is known to act as a catalyst in cycles of stratospheric reactions similar to those in which chlorine acts as a catalyst:

$$NO + O_3 \rightarrow NO_2 + O_2$$
$$NO_2 + O \rightarrow NO + O_2$$

producing a net reaction of:

$$O_3 + O \rightarrow 2O_2$$

Another ozone-destroying cycle involving oxides of nitrogen is the following:

$$NO + O_3 \rightarrow NO_2 + O_2$$
$$NO_2 + O_3 \rightarrow NO_3 + O_2$$
$$NO_3 + hv \rightarrow NO + O_2$$

in which the net reaction is:

$$2O_3 \rightarrow 3O_2$$

As scientists learn more about the chemical processes by which ozone is destroyed in the stratosphere, more options for combating this process become available. But the approach to problems of ozone depletion differs in some significant ways from that to acid rain issues. Regional environmental problems like acid deposition often require the cooperation of two or more nations. Reducing the damage caused by acid rain in the northeastern United States and eastern Canada, for example, has taken the efforts of both governments working in close cooperation. Global environmental problems, such as the issue of ozone depletion, are far more complex, calling for the mutual efforts of nations around the world. Achieving consensus for action in such circumstances is often profoundly difficult. Yet such consensus was achieved in this case, and the problem of ozone depletion has been, if not totally solved, at least dramatically reduced. As the table on page 76 shows, production of CFCs has decreased dramatically over the past seven decades.

Reduction of CFCs has come about as the result of an international effort that was begun at a meeting in Montreal, Canada, in September 1987. At that meeting, 24 nations and the European Community (a group of 12 nations that signed as a single entity)

◀ CFC PRODUCTION: 1930–2000 ▷

YEAR	CFC-11	CFC-12
1930	0	544
1935	45	998
1940	181	4,536
1945	363	20,094
1950	6,623	34,564
1955	26,263	57,606
1960	49,714	99,428
1965	122,833	190,056
1970	238,136	321,099
1975	314,068	380,973
1980	389,619	350,219
1985	326,814	376,339
1990	232,916	230,950
1995	32,683	82,822
2000	9,900	24,564

(Measurement expressed in metric tons)

worked out an agreement by which the production of ozone-depleting chemicals would be reduced over a specific period. The original Montreal Protocol on Substances That Deplete the Ozone Layer set a number of standards for CFC production, including freezing the emissions of CFCs at 1986 levels by 1990, cutting CFC emissions by 20 percent of 1986 levels by 1994, cutting CFC emissions by 50 percent of 1986 levels by 1999, and cutting CFC production by 50 percent by 1999.

The Montreal Protocol also established a research program to monitor the production and emissions of ozone-depleting chemicals and changes in the concentration of ozone in the stratosphere. As results of these studies became available, scientists concluded that the Montreal Protocol was too conservative and warned that stronger action was needed to protect the ozone layer. As a consequence, signatories to the Montreal Protocol (now numbering more than 100 nations) met again in London in 1990 and once more in Copenhagen in 1992, each time to consider more rigorous bans on the production of ozone-depleting chemicals. At the Copenhagen session, 78 nations agreed to an accelerated schedule for an end to the production of CFCs and other ozone-depleting chemicals. The new goal for a total phase-out of CFC production was set for January 1, 1996, and for halons, a group of CFC-like compounds that contain carbon and fluorine only, January 1, 1994.

What has been the effect of all these efforts? Unfortunately, there is no simple answer to that question. On the one hand, it is relatively simple to find out how much ozone-depleting substances are being produced each year and how much is being emitted into the atmosphere. Current evidence suggests that the efforts initiated with the Montreal Protocol are working very well indeed. Production of CFC-11 dropped by 97 percent during the period 1980–2000, and production of CFC-12 dropped by 93 percent during the same period. Reductions in emissions followed a similar pattern, with the release of CFC-11 and CFC-12 dropping by 84 percent and 85 percent, respectively, during the 1980–2000 period.

But does that mean that the *ozone hole* has started to disappear? That question is more difficult to answer. The concentration of ozone over the Antarctic, as measured at the Halley Bay station, did decrease from 1957 to 1972, but it appears to have remained essentially constant since that time. The problem is that changes in the atmosphere often take place very slowly. One cannot hope to make sudden and dramatic changes in the production and release of ozone-depleting chemicals on the Earth and see comparable changes in the atmosphere. Indeed, in its February 2003 report, the BAS research team posed the question, "Is the ozone hole recovering?" and then answered that question as follows:

> Recent measurements at surface monitoring stations show that the loading of ozone destroying chemicals at the surface has been dropping since about 1994 and is now about 6 percent down on that peak. The stratosphere lags behind the surface by several years and the loading of ozone depleting chemicals in the ozone layer is at or near the peak. The small size of this year's ozone hole is therefore nothing to do with any reduction in ozone depleting chemicals and it will be a decade or more before we can unambiguously say that the ozone hole is recovering. It will be the middle of this century or beyond before the ozone hole ceases to appear over Antarctica.

What does seem to be clear is that *without* the international agreements reached in Montreal, London, and Copenhagen, the problem of ozone depletion would probably have been much worse than it is today. The graph on page 79 shows the trends in ozone depletion (as measured by the concentration of chlorine in the stratosphere) that would have been seen in the absence of no agreement at all, with the Montreal Protocol alone, and with later amendments to that agreement.

One of the most serious challenges to arise in the effort to stop ozone depletion has been the search for chemicals that can be used in place of CFCs in their many industrial applications. The most promising substitutes seem to be a class of compounds known as hydrochlorofluorocarbons (HCFCs). HCFCs are similar to CFCs in that they contain carbon, chlorine, and fluorine, but they also include hydrogen.

Although HCFCs are less satisfactory than CFCs in many industrial applications, they have one major advantage: They tend to be more stable in the stratosphere, decomposing less easily, and they

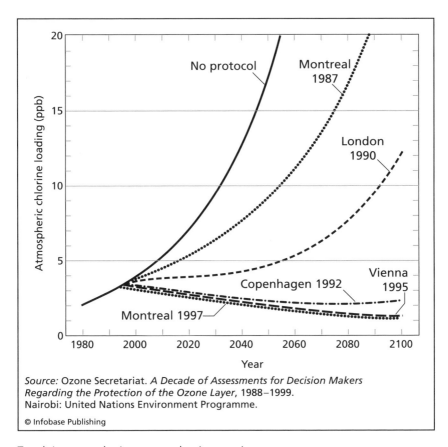

Source: Ozone Secretariat. *A Decade of Assessments for Decision Makers Regarding the Protection of the Ozone Layer*, 1988–1999. Nairobi: United Nations Environment Programme.

© Infobase Publishing

Trends in stratospheric ozone under six scenarios

are, therefore, less likely to produce chlorine radicals that can attack ozone. A compound's relative effectiveness in destroying ozone is measured as its *ozone-depleting potential,* or ODP, as compared with the ODP of CFC-11, which is arbitrarily assigned a value of 1.0 for its tendency to attack and destroy ozone in the atmosphere. The table on page 80 shows ODP values of several ozone-depleting chemicals. As the table indicates, HCFCs have considerable advantage over CFCs in this regard.

Global Climate Change

If the attempt to reduce ozone depletion can be said to be largely a success, and the battle against acid rain at least partly won, efforts

◁ OZONE-DEPLETING POTENTIAL (ODP) OF COMMON CFCS AND HCFCS ▷

COMPOUND	ODP
CFC-11	1.0
CFC-12	1.0
CFC-113	0.8
CFC-114	1.0
CFC-115	0.6
HCFC-22	0.055
HCFC-123	0.02
HCFC-124	0.022

to deal with massive changes in the atmosphere that cause global warming and climate change must be said thus far to have been largely unsuccessful.

The term *global warming* refers to a trend in which the average annual temperature of the Earth's atmosphere increases over long periods, that is, over many decades. As such, it reflects a significant and lasting change in the Earth's climate, not simply short-term alterations in its weather patterns. Most scientists agree that this trend is a consequence of chemical changes that take place on Earth's surface, primarily the combustion of coal, oil, and natural gas, although a variety of other chemical changes produced by human activities contribute to the process also.

Many experts prefer to call this trend *climate change* since fluctuations in temperature, precipitation, and other climatic variables usually do not occur to the same extent over all parts of the globe. That is, even though the Earth's average annual temperature seems to be increasing, these increases are more pronounced in some areas in others. Indeed, average temperatures may actually be decreasing in some specific regions of the planet.

Fluctuations in the Earth's average annual temperature over long periods are a normal and natural aspect of the planet's climate patterns. There is abundant evidence that at some times in the past the Earth has been much colder than it is now and at other times it has been much warmer.

For example, written records and archaeological evidence confirm that climatic conditions in Iceland, Greenland, Scandinavia, and North America were significantly milder during the first millennium of the common era. Iceland was settled in 874 C.E. by Vikings from Norway, one of whom, Erik the Red, established the first colonies in Greenland a century later in 986. During this period, conditions were apparently warm enough to permit the establishment of thriving communities and farms that supported more than 3,000 people. Greenland apparently earned its name, in fact, because of the lush environment early settlers first encountered in some parts of the subcontinent.

Later voyages by Viking explorers to North America found farms and vineyards in Labrador and other northerly regions that are much too cold for such enterprises today. During the same period, the Inuit were apparently able to fish in portions of the Arctic Sea that are now filled with ice. Similar conditions existed in northern Europe, where grapes grew successfully throughout Great Britain and farms were established at high elevations throughout most of Scandinavia.

Periods of warming, such as those experienced by Viking explorers, typically occur when relatively modest changes in the Earth's average annual temperature take place. For example, researchers believe that the warming conditions of the ninth and 10th centuries occurred when the Earth's average annual temperature increased by only about 3.5°F (2°C).

By the middle of the second millennium, changes began to occur in the Earth's climate, with temperatures dropping by 3.5°F–7°F (2°C–4°C). Scientists now refer to this period, which lasted from about 1400 to about 1850 in Europe, as the Little Ice Age. During the Little Ice Age, settlements in Greenland, Iceland, North America, and Scandinavia had to be abandoned as the climate became too cold to support agriculture. Alpine glaciers began to move down from the mountains, covering villages and filling in valleys that had been green and lush only a few centuries earlier. Most of the Netherlands's canals were filled with ice, disrupting the nation's system of transportation. Sea ice began to fill up much of the North Atlantic, essentially destroying the fishing industry in Iceland and many parts of Scandinavia. In China the thriving orange groves of Jiang-Xi province, which had remained luxuriant for more than three centuries, were frozen and destroyed.

The cycle of warming and cooling just described is only the most recent of many similar periods of climate change. Scientists now believe that Earth has gone through many such changes, dating back to the planet's very beginning about 4.6 billion years ago. They have constructed a chronology of climate change that can be divided into seven major cycles of warming and cooling known as ice eras. Each of these eras is characterized by a relatively short period of about 50 million years during which the Earth's annual temperature has been significantly cooler than average.

Virtually nothing is known about the first six of these ice eras because they occurred so long ago. But the final era, which began about 65 million years ago, is relatively well understood and is known to have itself consisted of six distinct warming and cooling trends, known as ice epochs. Finally, each ice epoch can be further subdivided into shorter cycles, known as ice ages. The last ice epoch, which began about 2.4 million years ago, has been well studied and found to consist of 23 ice ages.

How is it possible to explain these dramatic changes in Earth's climate? The answer to that question was provided by the Serbian mathematician Milutin Milankovitch (1879–1958). Over a period of three decades, between 1912 and 1941, Milankovitch investigated the effects of three long-term astronomical variations responsible for Earth's climate. The first of these variations is a change in the shape of the Earth's orbit around the Sun. Over a 100,000-year period, that orbit changes from a nearly perfect circle to an elongated ellipse. When it travels in a circular orbit, the Earth receives approximately the same amount of solar energy year round. In an elliptical orbit, the sunlight is significantly more intense at some times of the year than at others.

The second variation is in the Earth's tilt relative to its orbit around the Sun. That tilt varies from a maximum of 24.5 degrees to a minimum of 21.5 degrees over a 41,000-year period. The angle at which sunlight strikes the Earth's surface—and, therefore, the amount of heat absorbed by the surface—varies according to the angle of tilt.

A final variation involves the direction at which the Earth's axis points. Today, the axis points at the star known as Polaris, the North Star. But very slowly over time, the orientation of the axis changes, pointing in a slightly different direction. After about 12,000 years, the axis will be pointing toward the star known as Vega, which will then become the new "North Star." This 23,000-year variation is known as axial precession, or precession of the equinoxes, and because of it Earth's surface receives different amounts of solar radiation over the 23,000-year period.

Milkanovitch's great achievement was his ability to show in mathematical detail how the combination of these three astronomical factors could explain changes in the amount of heat energy received by the Earth and, hence, the long-term changes in annual average temperature that were responsible for global cooling and warming.

A knowledge of the astronomical variations identified by Milkanovitch is essential to understanding overall trends in climate change. But a number of other factors—most of which have a chemical basis—also affect climate change. One of these factors is the process by which the planet captures and stores heat from sunlight. Some of the earliest research on this topic was conducted by the French mathematician Jean-Baptiste Fourier (1768–1830). As early as 1807, Fourier began to write about the atmosphere as a giant greenhouse in which sunlight is captured and converted into heat energy. The atmosphere acts, Fourier said, as the windows in a greenhouse do. It is transparent to sunlight, which it allows to pass through on its way downward toward the Earth. But it prevents heat radiation reflected off the ground from passing outward, back into space.

Although Fourier's "greenhouse" analogy is not strictly correct, it provides a simple explanation of how the atmosphere traps heat that is still generally accepted. Fourier placed relatively little emphasis on the "greenhouse effect" in long-term climatic variations, however, as he believed that astronomical factors were far more important in determining these effects. For example, he made no effort to explain the chemical process by which heat is retained in the atmosphere.

The first attempt to solve that problem was made by the English physicist John Tyndall (1820–93) in the early 1860s. Tyndall studied the absorption of infrared radiation ("heat") by various substances found in the atmosphere, including nitrogen, oxygen, carbon dioxide, and water. He found that water was by far the most efficient absorber of infrared radiation, with carbon dioxide the next most efficient substance. Water, said Tyndall, "acts more energetically upon the terrestrial rays than upon the solar rays; hence, its tendency is to preserve to the earth a portion of heat which would otherwise be radiated into space." The same could be said for carbon dioxide, he believed, but to a lesser extent. Tyndall concluded from his research that changes in the concentration of water, carbon dioxide, and other atmospheric gases might be responsible for "all the mutations of climate which the researches of geologists reveal."

The role of carbon dioxide in global climate patterns was also a topic of great interest to the Swedish chemist Svante Arrhenius (1859–1927). During the early 1900s, Arrhenius became interested in ice ages and how they might have been produced. He eventually concluded that changes in the amount of carbon dioxide released by natural processes might account for significant increases and decreases in the Earth's average annual temperature. He calculated that a decrease of about 7°F (4°C) would be sufficient to bring about an ice age, and conversely, an increase of the same amount would cause the end of an ice age.

Arrhenius recognized that carbon dioxide released from anthropogenic sources, primarily the burning of coal, would contribute to these changes. But he believed that the amount of carbon dioxide from anthropogenic sources at the time of his writing was so small as to have little or no effect on climatic changes. In fact, he predicted that it would take 3,000 years for the carbon dioxide released from anthropogenic sources to have any effect at all on climate. Of course, his prediction was based on the rate of coal combustion in 1900, a rate that was even then increasing quite rapidly.

Arrhenius's analysis of the "greenhouse effect" did not arouse much concern among fellow scientists or the general public. In fact, the world was just recovering from the Little Ice Age, and many people thought that a warmer climate was not necessarily a bad thing. One of Arrhenius's colleagues, the great German physical chemist Hermann Walther Nernst (1864–1941), even suggested the possibility of setting fire to unused coal seams in order to release more carbon dioxide and increase the Earth's annual average temperature.

The English steam engineer Guy Stewart Callendar (1897–1964) held a similar view. In the 1930s, he made the first attempt to show that human activities were, in fact, responsible for significant changes in the concentration of carbon dioxide in the atmosphere and, hence, for changes that might be taking place in the Earth's climate. As did Arrhenius, Nernst, and other earlier scientists, Callendar suggested that these changes were, on balance, desirable since they were likely to benefit agriculture in the north temperate zone and would act as a safeguard against the onset of another ice age.

Whatever messages Tyndall, Arrhenius, Callendar, and their colleagues may have had about climate change, they were generally not regarded as "warnings" to the general public about the threats of a warmer planet. To the contrary, between 1940 and 1965 the planet's annual average temperature decreased slightly, about 0.5 °F (0.3 °C); the decrease was sufficiently great in some regions (up to 7 °F; 4 °C), to cause some observers to warn about the beginning of a new ice age on Earth.

Discussions of climate change reached a turning point toward the end of the 1950s, to some extent as a result of new data obtained from International Geophysical Year studies on the Earth's climate. By far the most important factor in this change, however, was the research of Charles David Keeling (1928–2005), then a postdoctoral student at the Scripps Institution of Oceanography, at La Jolla, California. In 1957, Keeling began to measure the concentration of carbon dioxide in the atmosphere above the volcano Mauna Loa in Hawaii and at the South Pole. It took more than a decade for a clear trend to emerge from those data. But by the time Earth Day 1970 had arrived, scientists were beginning to recognize that the composition of the Earth's atmosphere was changing.

Keeling summarized those changes in a graph that has now become one of the most famous diagrams in modern scientific history, the "Keeling curve" (see the graph below). The curve shows a gradual but regular increase in the concentration of carbon dioxide at Keeling's two monitoring stations—which presumably extends throughout the Earth's atmosphere. The annual vertical fluctuations in the graph reflect the regular variations of carbon dioxide concentrations *within* each year, increasing during one season and decreasing during another.

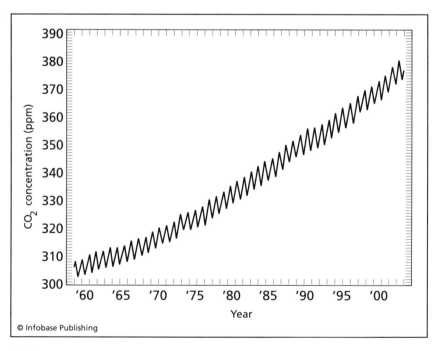

© Infobase Publishing

Keeling curve

By the end of the 1970s, a large portion of the scientific community, many governmental and political leaders, and a significant fraction of the general public were convinced that climate change had become a major environmental issue. In 1977 David Slade, a manager in the U.S. Energy Research Development Administration (later the Department of Energy), called a meeting of scientists to discuss a plan of research on the role of carbon dioxide in climate change. A year later, President Jimmy Carter's science adviser, Frank Press, asked the U.S. National Academy of Sciences to conduct a study of the greenhouse effect and the role of anthropogenic carbon dioxide in that effect. The panel later reported that, on the basis of current trends, anthropogenic carbon dioxide releases might lead to an annual increase in average global temperatures by 6°F ± 3°F (3°C ± 1.5°C). Also in 1979, the United Nations's World Meteorological Organization sponsored the First World Climate Conference in Geneva, Switzerland, a meeting devoted to the study of global climate change, drought, and related environmental issues.

During the mid-1970s, another very important discovery was announced by the Indian-born American meteorologist Veerabhadran Ramanathan (1944–   ), whose contributions to the field of climate change are discussed in the sidebar on page 88. Ramanathan found that CFCs and other ozone-depleting gases were also strong absorbers of infrared radiation. In fact, some CFCs were more than 10,000 times as efficient as heat absorbers as carbon dioxide itself. It suddenly became clear that concerns about climate change could not focus on carbon dioxide alone but must extend to *any* chemical compound with the ability to absorb heat radiated from the Earth. Today, all such gases are classified together as *greenhouse gases.* Any discussions about the nature of global warming and efforts to deal with that problem involve not only the release of carbon dioxide into the atmosphere but the release of *all* greenhouse gases.

Research on global climate change poses some of the most daunting challenges to scientists of any environmental problem. It involves many complex human and natural factors interacting in ways that are often poorly understood by scientists, requiring researchers to

◄ VEERABHADRAN RAMANATHAN (1944–) ►

Scientists have known for more than a century that the presence of carbon dioxide in the atmosphere is a major reason that the Earth is able to retain heat, providing a hospitable environment for plants and animals that live on the planet. They have also known for some time that the release of carbon dioxide into the atmosphere by human activities, such as the burning of fossil fuels, was likely to enhance the atmosphere's heat-trapping properties and, possibly, to increase Earth's annual average temperature. But few scientists considered the possibility that gases other than carbon dioxide might be as efficient, or even more efficient, at trapping heat until 1985, when Veerabhadran Ramanathan and his colleague, Ralph Cicerone, proved it was so.

Veerabhadran Ramanathan was born in Madras (now called Chennai), India, on November 24, 1944. He earned his bachelor of engineering degree from Annamalai University in 1965, his master of science degree at the Indian Institute of Science in Bangalore in 1970, and his doctorate in atmospheric sciences (planetary atmospheres) from the State University of New York at Stony Brook in 1974. After spending a year as a research fellow at the National Aeronautics and Space Administration's (NASA's) Langley Research Center, he began a long affiliation with the National Center for Atmospheric Research (NCAR) in Boulder, Colorado.

It was there that Ramanathan and Cicerone discovered the potential of chlorofluorcarbons (CFCs) to trap atmospheric heat. Indeed, they demonstrated that some CFCs were 10,000 times as efficient as carbon dioxide in capturing infrared radiation from the Earth's surface. The announcement

deal with a variety of questions. For example, what is the long-term fate of higher concentrations of carbon dioxide in the atmosphere, observed by Keeling and others? Will the gas remain in the air for dozens or hundreds of years? Or will it be absorbed by the oceans or used up during photosynthesis by plants?

In spite of the many questions about possible future climate changes, many authorities now accept a general scenario that they think can reasonably predict future climate trends. It is based on a number of assumptions about climate, some of which can be reshowed that a family of compounds already in bad repute because of their effect on the ozone layer—the CFCs—posed another and equally dangerous risk to the planet.

Since 1990, Ramanathan has been Victor C. Alderson Professor of Applied Ocean Sciences and Professor of Climate and Atmospheric Sciences at the Scripps Institution of Oceanography in San Diego. In 1991 he was appointed director of the Center for Clouds, Chemistry, and Climate at Scripps, and in 1996, he became director of the Center for Atmospheric Sciences at the institution.

Ramanathan's primary research interests have been in the fields of climate dynamics, global warming, the greenhouse effect, global climate models, and the effects of clouds and aerosols on climate. In 2003, Ramanathan reported some interesting findings resulting from his most recent research on cloud patterns over the Indian Ocean. He announced that an enormous brown cloud more than 1.6 miles (three kilometers) thick had formed over the Indian Ocean from particulates formed from automotive exhaust and the burning of wood. The cloud was unlike typical clouds, in which water droplets typically become large enough to coalesce, condense, and fall to Earth as precipitation. The Indian Ocean clouds, Ramanathan pointed out, show little or no tendency to settle out. Instead, they are likely to remain suspended in the atmosphere for long periods, significantly affecting the climate of the region surrounding the Indian Ocean.

Ramanathan has been awarded many honors, including the Volvo Environmental Prize in 1997 and the Rossby Medal of the American Meteorological Society in 2002. He was elected to the National Academy of Sciences in 2002.

garded as essentially proved, others as probably true, and still others as possibly true, but still uncertain.

One point about which there is essentially no dispute is the change in carbon dioxide concentration in the atmosphere. Studies seem to show conclusively that the amount of carbon dioxide increased from about 280 ppmv during the Industrial Revolution to about 380 ppmv in early 2006. Most scientists agree that this increase is the result of increased use of fossil fuel by humans, although a small number of authorities dispute this conclusion and suggest that natural variations in biological processes on Earth may account for the increase.

Virtually all scientists also accept the fact that the past three decades has been a period of distinct warming in Earth's climate. Measurements indicate that the 10 warmest years in the 20th century were recorded in the 1980s and 1990s. The warmest of those years, 1998, may have been the warmest year since the end of the Little Ice Age. That warming trend has continued into the first decade of the 21st century. The average global temperature has increased by about $1°F$ ($0.6°C$) over the last century. These data have not been challenged by any leaders in the field of meteorology or climatology.

Less certainty exists about the possible effects of these increased temperatures. Most scientists agree that, for two reasons, the volume of the oceans is likely to increase. First, many large ice packs, such as those found in the Antarctic, are likely to melt. Second, increases in temperature will cause water in the oceans to expand. As a consequence, sea levels are likely to rise and inundate low-lying coastal areas around the world.

Experts also tend to agree that warmer temperatures will increase the rate at which water evaporates from the oceans, resulting in an increase in cloud formation. Some types of clouds ("white" clouds) may reflect more sunlight back into space and reduce global warming, while other types of clouds ("black" clouds) may absorb sunlight, further increasing the amount of sunlight trapped by the atmosphere. Both of these scenarios are possible, and no one can yet say which one will predominate.

Differences of opinion exist as to the effects of increased temperatures, more extensive oceans, and a greater volume of cloud cover on weather patterns. Most authorities agree that the number and severity of storms will increase, that some regions will have greater rainfall and some less, and that some regions will become warmer and others cooler. Beyond these general observations, however, a considerable difference of opinion exists as to the specific changes in weather than global climate change may produce.

The greatest differences of opinion occur as to the way climate change may affect biological life on Earth. In particular, some experts believe that the geographic range in which crops can be grown will increase. They point out that crop distribution patterns a century or two from now may be very different from what they are today. They also believe that public health systems may face very different challenges than those encountered today. Weather conditions may encourage the spread of disease-causing organisms (such as mosquitoes), which, in turn, will extend the areas in which tropical and subtropical diseases may exist.

After two decades of research on climate change, a broad range of opinions still exists as to whether global warming is taking place, what its possible causes are, what effects it may have on the environment and on humans, and what, if anything, should be done to prevent its continuation. Spokespersons for the extremes in this debate—as well as for every position in between those extremes—can easily be found. For example, the Australian John McLean, who says he has had an "amateur interest in global warming" for many years, has written a paper entitled "The Disputed Science of Global Warming," in which he asserts:

> (1) Any current warming of the earth is small and is probably quite normal climate variability, (2) There is no noticeable increase in the frequency of extreme weather events, (3) Talk of rising sea levels is alarmist and not supported by data, (4) Despite claims to the contrary, research shows that temperatures and carbon dioxide levels have been higher than today, (5) The current level of carbon dioxide is no cause for alarm, . . . and (7) An increase in the level of carbon dioxide is not the cause of global warming.

At the opposite extreme, President Bill Clinton released a new report on climate change in November 2000 with the warning that "projected warming threatens serious harm to our environment and to our economy."

The consensus of scientists with expertise in climate and weather issues appears to be that global warming is of sufficient concern to demand some form of political action. They argue that it is more prudent to act now to reduce emissions of carbon dioxide and other greenhouse gases and reduce the risk of global warming than to delay further and possibly further increase the threat of serious climate disruptions.

That view has also carried the day among most of the world's political leaders. In 1997 representatives from 159 nations met in Kyoto, Japan, to negotiate a treaty that would require controls to reduce the amount of carbon dioxide and other greenhouse gases they released to the atmosphere. A similar treaty, based on *voluntary* quotas, had originally been signed as part of the 1992 United Nations Conference on Environment and Development in Rio de Janeiro, Brazil. But the passage of five years proved that voluntary restraints were essentially useless, as emissions of carbon dioxide and other greenhouse gases continued to rise in almost every nation of the world. The goal of the Kyoto conference was to persuade nations to agree to *compulsory* limitations on emissions of carbon dioxide and other greenhouse gases.

After some dramatic last-minute bargaining, a draft document was accepted by the conference and signed by all who attended. The final document called for reductions in carbon dioxide and other greenhouse gas emissions ranging from 6 percent below 1990 levels for Japan to 8 percent below those levels for members of the European Union. (The United States was assigned a 7 percent reduction.) The treaty was scheduled to go into effect when 55 nations accounting for at least 55 percent of all global carbon dioxide emissions had ratified the treaty.

As of July 2006, 164 nations accounting for 61.6 percent of the world's carbon dioxide emissions had ratified or accepted the treaty. About 30 (mostly small) nations have never taken a position on the treaty. These nations include Afghanistan, Andorra, Angola, Brunei, Central African Republic, Chad, Comoros, Gabon, Iraq, Saint Kitts and Nevis, San Marino, Sao Tome and Principe, Serbia, Sierra Leone, Tajikistan, Timor-Leste, Tonga, Turkey, Zimbabwe, Republic of China (Taiwan), and Vatican City. Only two nations have signed but declined to ratify the treaty, Australia and the United States.

Debate over treaty ratification was especially intense in the United States, where many observers felt that cutting back on emissions of carbon dioxide would place a huge hardship on the economy. One opponent of the treaty, Gail McDonald, president of the industry-based Global Climate Coalition, announced after the Kyoto conference that reducing carbon dioxide emissions would result in "canceling an expected 26 percent increase in America's economic growth." Reflecting this view, President George Bush announced in March 2001 that the treaty would not be sent to the Senate for ratification and that it was, therefore, for all intents and purposes, "dead."

A year later, Bush announced his own approach to the problem of climate change. In February 2002, he outlined a voluntary system by which industries would be encouraged to reduce the emission of greenhouse gases by 18 percent by the year 2010. In addition, $4.6 billion would be allotted to the nation's climate change effort in the next five years, 65 percent of which would go to research on the problem and development of new technologies.

A panel of 17 environmental experts convened by the National Academy of Sciences adopted an unfavorable report on the president's plan, however. They said that the plan lacked "most of the basic elements of a strategic plan: a guiding vision, executable goals, clear timetables and criteria for measuring progress." They were also concerned that the plan missed the opportunity to cooperate with other countries on research on climate change issues.

By the end of 2004, the debate over climate change was essentially stalled. On the one hand, climate researchers continued to report on problems that appeared to be connected with global warming. For example, researchers from the Norwegian-based Nansen Environmental and Remote Sensing Center predicted that Arctic sea ice will have essentially disappeared by the end of the 21st century. And phenologists (scientists who study the effect of climate on breeding patterns in animals) announced that breeding cycles have begun to begin at a significantly earlier date and to spread out over wider geographical areas as a result, they believe, of increased annual global temperatures. And, finally, meteorologists reported that 2002 was the second-warmest year in recorded history.

On the other hand, many government officials and leaders of industry continue to argue that there are still too many unanswered questions about climate change to initiate social and political action. In December 2002, for example, the White House science and technology adviser John Marburger told the press that the Bush administration was still not ready to consider legislation dealing with greenhouse gas emissions. "What we are arguing," he said, "is that we need more information to have a clearly articulated regulatory policy that is practical, that's affordable and doesn't put the economy at risk."

4

CHEMISTRY OF
WATER POLLUTION

Water pollution occurs in many different forms, is produced in a variety of ways, and has a range of effects on the biological and physical environment. Consider some common examples:

➤ A river dashing down a steep mountainside cuts into its rocky bed and carries away sand, silt, and pebbles. When the river reaches flat ground, it deposits these materials on the river bottom.

➤ A farmer spreads herbicides, pesticides, and fertilizer on her land, knowing the increase in crop value this practice will produce. During the next rain, some of those chemicals are washed away into the nearest lake, where they remain suspended for weeks or months.

➤ A small crack develops in an underwater pipe that carries oil from an offshore drilling rig to a holding tank on land. Crude oil seeps out of the crack and into the ocean, where marine plants and animals are exposed to its toxic effects.

Pollution problems differ for various bodies of water. For example, the most serious form of pollution for rivers and streams in the United States is siltation, which causes virtually no significant harmful effects in the oceans. The accumulation of toxic metals, on the other hand, is a relatively minor problem in rivers and streams, but a more important problem in estuaries.

Common Pollutants and Sources

Traditionally, the most serious water pollutants have been divided into seven major categories: (1) oxygen-depleting substances, (2) nutrients, (3) *sedimentation* and siltation, (4) pathogens, (5) *toxic organic chemicals,* (6) heavy metals, (7) acidity, and (8) heat. The table on page 97 shows the major pollutants and major sources of pollutants in various types of water in the United States. Although two of these categories—pathogens and heat—are not chemical forms of water pollution, no discussion of this topic is complete without some mention of their role. In addition, chemical principles may be involved in the elimination of these sources of water pollution.

This classification of water pollutants does not reflect one important point about the status of water pollution today, however. It fails to make clear the extent to which water pollution problems in the United States and the rest of the world are changing. Consider the following example.

Between 1999 and 2000, the U.S. Geological Survey (USGS) carried out a study of 139 streams and rivers in 30 states. The purpose of the study was to determine the concentration of certain chemicals usually not thought of as water pollutants. These chemicals included human and veterinary drugs (including antibiotics), natural and synthetic hormones, detergents and products of detergent degradation, plasticizers, insecticides, and fire retardants. A total of 95 chemicals belonging to these categories were targeted for study.

USGS researchers found that at least one of these chemicals was present in more than 80 percent of the rivers and streams examined. Half of the streams had seven or more of the chemicals, and about a third contained 10 or more. The most common substances encountered were coprostanol (a fecal steroid), cholesterol, N,N-diethyltoluamide (an insect repellent), caffeine, triclosan (a disinfectant), tri(2-chloroethyl) phosphate (a fire retardant), and 4-nonylphenol (a product of the degradation of detergents). None of the chemicals found occurred in very high concentrations. For the less common chemicals, concentrations sometimes ranged as low as less than 1

◄ MAJOR POLLUTANTS AND SOURCES OF POLLUTION IN U.S. WATERS ►

BODY OF WATER	MAJOR POLLUTANTS (IN ORDER OF IMPORTANCE)	MAJOR SOURCES OF POLLUTION (IN ORDER OF IMPORTANCE)
Rivers and streams	Pathogens	Agriculture
	Sedimentation	Hydro-modification*
	Habitat alteration	Habitat modification
	Oxygen-depleting substances	Urban runoff/storm sewers
Lakes	Nutrients	Agriculture
	Metals	Hydro-modification*
	Sedimentation	Urban runoff/storm sewers
	Oxygen-depleting substances	Nonpoint sources**
Estuaries	Metals	Municipal sewers
	Pesticides	Urban runoff/storm sewers

(continues)

◄ **MAJOR POLLUTANTS AND SOURCES OF POLLUTION IN U.S. WATERS** *(continued)* ➤

BODY OF WATER	MAJOR POLLUTANTS (IN ORDER OF IMPORTANCE)	MAJOR SOURCES OF POLLUTION (IN ORDER OF IMPORTANCE)
	Oxygen-depleting substances	Industrial discharges
	Pathogens	Atmospheric deposition
Wetlands	Causes of degradation	Sources of degradation
	Sedimentation	Agriculture
	Flow alterations	Construction
	Nutrients	Hydro-modification*
	Filling and draining	Urban runoff
Groundwater	Major sources of contamination	
	Underground storage tanks	Septic systems

BODY OF WATER	MAJOR POLLUTANTS (IN ORDER OF IMPORTANCE)	MAJOR SOURCES OF POLLUTION (IN ORDER OF IMPORTANCE)
	Landfills	Spills

*Changes in river, stream, coastal, and other water resources (such as changing the course of a river) to achieve some desirable outcome, such as reduction in flooding of adjacent lands.

**Forms of pollution that cannot be assigned to some specific source, such as an individual plant or group of factories or a broken pipe.

Source: 2000 National Water Quality Inventory. Washington, D.C.: Environmental Protection Agency, Office of Water, 2002. Available online: http://www.epa.gov/305b/2000report/.

ppb (part per billion). For other chemicals, the concentrations were somewhat higher.

The problem noted by USGS researchers is that virtually nothing is known about the potential effects on human or other animal health of most of these chemicals. Minimal safe standards have been set for only 14. Yet 33 of the substances are known to be active as hormones in the human body, and 46 are pharmaceutically active (that is, they produce druglike effects in one way or another). Thus it is difficult to say whether the concentrations observed in the study represent a threat at any level to humans or other animals. As illustrated in the sidebar on page 100 about the work of John Cairns, Jr., scientists are developing a better understanding of more familiar water pollutants, developing methods for controlling them, and improving the general quality of water resources. Yet they also face new and unexpected problems that are now beginning to appear.

◁ JOHN CAIRNS, JR. (1923–   ) ▷

In 1969, the French toxicologist René Truhaut (1909–94) suggested a name for a new and growing field of environmental research. He defined the term *ecotoxicology* for the study of the adverse effects of chemicals on natural species and populations. One of the leading scientists in that field has long been John Cairns, Jr., a researcher, teacher, and prolific author.

John Cairns, Jr., was born in the steel town of Conshohocken, Pennsylvania, on May 8, 1923. His parents encouraged him to consider attending college, a step that was unusual for high school graduates of Conshohocken. Cairns was accepted at Pennsylvania State University (PSU) in 1940 but had to withdraw two years later when the United States entered World War II. He served in the U.S. Navy for four years, receiving his discharge in 1946. He then enrolled at Swarthmore College (because PSU was unable to provide housing for married veterans), which awarded him a bachelor's degree in biology in 1947. He then began graduate studies at the University of Pennsylvania, from which he received his M.S. and Ph.D. degrees in biology in 1949 and 1953, respectively.

Cairns began working at the Academy of Natural Sciences in Philadelphia in 1948. His first job was as an assistant to Ruth Patrick, the senior curator at the academy. Since no formal courses in environmental pollution were then being taught in colleges and university, Cairns received most of his training through on-the-job research. His master's thesis, for example, was based on his academy work with Patrick, a study of the effects of pollution in the Conestoga River on microbial communities living in the river.

Oxygen-depleting Substances

Almost all living organisms, including those that live in water, need oxygen to survive. The concentration of dissolved oxygen needed can survive at relatively low concentrations of oxygen. For most fish, oxygen concentrations must remain in the range of 3–4 mg/L (milligrams of oxygen per liter of water). These levels are too low for larvae and juvenile fish, however, which require a minimum of 5–8 mg/L for survival.

When Ruth Patrick retired from the post of curator of limnology at the academy in 1961, Cairns was selected as her replacement. He held that position for five years before accepting an appointment as professor of zoology at the University of Kansas. In 1968, Cairns left Kansas to accept a post as research professor of zoology at Virginia Tech. Two years later, he became director of the University Center for Environmental and Hazardous Materials Study at Virginia Tech and, in 1972, was appointed University Distinguished Professor, a post he held until his formal retirement 24 years later.

Cairns has spent virtually his entire life studying and writing about the way in which ecosystems respond to stresses, especially those caused by human activities. He has focused his work on the way in which industrial wastes, pesticides, and other pollutants have damaged rivers, streams, lakes, and other aquatic systems and on the ways in which those systems can be restored to natural, nonpolluted, healthy conditions.

He is the author of 63 books and monographs, 28 bulletins, 304 chapters in books, 615 journal articles, 309 abstracts, and 137 editorials, book reviews, and congressional testimonies. Cairns has been awarded a number of honors, including election to the National Academy of Sciences, the American Philosophical Society, the American Academy of Arts and Sciences, and the Linnean Society of London. He has been awarded the United Stations Environmental Programme Medal, the B. Y. Morrison Medal of the American Chemical Society, the Life Achievement Award in Science of the Commonwealth of Virginia, and the Superior Achievement Award of the U.S. Environmental Protection Agency.

The amount of oxygen dissolved in water varies naturally as the result of a number of circumstances. For example, as water becomes warmer, it is able to hold less oxygen. Aquatic organisms are usually able to adjust to these normal fluctuations in oxygen concentration. Human activities, however, can produce rather dramatic changes in the amount of oxygen dissolved in water, creating a threat to the survival of aquatic organisms.

For example, any biodegradable product discarded into a river, lake, or stream begins to decay by reacting with oxygen dissolved in water. Examples include dead plants, animal wastes, leaves and grass clippings, agricultural wastes, sewage, and wastes from food-processing plants and other industrial operations. The greater the amount of these products discarded into a body of water, the more oxygen is used up as they decay, and the less oxygen there is for aquatic organisms.

Biodegradable materials decay because aerobic bacteria that live in water feed on these materials. As the supply of oxygen dissolved in water decreases, aerobic bacteria (those that require oxygen to survive) begin to die off, and anaerobic bacteria (those that do not require oxygen for their survival) begin to take over the process of decomposition. The waste products produced by these two forms of bacteria are, however, quite different. When aerobic bacteria decompose organic material, they produce carbon dioxide, nitrates, sulfates, carbonates, and other products that are odorless, colorless, and relatively harmless to water quality. By contrast, the products of anaerobic bacterial decomposition include methane, ammonia, hydrogen sulfide, and a variety of amines, all of which have unpleasant odors and tend to be toxic to humans and other animals.

Low oxygen concentration itself impairs water quality. Aquatic organisms differ significantly in their ability to survive in low-oxygen conditions. Many popular food fish, such as perch, bluegill, and trout, require relatively high concentrations of dissolved oxygen for their survival. On the other hand, carp, catfish, sturgeon, northern pike, certain varieties of bass, and sediment-dwelling aquatic worms are able to tolerate low-oxygen waters. In severely oxygen-depleted water, most species of fish are killed and only the hardiest forms of worms are able to survive.

The extent to which a water source has been contaminated by oxygen-depleting substances can be determined by measuring the amount of oxygen present in the water. The most common test of the amount of oxygen being consumed by bacteria as they decompose organic wastes is called *biological* (or *biochemical*) *oxygen demand,* or, more commonly BOD. In a BOD test, a sample of water is saturated with oxygen and allowed to incubate at a temperature of about 70°F (20°C) for five days. During that time, almost all of the nutrients in the water will have been oxidized. The amount of dissolved oxygen

◄ **VALUES FOR DIFFERENT TYPES OF WATER FOR BOD** ➤

TYPE OF WATER	BOD (MG/L)*
Pure water	0
Fresh, natural water	2–5
Sewage after primary and secondary purification	10–20
Metal processing	50
Domestic sewage	200
Textiles	200
Chemicals and pharmaceuticals	300
Paper and pulp manufacture	750
Food processing	750

*Milligrams of oxygen per liter of water

remaining in the water is then measured and the result expressed in milligrams of oxygen per liter of water (mg/L). Results obtained from the standard five-day BOD test are referred to as the BOD_5 values. Values for some types of water may range significantly, depending on a wide variety of conditions. For example, in one study of wastewater from paper and pulp plants in Germany, BOD values ranged from a low of 115 to a high of 1,400. Some typical BOD_5 values for various types of water are shown in the table on page 103.

Another common method used to measure oxygen-depleting substances in water determines *chemical oxygen demand* (COD). In this method, potassium dichromate and sulfuric acid are added to a sample of water. The potassium dichromate plays the same role in this test as aerobic bacteria; that is, it oxidizes organic material present in the water. The sample is heated to about 300°F (150°C) for two hours and then allowed to cool. At the end of that time, some portion of the chromium in potassium dichromate that was used to oxidize the organic matter in the water will have been converted from the reddish orange hexavalent (+6) state to the greenish trivalent (+3) state. Standard colorimetric methods are used for determining the quantity of chromium that has undergone this change, and hence the quantity of organic material oxidized during the reaction. This method involves a precise measurement of the colors of the original and final solution using a spectrophotometer, permitting a very accurate calculation of the amount of organic material present in the water sample.

The COD method is preferable to the BOD method in determining the presence of oxygen-depleting substances in water because it produces faster results, usually in a matter of hours rather than days. The one disadvantage of the COD method is that it measures some organic substances in water that are not metabolized by aerobic bacteria. For this reason, the BOD and COD values obtained for the same sample of water may differ slightly.

A third method for estimating the presence of oxygen-depleting substances is determines *total organic carbon* (TOC). In this method, a sample of water is taken and all dissolved solids collected from it. These solids are then heated to high temperatures, of the order of 1,800°F (1,000°C), until the solids have all been converted to gaseous products. The amount of carbon dioxide produced during this process is then measured and used to estimate the amount of oxygen-depleting substances present in the sample. With certain automated forms of this process, results can be obtained in as little as 15 seconds, making it by far the fastest method for determining oxygen-depleting substances. On the other hand, TOC measures an even larger range of substances than does either BOD or COD. Nonetheless, its results provide a good indication of the degree to which a sample of water has been polluted by oxygen-depleting substances.

Nutrients

Lakes, ponds, and other bodies of water normally evolve over time. When such bodies are first formed, they are typically relatively rich in oxygen and poor in nitrogen and phosphorus. Over time, organic matter from dead plants and animals runs off into the lake or pond, where it is decomposed by bacteria. Concentrations of nitrogen and phosphorus begin to increase, encouraging the growth of simple plant life. Eventually more complex plants begin to grow in the lake and sediments begin to accumulate on the lake bottom. The lake or pond evolves from a relatively pure body of water into a marsh or swamp, and eventually into a meadow. This process is known as *eutrophication*.

The evolution of a lake or pond into dry land depends on the presence of nutrients in the water. The term *nutrients* refers to elements and compounds that are necessary for the growth of plants. Nutrients are commonly divided into two categories: major nutrients and minor nutrients, also known as *micronutrients*. Despite some differences in the way that various elements and compounds are classified, carbon, nitrogen, and phosphorus are always regarded as major nutrients. Some authorities also list potassium, sulfur, calcium, magnesium, and/or iron as major nutrients. Micronutrients include aluminum, boron, chlorine, copper, manganese, molybdenum, silicon, and zinc.

Carbon and nitrogen are generally available to aquatic ecosystems in abundance. The major source of carbon is carbon dioxide in the air and water, which is converted to organic carbon by phytoplankton in the water. Nitrogen is obtained from nitrogen-fixing algae, which convert compounds of nitrogen from runoff into the lake or pond into nitrates. Of all the major nutrients, only phosphorus is likely to be in limited supply. For this reason, it is the amount of phosphorus in a lake or pond that determines the rate at which eutrophication occurs. Because of this special role, phosphorus is said to be the *limiting factor* in the process of eutrophication.

The accumulation of nitrogen compounds in bodies of water, like Lake Superior in the Catskill Mountains of New York shown here, contributes to the growth of plants and algae, resulting in the rapid eutrophication of the lake. (Michael P. Gadomski/Photo Researchers, Inc.)

Under normal circumstances, the eutrophication of a lake or pond is a very slow process, requiring hundreds or thousands of years. That rate may be altered, however, by human activities. For example, runoff from farmlands, municipal sewage, and industrial wastes may contain compounds of phosphorus. When these materials empty into a lake or pond, they may dramatically increase the amount of phosphorus present and, hence, the rate at which eutrophication occurs. It is not unusual today for anthropogenic sources to be responsible for at least 90 percent of all the phosphorus found in a body of water. Under these circumstances, eutrophication may occur in a fraction of the normal time.

One of the primary culprits in the eutrophication of lakes and ponds is phosphorus from synthetic detergents, often known as *syndets*. Since the 1930s, syndets have been a highly desirable alternative to natural soaps for a variety of cleaning purposes. They tend to be complex mixtures of the cleaning agent itself, "builders," brighteners, antifoaming agents, artificial odors, antiredeposition agents, bleaches, and enzymes.

The problematic agent in this list are builders, compounds that sequester ("capture") mineral ions such as calcium and magnesium that would otherwise reduce the sudsing properties of a cleaning agent. One of the most effective builders ever discovered, and one that was widely used for many years, is sodium tripolyphosphate (TPP). The structure of this molecule is such that it can surround and trap ions (such as Ca^{2+} and Mg^{2+}) that are responsible for the "hardness" in water (which reduces the effectiveness of a detergent).

The problem with TPP is that it is often the single most important source of phosphorus in wastewater and sewage that escapes into lakes and rivers. It may, therefore, be one of the primary reasons for the faster rate of eutrophication in lakes and ponds.

One common step in the treatment of sewage is aeration, a process by which air is pumped through water, destroying the bacteria contained in it and converting them to carbon dioxide, water, and other harmless products. (Rosenfeld Images Ltd. /Photo Researchers, Inc.)

Concerns about the effect of TPP on eutrophication have led many states, cities, and regional governments to ban the use of the compound in syndets. Such bans have caused serious problems for detergent manufacturers, however, because no entirely satisfactory substitute for TPP has yet been found. Two promising candidates are the sodium salt of nitrilotriacetic acid, $3Na^+,N(CH_2CO_2)_3^-$, or NTA and ethylenediaminetetraacetic acid (EDTA). Both of these compounds act in much the same way as TPP, that is, by sequestering metal ions. Other builders that have been incorporated into *syndet* formulations include sodium carbonate, synthetic zeolites, borates, and organic polymers known as polycarboxylates.

Detergent manufacturers have been reluctant to stop using TPP in their syndet formulations, however. For one thing, they are not convinced that TPP is as much of an environmental threat as some scientists have suggested. Also, they point out that many of the alternatives available pose problems of their own. For example, there is some evidence that NTA may be carcinogenic in rats. In response to that information, the U.S. Environmental Protection Agency (EPA) banned the use of NTA in detergents in 1970. A decade later, however, the EPA reversed course and once more permitted its use in 1980.

Nonetheless, as of the mid-1990s, detergent manufacturers had essentially given up the battle to retain TPP in their syndet formulations, and they generally stopped producing syndets that contained the troublesome compound. As a result of the industry's action, phosphorus levels in most bodies of water began to drop dramatically in the late 1990s and are now approaching zero in some locations.

Sedimentation and Siltation

Running water erodes the ground over which it runs. Its efficiency at tearing off and breaking apart pieces of the surface is a function of its velocity. That is, the faster the water runs, the more effective it is at eroding the ground. Running water also dissolves some materials in the ground. Thus, a river contains both dissolved substances and substances held in suspension. The faster the water is moving, the greater the volume of materials held in suspension.

As a river or stream slows, it loses some of its ability to keep solids in suspension, and they begin to settle out. Heavier particles such as pieces of gravel and sand settle out first, and lighter particles, such as pieces of silt, settle out later. As a river or stream reaches a lake or ocean, it slows enough that essentially all of its suspended materials are deposited on the lake or ocean bottom. This process is referred to as *sedimentation* or *siltation*. A distinction is sometimes made between these two terms depending on the size of particles deposited, but they are often used interchangeably.

A variety of human activities increase erosion and sedimentation rates. For example, soil typically erodes from cultivated land five to 10 times as fast as from noncultivated land. Construction sites lose soil 100 times as fast and mined land more than 500 times as fast as land that is undisturbed. Besides greatly increasing water pollution, this erosion accelerates the loss of valuable farmland. By some estimates, as much as 3.3 billion tons (3 billion metric tons) of topsoil is lost to such processes in the United States each year. Overall, the major anthropogenic sources of erosion (and, as a consequence, sedimentation) are certain types of agriculture (such as row cropping), livestock operations, logging, flooding from developed land, and construction projects.

Although the erosive action of running water on soil and rock produces the majority of sediments, they may also result from a variety of chemical processes that take place in water. For example, carbon dioxide dissolved in water may react with calcium ions to form insoluble calcium carbonate:

$$CO_2(aq) + H_2O \rightarrow H^+(aq) + HCO_3^-(aq)$$
$$Ca^{2+}(aq) + 2HCO_3^-(aq) \rightarrow CaCO_3(s) + CO_2(aq) + H_2O$$

Bacterial action also results in the formation of sediments. For example, some aquatic bacteria obtain energy from the conversion of ferrous ion to ferric ion:

$$4Fe^{2+}(aq) + 4H^+(aq) + O_2(g) \rightarrow 4Fe^{3+} + 2H_2O$$

The ferric ion produced in this reaction then reacts with water to form insoluble iron(III) hydroxide:

$$Fe^{3+}(aq) + 3H_2O \rightarrow Fe(OH)_3(s) + 3H^+(aq)$$

Finally, human activities may result in increased sedimentation in lakes and the oceans. Phosphate from wastewater may react with Ca^{2+} ions in water to form the insoluble mineral hydroxyapatite:

$$5Ca^{2+}(aq) + OH^-(aq) + 3PO_4^{3-}(aq) \rightarrow Ca_5(OH)(PO_4)_3(s)$$

Sedimentation and siltation can have a number of harmful effects on the environment. For example, as sediments accumulate in a river, stream, harbor, bay, or other body of water, they may disrupt transportation on the water and limit its use for swimming, fishing, boating, and other recreational activities. In some bodies of water, dredging has become a virtually nonstop operation in order to keep them open to shipping and other commercial and recreational operations. The U.S. Army Corps of Engineers alone dredges more than 78 million cubic yards (60 million cubic meters) of sediment each year at an annual cost of nearly $200 million.

Sediments also represent a serious threat to various forms of aquatic life. One direct effect occurs when sand, mud, silt, and other sediments settle on the bottom of a lake, river, estuary, or other body of water, smothering fish eggs and bottom-dwelling organisms. Sediments also clog fish gills and the filters in certain types of shellfish, often resulting in their death. The turbidity caused by sediments may make it difficult for aquatic organisms to locate food and may limit the amount of sunlight needed to carry out photosynthetic processes. Sediments may, for example, settle on the leaves and stems of aquatic plants, reducing the amount of light that reaches those plants.

A less direct effect of sedimentation is the tendency of particles of sand, silt, mud, clay, and other sediments to adsorb pesticides, bacteria, toxic metals, and other harmful substances. The U.S. Environmental Protection Agency has estimated that of the 300 million cubic yards (228 million cubic meters) dredged in the United States each year, up to 12 million cubic yards (9 million cubic meters) are so badly contaminated that they require special handling.

Sediments constitute one of the two most serious forms of water pollution (the other are oxygen-depleting substances). The 2002

National Water Quality Inventory found that more than 30 percent of the rivers and streams studied and more than 20 percent of the lakes studied had to be classified as "impaired" because of sedimentation problems.

The principle that guides efforts to reduce sedimentation and siltation as causes of water pollution is to reduce the flow of water over cultivated land or land that has otherwise been disturbed, such as during construction. A number of farming techniques, such as contour and strip farming and terracing, are well known to reduce soil erosion. To the extent that more farmers adopt such techniques, problems of sedimentation and siltation will be reduced.

Pathogens

Pathogens are disease-causing microorganisms. They fall into five major categories: bacteria, viruses, fungi, protozoa, and parasitic worms. When pathogens are present in water, they may cause a wide variety of diseases, generally known as *waterborne diseases,* including botulism, campylobacteriosis, cholera, cryptosporidiosis, cyclosporiasis, dysentery, giardiasis, hepatitis A, salmonellosis, shigellosis, and typhoid. One of the pioneers in the study of pathogens as water pollutants was Ruth Patrick, whose biography is outlined in the sidebar on page 112.

Pathogens may be spread in a variety of ways. One of the most common mediums is water. In a typical pattern, an infected person sheds a disease-causing organism in her or his feces or urine, which then escapes into the public water supply. When some other person or group of people use that water, the pathogen is passed on to new hosts, who may then contract the disease.

Waterborne diseases are relatively rare in nations that have modern water purification systems. During the period 1999–2000, for example, a total of 39 incidents of *waterborne disease* were associated with drinking water in 25 U.S. states. These incidents affected 2,068 persons, of whom two died. In the 22 cases in which the cause of the outbreak was identified, 20 were due to pathogens and two to chemicals. The most common disease noted was gastroenteritis. About three-quarters of the incidents were found to be related to the

◄ RUTH PATRICK (1907–   ) ➤

How does one know whether a body of water is polluted? In some cases, the answer to that question is easy. Just looking at a river or stream sometimes reveals the presence of dead plants and animals, discarded tires and plastic bottles, oil films, and other obvious evidence of pollution. But detecting pollution is not always that easy. Water that looks crystal clear and pure may sometimes harbor disease-causing organisms, toxic chemicals, or other materials that make it unsafe to drink or use. One of the pioneers in developing methods for detecting water pollution is Ruth Patrick.

Ruth Patrick was born in Topeka, Kansas, on November 26, 1907. She became interested in science early in her life when her father gave her a microscope at the age of seven. He set a challenge for her that was to guide much of her adult life: "Read and improve your mind."

Patrick attended Coker College, from which she received her bachelor of science degree in 1929. She then earned her master's and doctoral degrees in botany from the University of Virginia in 1931 and 1934, respectively. The subject of Patrick's doctoral thesis were diatoms, single-celled organisms that are ubiquitous in bodies of water around the world. It was her early work with diatoms that opened up for her the possibilities of using these tiny organisms—along with a host of other plants and animals—in determining the quality of a body of water.

Patrick left Virginia at a time when employment opportunities for women in science were slim. She taught briefly at the Pennsylvania School of Horticulture and worked as a technician at Temple University, while volunteering her time at the Leidy Microscopical Society of the Academy of Natural Sciences. She had to volunteer at the Leidy because, at the time, women were not paid to work at the academy. That situation changed in 1937, however, when Patrick was appointed curator of the Leidy, a post she held for 10 years. During that time, she catalogued the society's collection of diatoms and added many specimens of her own to its holdings. Largely as a result of her work, that collection remains "unique in the world of dia-

use of groundwater, primarily from water taken from private wells. During the same period, 59 outbreaks of waterborne illness resulting from exposure to contaminated recreational water sources were reported. These outbreaks affected 2,093 persons, none of whom died.

tom research," as Dr. Charles Reimer of the Academy of Natural Sciences has written.

Beginning with a paper published in 1948, "Factors Affecting the Distribution of Diatoms," Patrick developed a general concept for determining the pollution of water that has come to be known as the *Patrick principle*. According to that principle, the quality of a body of water and the changes caused by human activities on that water can be determined by the type and number of organisms found there. The principle does not mean that one can simply go to a lake or river and count the number of bacteria, frogs, or other organisms living there. Instead, it suggests that one must be able to compare the current state of a particular ecosystem with the "pure" or "natural" state of that ecosystem.

In 1947, Patrick established a new department of limnology (the study of lakes, ponds, and streams) at the academy, a department that is now known as the Patrick Center for Environmental Research. The purpose of the department has been to study the structure and function of freshwater ecosystems, including rivers, lakes, and wetlands, along with the impact of human activities on these systems. Patrick served as curator of the center and chair of the Department of Limnology at the academy for more than decades. In 2003, at the age of 94, she still held the titles of Senior Scientist and Francis Boyer Chair of Limnology at the academy.

Patrick has been awarded a number of honors, including the Chairman's Medal of the Heinz Family Foundation, which honors lifetime achievement in the natural sciences; the National Medal of Science (1996); the American Society of Limnology and Oceanography's Lifetime Achievement Award (1996); the Benjamin Franklin Award for Outstanding Scientific Achievement of the American Philosophical Society (1993); the Gold Medal of the Royal Zoological Society of Antwerp, Belgium (1978); and the John and Alice Tyler Ecology Award (1975). She was elected to the National Academy of Sciences in 1970. The Ruth Patrick Science Education Center, in Aiken, South Carolina, is named in her honor.

The two-year period for which these results were reported saw a small but significant increase in the number of waterborne incidents for drinking water. This increase has been attributed to the spread of microorganisms resistant to disinfectants commonly used in municipal water treatment plants. The most common of these pathogens is the parasite *Cryptosporidium,* which was responsible for the largest single outbreak of a waterborne disease in the United States in 1993. That incident affected more than 400,000 people.

By contrast with that in the United States, the incidence of waterborne diseases in less-developed nations is very large, responsible for the deaths of millions of people annually. For example, the World Health Organization estimates that about 4 billion people worldwide are currently infected with some form of dysentery. Of this number, 3 million to 4 million will die each year. The difference in the threat posed by waterborne diseases in developed and less-developed nations results almost entirely from the accessibility of pure, clean water in developed nations.

Tests for most disease-causing organisms are available. But they are generally slow and expensive. Also, in most developed countries, the level of any given pathogen in a sample of water is likely to be very low. As a result, tests for individual pathogens are rarely carried out, except in the case of outbreaks like those just described. Instead, the usual method for testing for the presence of pathogens in water is to test for *coliform bacteria.*

Coliform bacteria are common microorganisms found in the intestinal tract of warm-blooded animals and in the soil and plants. The intestinal type is known as *fecal coliform bacteria,* while the most common type of soil and plant coliform bacteria is the bacterium *Aerobacter aerogenes.* Fecal coliform bacteria are easy to test for, and they are present in water at any given time and place in much larger numbers than are pathogens. If large numbers of fecal coliform bacteria are present in a sample of water, it is likely that pathogens are present as well.

In the test for fecal coliform bacteria, a sample of water is incubated at 112°F (44.5°C) for about 24 hours. If bacteria are present, the person conducting the test counts the number of colonies formed or looks for carbon dioxide gas in the incubation tube. This test is specific for fecal coliforms because they are members of a group of coliform bacteria known as thermotolerant that survive at temperatures of 112°F (44.5°C) or more; other types of coliforms do not.

Treatment with chlorine, in one form or another, kills the vast majority of pathogens in water, and such treatment is now a standard procedure in any modern water treatment plant. Chlorine-resistant pathogens such as certain types of viruses and the parasite *Cryptosporidium* can be killed with a variety of techniques, including use of small-pore filters and treatment with ultraviolet radiation or significantly increased levels of chlorine. These treatments, as data presented indicate, have largely reduced the problem of pathogens as water pollutants in most developed nations. The lack of such treatments in most developing nations, however, means that pathogens in water continue to pose a serious problem for the majority of the world's population.

Toxic Organic Chemicals

The term *toxic organic chemicals* (TOCs) refers to a large group of synthetic compounds that contain the element carbon. These compounds are sometimes known as synthetic organic compounds (SOCs) or as *persistent organic pollutants* (POPs). The vast majority of toxic organic chemicals of interest to environmental scientists are compounds produced for use in agriculture and public health. These are toxic to plants and animals, interfere with the growth of crops, or spread disease. They include pesticides, insecticides, fungicides, and herbicides such as para-dichlorodiphenyltrichloroethane (DDT), dichlorodiphenyldichloroethylene (DDE), chlordane, lindane, toxaphene, endrin, dieldrin, heptachlor, 1,4 dichlorobenzene, malathion, carbofuran (Furadan), carbaryl (Sevin), aldicarb, atrazine, pentachlorophenol, and tetrachlorophenol. Two other groups of compounds included in the category of toxic organic chemicals are the polychlorinated biphenyls (PCBs) and *dioxins.* (These substances are discussed in chapter 5.)

Many TOCs were first synthesized in the mid-20th century. Initially they were widely regarded as "wonder chemicals." They were very effective in killing the pests and weeds that compete with farmers for crops. With the use of these products, crop yields increased enormously in what came to be called the green revolution, which swept through much of the world in the 1960s and 1970s. The green revolution was a movement in which agricultural scientists applied modern principles of genetics and breeding, such as new types of seeds and pesticides, to improve crops grown primarily in less-developed countries.

Pesticides were also valuable in bringing about the control of many insect-transmitted diseases. The use of DDT against the anopheles mosquito in the 1950s and 1960s, for example, was responsible for dramatic decreases in malaria infection rates in many parts of the world. The number of malaria cases in Venezuela dropped from more than 8 million in 1943 to 800 in 1958. Comparable results were reported in Italy, where the number of malaria cases dropped from 411,502 in 1945 to 37 in 1968, and in Taiwan, where the incidence dropped from more than 1 million cases in 1945 to just nine in 1969.

It soon became obvious, however, that these "wonder chemicals" pose some serious environmental hazards. Because they are synthetic products, the microorganisms that normally degrade natural products do not affect them. Therefore, they tend to persist in the soil on which they are sprayed for long periods. They eventually become part of groundwater or are washed into lakes and rivers by rain. In the water, they are toxins that threaten aquatic organisms.

Toxic organic chemicals can harm organisms in a variety of ways. Many animals simply become ill after feeding on poisoned plants. Others survive but are then eaten by larger animals that prey on them. The toxins accumulate in predators' bodies over time as they consume affected prey animals. Thus, the concentration of a toxic chemical tends to increase as it moves up the food chain in a process known as biomagnification. In one study, for example, the concentration of DDT was found to be 0.25 ppm in the phytoplankton in a body of water, 0.123 ppm in zooplankton, 1.04 ppm in small fish, 4.83 ppm in larger fish, and 124 ppm in birds that fed on the fish.

A vast number of studies now document the biological effects of TOCs on a variety of organisms. According to a detailed compilation prepared by independent consultant Bernard Windham, the effects scientists have identified include the following:

➤ Eggshell thinning and deformities in certain species of fish-eating birds

➤ Abnormal thyroid function in fish and birds

➤ Abnormal hormone levels in birds, alligators, and mammals

➤ Decreased fertility in birds, fish, shellfish, otters, and minks

➤ Emasculation and feminization of male fish, birds, turtles, alligators, otters, minks, beluga whales, polar bears, and panthers

➤ Defeminization and masculation of female fish, gastropods, turtles, birds, and mammals

➤ Damage to immune functions in birds and mammals

➤ Birth defects and high infant mortality rate in mammals

➤ Behavioral changes in birds

➤ Abnormal sex organs in birds, turtles, alligators, and sturgeon

➤ Low testosterone levels and undescended testes in alligators and panthers

By the 1960s, concern about the use of at least some TOCs had reached a point that governments around the world began to consider banning their use for at least some purposes. In the United States, for example, the Environmental Protection Agency announced a ban on the use of DDT for most purposes in 1972. Today, a number of TOCs are banned from use in all or many applications. For example, the pesticides dieldrin, aldrin, and endrin are banned for agricultural use in more than 60 countries around the world. In some cases, a toxic organic chemical is allowed to be used in specific applications. In the United States, for example, dieldrin was banned from agricultural use in 1974 but was permitted for use in mothproofing and termite treatments until 1987, when it was then banned for those purposes also.

Thirty years after bans on many toxic organic chemicals first went into effect, their levels in the environment in many developed countries had decreased substantially. For example, health scientists and environmentalists now believe that concentrations of DDT remaining in soils and water in the United States are so low as to pose no threat to human health or to the health of other animals.

Such is not necessarily the case in other parts of the world, however. Pesticides, DDT in particular, are among the most effective agents known for the prevention of malaria. Some nations have accepted the environmental risks posed by DDT and other TOCs as a reasonable trade-off for the protection they offer against malaria and other infectious diseases. At the beginning of the 21st century, then, DDT and other toxic pesticides were still being used in the public health programs of a number of countries around the world.

Toxic organic chemicals continue to pose a dilemma for public health officials, environmentalists, and government officials around the world. On the one hand, many individuals and groups continue to push for an outright ban on the use of such chemicals everywhere in the world. They argue that the risks they pose are too great to permit their continued use. Other individuals and groups point to the lifesaving value of such chemicals and insist that their use be permitted.

These two positions were in conflict in 2001 when representatives from 127 nations met in Stockholm to consider a universal ban on 12 TOCs, commonly known as the "dirty dozen." The dirty dozen includes aldrin, chlordane, dieldrin, DDT, endrin, heptachlor, hexachlorobenzene, and Mirex. After extended discussion and debate, representatives adopted a final document now known as the Stockholm Convention on Persistent Organic Pollutants. The document was signed on May 22, 2001, and entered into force on May 17, 2004, at which point the required minimum of 50 nations had ratified the treaty.

The Stockholm treaty completely banned the production and use of some TOCs (such as endrin and toxaphene), while permitting the use of other TOCs for specific purposes (such as aldrin as an insecticide and dieldrin in certain agricultural operations). In addition, a number of nations requested exceptions that would allow them to use otherwise-banned compounds in public health programs. By 2003, more than 20 nations had taken advantage of that exception and were using certain pesticides, usually DDT, to spray for the anopheles mosquito. Those 20 nations included Ethiopia, Eritrea, Madagascar, Mauritius, Morocco, Namibia, South Africa, Sudan, Swaziland, and Zambia.

Discussions at Stockholm and since concerning the use of TOCs illustrate the divergence of views about these compounds. Some critics point out that the number of human lives lost as a result of exposure to such compounds is very small indeed. There is, for example, no record of any human who ever died of ingestion of DDT in the United States. By contrast, the number of lives that can be saved by using some TOCs in pest-elimination programs is enormous. One example that has been cited is Sri Lanka. In 1946, before DDT was generally available, the nation had 2.8 million cases of malaria, 12,500 of which resulted in death. After the government began spraying with DDT, the number of malaria cases dropped to 17 in 1963, with no deaths. Five years later, after DDT had been banned in the country, the number of malaria cases rose once again, reaching 500,000 in 1968, with 113 deaths.

Given these conflicting views about the benefits and risks of TOCs to human health and the environment, debate about the use of these compounds is likely to continue for some time.

Heavy Metals

The term *heavy metal* in environmental chemistry has traditionally been used to describe certain elements and compounds that are hazardous to the health of humans and other animals. Some elements included in this definition are arsenic, beryllium, cadmium, chromium, lead, and mercury.

A number of objections have been raised to the use of the term. In the first place, the list of so-called heavy metals usually includes some elements that are not even metals, such as the semimetals arsenic and antimony. Also, some of the "heavy metals" are not really very "heavy" by almost any standard. Beryllium, for example, has an atomic mass of about 9, and aluminum, an atomic mass of about 27. Yet both are often classified as "heavy metals." For these reasons, some authorities now prefer the term *toxic metals* to the more traditional term *heavy metals.* Either term can refer to elements in both their free and combined states. The table on pages 120–121 provides an overview of the sources and health effects of some heavy metals,

◄ **BACKGROUND INFORMATION ON**
   SOME HEAVY METALS ➤

METAL	MAJOR SOURCE(S)	HEALTH EFFECT(S)	DRINKING WATER STANDARDS*
Arsenic	Mining, pesticides, power generating plants	Carcinogenic(?)	10 ppb
Beryllium	Power generating plants	Toxic, carcinogenic(?)	4 ppb
Cadmium	Mining, industrial wastes, water pipes, electroplating plants	Kidney damage, hypertension, toxic to aquatic organisms	5 ppb
Chromium	Electroplating plants	Carcinogenic (as Cr^{6+})(?), essential to human health in trace amounts	100 ppb
Copper	Electroplating plants; mining, industrial, and municipal wastes	Essential to human health in trace amounts; toxic to plants at moderate levels	1.3ppm

METAL	MAJOR SOURCE(S)	HEALTH EFFECT(S)	DRINKING WATER STANDARDS*
Lead	Gasoline emissions, industrial wastes, mining, water pipes	Anemia, damage to kidneys and nervous system	0
Manganese	Mining, industrial wastes	Toxic to plants in high concentrations	None established
Molybdenum	Industrial wastes	Essential to plants; may be toxic to animals	None established
Selenium	Agricultural runoff	Essential at low levels, toxic and carcinogenic (?) to animals at higher levels	50 ppb

*The Environmental Protection Agency has been authorized by provisions of the Safe Drinking Water Act of 1974, as amended in 1986 and 1996, to establish drinking water standards. Those standards are listed in this column.

along with current standards for their presence in drinking water in the United States, as established by the Environmental Protection Agency.

As this table suggests, the environmental hazard posed by heavy metals varies significantly. Some of the elements listed in that chart are among the most hazardous substances released to the environment. The EPA has classified four of the heavy metals—arsenic, lead, mercury, and cadmium—among the top 25 most hazardous chemicals present in the environment in the United States. (Of the remaining substances on that list 18 are toxic organic chemicals; one is another heavy metal, chromium; one is white phosphorus; and the last is creosote produced from coal tar.)

Heavy metal poisoning is hardly a new phenomenon in human civilization. Scholars have studied in considerable detail the effect of lead poisoning, which was apparently rampant, on the Roman civilization. Pipes used to conduct water to local homes in Rome and other imperial cities were made of lead, which continually dissolved in the water that passed through the pipes. People who drank the water gradually accumulated significant levels of lead, and this lead poisoning resulted in a variety of health problems, including gout

The pollution of waterways is sometimes difficult to see and, at other times, dramatically obvious, as in the pollution of the King River, in Tasmania, by waste copper. (Patrick Fagot/Photo Researchers, Inc.)

and sterility among men, infertility and stillbirths among women, and jaundice, palsy, dropsy, mental disorders, madness, and death among both adults and children.

Another familiar historical case of heavy metal poisoning occurred in the mid-19th century, when hatters used a solution of mercury(II) nitrate to help shape the hats they made. When the mercury was inhaled or ingested, it caused damage to a hatter's nervous system; frequently mental disorders resulted. Thus originated the expression "mad as a hatter."

In the modern world, such dramatic examples of health problems resulting from exposure to heavy metals are relatively rare. In fact, those cases occur almost exclusively as the result of accidental massive exposure to a heavy metal or to long-term exposure to lower levels of the metal. For example, workers exposed to the element beryllium or its compounds are at risk for a disorder known as berylliosis. The condition is characterized by shortness of breath and inflammation, swelling, and scarring of the lungs. These symptoms most commonly develop over a period of many years, during which time finely divided particles of beryllium gradually accumulate in the lungs, irritating tissue and reducing the lungs' ability to transmit oxygen to the bloodstream. The EPA has estimated that, in up to 6 percent of all workers exposed to beryllium, berylliosis eventually develops.

Humans may also be put at risk from heavy metals by the accidental or intentional discharge of industrial wastes into public water supplies. Perhaps the most famous example of this kind of release occurred during the 1950s. A company producing plastics in Minimata, Japan, routinely discharged its wastes into the adjacent bay. Those wastes contained mercury, which was ingested by shellfish living in the bay. The shellfish, in turn, were a major source of food for people living on the bay. Over time, the mercury slowly poisoned hundreds of residents of the area, who suffered elevated rates of stillbirths, serious birth defects, kidney damage, and damage to the neuromuscular system, resulting in insanity and death. More than 50 years after the incident, Minimata Bay is still considered unsafe for fishing.

The Environmental Protection Agency is required by law to conduct a survey of water quality conditions in the United States every other year. This survey reports the primary water pollutants and their sources for rivers and streams, lakes, estuaries, groundwater, and other bodies of water. In the last survey published, released in 2000, metals were the leading cause of pollution in estuaries, affecting about a quarter of the 31,072 square miles (80,476 square kilometers) surveyed; the second most important cause of pollution in lakes, affecting about 22 percent of the 17.3 million acres (7 million hectares) surveyed; and the sixth most important pollutant in rivers and streams, affecting about 6 percent of those surveyed.

Acidity

Abnormally low pH values (acidic conditions) of surface or groundwater have little or no effect on human activities. Excess acidity (or, much less commonly, excess alkalinity) may have quite serious effects on aquatic life, however. As described in chapter 3, fish eggs, fry and immature fish, and some species of mature fish are especially susceptible to pH values of less than about 4.0 (or more than about pH 9.0).

Acidity problems tend to be localized in bodies of water near industrial operations that discharge acidic materials or near active or abandoned mines. Acids form when water flows through all kinds of mines, including coal mines and mines for the extraction of various metals. Probably the most common acid-forming process in such cases occurs when iron pyrites (FeS_2), found in coal seams and in many metal mines, is oxidized by atmospheric oxygen or oxygen dissolved in water to produce iron(II) sulfate:

$$2FeS_2 + 7O_2 + 2H_2O \rightarrow 2Fe^{2+} + 4SO_4^{2-} + 4H^+$$

$$4Fe^{2+} + O_2 + 4H^+ \rightarrow 4Fe^{3+} + 2H_2O$$

$$4Fe^{3+} + 12H_2O \rightarrow 4Fe(OH)_3 + 12H^+$$

$$FeS_2 + 14Fe^{3+} + 8H_2O \rightarrow 15Fe^{2+} + 2SO_4^{2-} + 16H^+$$

Notice that sulfuric acid (H_2SO_4) is formed at two different points in this process, once during the oxidation of iron pyrites itself and once during the reaction between the iron(III) ion and iron pyrites.

The amount of sulfuric acid produced in this sequence of reactions and the volume of the water into which it is discharged determine the pH of that water. In some cases, the solution is sufficiently dilute that the pH is near that of unpolluted water, just under 7.0. But in many cases, the pH can drop much lower, often to 3 or less. People have observed pH levels of 2 or less, a level of acidity at which virtually no aquatic life can live.

As the acidity of a river or lake increases, it can trigger a secondary effect. Metals that are normally tied up as compounds in the ground become soluble and enter the water. In such cases, the combined effects of low pH and increased metal concentration are even more harmful to aquatic organisms than the sum of the two effects taken separately. For example, many fish are able to survive in water with a pH of less than 5.0. But if the water contains a small amount of iron, as little as 1 ppm, fish will begin to die at a pH as high as 5.5.

A number of methods have been devised to reduce acid mine drainage (AMD) and, therefore, the harmful environmental effects it may cause. One of the simplest approaches (at least in theory) is to divert the flow of water that would normally pass through or over a mine. The principle is that in the absence of water much less sulfuric acid forms and what little is produced is not likely to be carried into lakes, rivers, and other bodies of water.

A very different approach is to inundate the land in and around a mine, washing away and/or dissolving out pyrites and other acid-forming minerals. These waters are then diverted into large holding ponds where they are allowed to remain undisturbed. When isolated in this way, acid-producing substances are prevented from entering the natural environment.

Another method of preventing acid mine drainage is to construct barriers around the mine itself. The most important single source of AMD are abandoned coal mines. In some cases, the entrances to those mines can be sealed or barriers can be constructed to prevent the outflow of acidic water from the mines into lakes and streams. Finally, abandoned mines can sometimes simply be filled with sand, gravel, fly ash, or other materials, effectively immobilizing any potential acid-producing substances remaining within them.

Heat

The largest single use of water consumed in the United States is for cooling purposes. Electrical power generating plants and a great many different industries withdraw water from rivers, streams, lakes, and oceans to carry away heat produced during the generation of electricity or various industrial operations. That water is then returned to the source from which it was taken, usually with a temperature somewhat higher than it was originally. In 1995, the latest year for which data are available, 39 percent of all the fresh water consumed in the United States was used for cooling operations (the second most important use, by about 1 percent, after irrigation), and 95 percent of all the saline water used went for the same purpose.

The addition of heat to a body of water, a condition known as *thermal pollution,* represents virtually no problem for humans. In fact, thermal pollution can even have certain advantages. For example, water heated by such processes can be used to spray on fruit trees to prevent damage from frost. It can also be used, under controlled circumstances, in aquaculture, the controlled cultivation of fish and seafood.

By contrast, thermal pollution can have some significant effects on the natural ecosystem. As the temperature of water rises, its ability to hold dissolved oxygen declines. The graph shows how the solubility of oxygen varies with temperature. Since fish are cold-blooded animals, they are unable to regulate their own temperatures, and

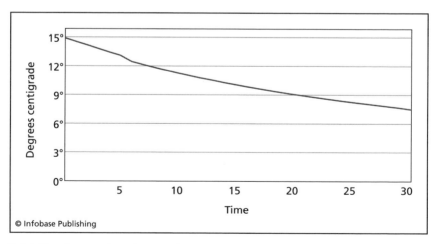

Solubility of oxygen in water at various temperatures

◄ TEMPERATURE EFFECTS ON VARIOUS FISH SPECIES ►

SPECIES	A	B	C	D
Sockeye salmon	64°F (18°C)	72°F (22°C)	50°F (10°C)	55°F (13°C)
Brook trout	66°F (19°C)	75°F (24°C)	48°F (9°C)	55°F (13°C)
Rainbow trout	66°F (19°C)	75°F (24°C)	48°F (9°C)	55°F (13°C)
Atlantic salmon	68°F (20°C)	73°F (23°C)	41°F (5°C)	52°F (11°C)
Small-mouth bass	84°F (29°C)	n/a	63°F (17°C)	73°F (23°C)
Bluegill	90°F (32°C)	95°F (35°C)	77°F (25°C)	93°F (34°C)
Channel catfish	90°F (32°C)	95°F (35°C)	81°F (27°C)	84°F (29°C)
Large-mouth bass	90°F (32°C)	93°F (34°C)	97°F (21°C)	81°F (27°C)

A = maximum weekly average temperature for growth of juveniles
B = maximum temperature for survival of short exposure
C = maximum weekly average temperature for spawning
D = maximum temperature for embryo spawning
Source: U.S. Environmental Protection Agency, Office of Water. *Volunteer Stream Monitoring: A Methods Manual,* chapter 5: "Monitoring and Assessing Water Quality," available online at http://www.epa.gov/OWOW/monitoring/volunteer/stream/vms53.html.

variations from their ideal environmental conditions may result in illness, death, and reproductive problems. The chart on page 127 shows the considerable range in the ability of various fish species to survive differing water temperatures.

In addition to fish kills, changes in water temperature may induce significant changes in the aquatic ecosystem overall, causing an increase in the growth of blue-green algae and a decrease in the growth of green algae, more common in rivers, streams, and lakes at normal temperatures. Rapid algae blooms produced by increased temperatures may themselves contribute to the die-off of fish in the body of water.

A number of methods can be used to control thermal pollution. Many environmentalists point out that one approach is for consumers and industries simply to reduce the amount of electricity they use and waste, allowing power plants to reduce the amount of electricity they generate. Another approach is to discharge heated water in places that are less ecologically sensitive, that is, bodies of water that contain fewer fish, shellfish, and other aquatic organisms that are affected by heated water. For example, heated water can be used to heat homes, office buildings, and other structures.

At one time, the most common method for disposing of heated water was to discharge that water into large, artificial *cooling ponds.* In some cases, heated water is simply allowed to flow into the cooling pond, while in other cases, it is sprayed into the air over the pond. As the water evaporates from such ponds or during the spraying process, it releases water vapor and thermal energy into the atmosphere. The cool water remaining behind can then be discharged into natural ponds, lakes, rivers, streams, or the ocean.

The problem with cooling ponds as a method of controlling thermal pollution is that they require that very large land areas be taken out of productive use and devoted to unproductive cooling ponds. Because of this problem, most heated water is now cooled by discharging it into cooling towers, like that shown in the diagram. Cooling towers are very large structures through which heated water is pumped. Some of the warm water evaporates, as in a cooling pond, allowing water vapor and thermal energy to escape into the atmosphere. In some cases, air is forced upward through the hot water (as shown in the diagram on the adjoining page), while in other cases, the hot water is allowed to evaporate naturally.

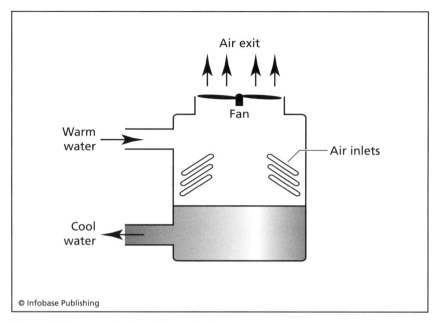

Air exit

Fan

Warm
water

Air inlets

Cool
water

© Infobase Publishing

Schematic diagram of a forced air cooling tower

Cooling towers vary dramatically in their size, with some able to handle no more than about 2,000 gallons per minute (7,500 liters per minute), and the largest able to process more than 100,000 gallons per minute (400,000 liters per minute). The least efficient of such plants reduce the temperature of the water they process by less than 10°F (5°C), and the most efficient, by more than 30°F (16°C).

The Clean Water Act Amendments of 1990 required the Environmental Protection Agency to prepare a biennial report for Congress on the quality of rivers, streams, lakes, ponds, estuaries, wetlands, groundwater, and other bodies of water in the United States. The table on page 130 summarizes the trends reflected in three of the five reports prepared thus far. With few exceptions, these reports document relatively modest changes (both improvement and deterioration) in the nation's waters. Although environmental chemists continue to learn a great deal more about the nature of water pollution, its effects on plants and animals, and methods by which pollution can be controlled, that knowledge appears to have had relatively minor effect on the actual water quality in the United States.

◢ SUMMARY OF WATER QUALITY IN THE UNITED STATES, 1992, 1996, AND 2000 ◢
◣

BODY OF WATER	SURVEY YEAR	GOOD	THREATENED	IMPAIRED
Rivers and streams	1992	56%	6%	38%
	1996	56%	8%	36%
	2000	53%	8%	39%

(continues)

BODY OF WATER	SURVEY YEAR	GOOD	THREATENED	IMPAIRED
Lakes, reservoirs, and ponds	1992	43%	13%	44%
	1996	51%	10%	39%
	2000	47%	8%	45%
Estuaries and shoreline waters	1992	56%	12%	32%
	1996	58%	4%	38%
	2000	45%	4%	51%

Sources: National Water Quality Inventory Report to Congress, 1992, 1996, 2000. Available online at http://www.epa.gov/305b/.

5
CHEMISTRY OF SOLID WASTE DISPOSAL

In the mid-1980s, the city of Philadelphia was experiencing a problem common to many urban areas in the United States. The city had run out of places to dispose of some of its solid wastes. One batch of wastes that posed a special problem consisted of ash produced at the city's Roxborough incinerator. These wastes contained hazardous chemicals, which made them unacceptable to other "host" states, such as Ohio, Virginia, South Carolina, and Georgia, which had been receiving wastes from other urban areas on the East Coast.

In an effort to solve this problem, a contractor for the city hired the 466-foot (142-meter) barge *Khian Sea* to transport the wastes to an artificial island in the Bahamas. It set sail for the islands on September 5, 1986. En route to his destination, the captain of the *Khian Sea* received word from the Bahamian government that it had not given permission to dump the wastes in its nation, and the vessel would not be allowed to dock within its waters.

At that point, the barge began its search for some nation that *would* allow it to dock and unload its cargo. Between September 1986 and December 1987, it visited Bermuda, Puerto Rico, the Dominican Republic, Honduras, Guinea-Bissau, and the Netherlands Antilles, all of which refused to accept Philadelphia's wastes. In late 1987, the ship finally received word that the Haitian government had agreed to accept its cargo. The *Khian Sea* arrived in Haiti on January 20, 1988, and began unloading its wastes, now redesignated as "fertilizer," in the port of Gonaïves. Only when environmentalists began to complain about the dumping of these wastes in Haiti did the government order the ship's captain to discontinue his dumping of the fertilizer/wastes.

Once again, the barge set sail, now carrying a reduced load of about 12,000 tons (11,000 metric tons) of wastes/fertilizer. This time, under the new name of the *Felicia,* it traveled to Sri Lanka, Indonesia, and the Philippines in an attempt to find a final resting place for Philadelphia's wastes. At each port, the barge was turned away, and the *Khian Sea/Felicia* set sail on its final journey in November 1988—this time under the name of the *Pelicano*—from the Philippines for Singapore. When it arrived in Singapore, it was no longer carrying its cargo, which had "disappeared" mysteriously at sea. In June 1993, William P. Reilly and John Patrick Dowd, officers of Coastal Carriers, Inc., operators of the *Khian Sea/Felicia/Pelicano,* were convicted of perjury and sentenced to prison. No one was ever convicted of dumping wastes on a Haitian beach or in the Pacific Ocean between the Philippines and Singapore.

An Overview of Solid Wastes

The term *solid waste* is a very comprehensive term that can be difficult to define precisely. The United States Code of Federal Regulations (Chapter 1, Part 261, of Title 40) provides the legal definition. That document defines *solid wastes* rather simply as "any discarded material that is not excluded" by other provisions of the chapter. Those provisions refer primarily to liquid wastes, such as sludge and domestic wastewater. The U.S. Army provides a somewhat more detailed definition of the term: "any garbage, refuse, sludge, or other discarded material resulting from industrial, commercial, institutional, and residential activity. Discarded materials include those that are disposed of, abandoned, recycled, or are inherently waste-like."

About 8.25 billion tons (7.5 billion metric tons) of solid wastes are generated in the United States each year. The single most important

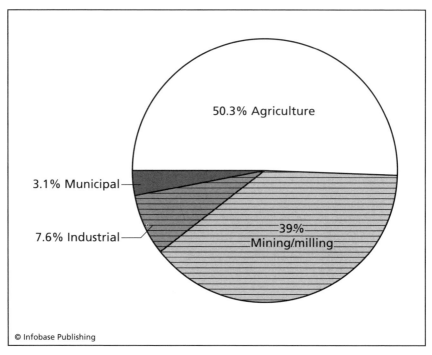

50.3% Agriculture

3.1% Municipal

7.6% Industrial

39%
Mining/milling

Sources of solid wastes in the United States

sources of these wastes are agriculture and lumbering. As the graph shows, about half of all the solid waste generated in the United States is from these two sources. Another 39 percent of all wastes are generated by mining industries. As important as these sources are in terms of volume, they are relatively unimportant in terms of their environmental impact. Most wastes produced by agriculture and lumbering, for example, tend to remain on the ground until they are biodegraded and their components returned to the earth. Mining operations do have some significant environmental impacts (see chapter 4), but the vast majority of the wastes produced during these operations consist of soil and rock, which are simply displaced from one part of the Earth to another. This process of displacement often results in increases in water pollution and soil erosion and a less attractive environment, but they generally do not pose hazards to the health of humans or other animals.

It is the roughly 7 percent of solid wastes produced by industrial and energy-generation operations and the 3 percent produced by nonindustrial human activities that present the most serious environmental problems in the United States today. These fall into three large categories: (1) pure volume of wastes, (2) hazardous wastes, and (3) radioactive wastes. Each type of solid waste poses its own set of problems and requires its own set of solutions.

Municipal Solid Wastes

The term *municipal solid wastes* (MSW) is used to describe the wide range of waste materials produced by individual, family, and community activities. The graph shows the approximate composition of the municipal solid waste found in the United States today.

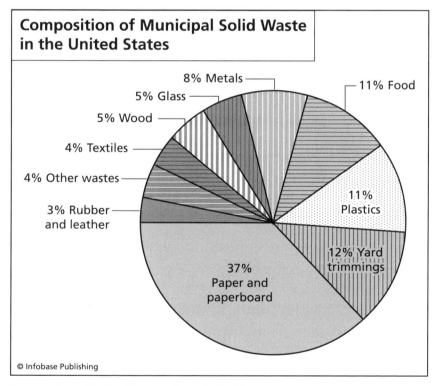

Sources of municipal solid wastes in the United States

◄ MUNICIPAL WASTES GENERATED, 1960 TO 2000 (IN PERCENTAGE OF TOTAL WASTES) ►

MATERIALS	1960	1970	1980	1990	1995	1998	1999	2000
Paper and paper-board	34.0	36.6	36.4	35.4	38.6	37.7	38.2	37.4
Glass	7.6	10.5	10.0	6.4	6.1	5.7	5.6	5.5
Metals	11.7	10.2	8.3	6.2	5.5	5.5	5.8	5.8
Plastics	0.4	2.4	4.5	8.3	8.9	10.0	10.4	10.7
Rubber and leather	2.1	2.5	2.8	2.8	2.9	3.1	2.7	2.7
Textiles	2.0	1.7	1.7	2.8	3.5	3.9	3.9	4.0

MATERIALS

	1960	1970	1980	1990	1995	1998	1999	2000
Wood	3.4	3.1	4.6	6.0	4.9	5.4	5.4	5.5
Other	0.1	0.6	1.7	1.6	1.7	1.7	1.7	1.7

WASTES

	1960	1970	1980	1990	1995	1998	1999	2000
Food scraps	13.8	10.6	8.6	10.1	10.3	11.2	10.9	11.2
Yard trimmings	22.7	19.2	18.1	17.1	14.0	12.4	12.0	12.0
Miscellaneous nonorganic wastes	1.5	1.5	1.5	1.4	1.5	1.5	1.5	1.5

Source: Office of Solid Waste and Emergency Response, *Municipal Solid Waste in the United States: 2001 Facts and Figures*, October 2003.

Trends in solid waste generation have changed in some important ways over the past four decades. As the table on pages 136–137 shows, the contribution to the total solid waste volume for most constituents stayed about the same between 1960 and 2000 (the last year for which data are available). The two exceptions are metals, whose share of the MSW had dropped from about 12 percent in 1960 to less than 6 percent in 2000, and plastics, which made up only 0.4 percent of all MSW in 1960 and now constitute nearly 11 percent of all such wastes.

This change is significant in that most components of MSW are either biodegradable or recyclable with relatively modest effort. For example, glass, paper, and metals have been recycled for decades. By contrast, the recycling of plastics is more difficult partly because there are so many different kinds of plastic and partly because some plastics (thermosetting plastics) cannot be remelted, an important first step in any recycling process.

In some ways, the most significant single fact about municipal solid wastes is the rate at which they are increasing in volume in the United States. The table on pages 136–137 shows that the total amount of MSW in the United States increased between 1960 and 2000. Notice that the weight of all MSW increased during that period from just less than 90 million short tons (82 million metric tons) in 1960 to more than 230 million short tons (209 million metric tons) in 2000, an increase of more than 150 percent in just 40 years. Of course, the U.S. population increased significantly during this period. But the amount of MSW generated per person still increased from about 2.7 pounds (1.2 kilograms) per person in 1960 to 4.5 pounds (2.0 kilograms) per person in 2000.

Municipal Solid Waste Disposal: Landfills

What do communities do with all of these wastes? Traditionally, the most common method of disposal is dumping on or in the land. Since the 1960s, however, two other methods of waste disposal have become increasingly popular: incineration and recovery (recycling).

At one time, the guiding principle behind waste disposal in most parts of the world was (figuratively) to "throw it out the window." That is, communities searched for open space that was not being used for any productive purpose, and that was not likely to be so used, and set that space aside as a "dump." A dump is legally defined in the United States as "any facility or site where solid waste is disposed of which is not a sanitary landfill" (25 U.S.C. 3902, sec. 3). Thus, a municipal dump could be established in an old gravel pit, at a dried-up lake, in the corner of someone's pasture, or at any other nonproductive site in the area.

Open dumps pose a number of environmental problems, however. For example, they tend to attract rats, flies, gulls, insects, and other undesirable animals. Those animals not only are unsightly but also transmit a variety of diseases. In addition, open dumps tend to produce offensive odors that are carried to nearby residents. Dumps also tend to catch fire spontaneously, filling the air with additional unpleasant odors, as well as noxious and toxic fumes from burning rubber, plastic, and other synthetic chemicals.

But perhaps the most serious threat posed by open dumps is the leachate they release to groundwater and surrounding surface waters. Leachate is a solution and/or suspension formed when rainwater runs over and through an open dump, dissolving or picking up noxious and/or hazardous chemicals, disease-causing organisms, and other dangerous substances. This solution and/or suspension then seeps into the groundwater or runs off into adjacent rivers, lakes, and streams, contributing to the pollution of these bodies of water.

About 80 percent of all municipal solid waste was disposed of in open dumps until 1970, when amendments to the 1965 Solid Waste Disposal Act discouraged and, in some cases, outlawed the practice. An important objective of those amendments was to encourage communities to make use of *landfills,* rather than dumps, for their waste disposal programs.

A landfill is a site for the storage of wastes that is one step improved over an open dump. It normally consists of a hole in the ground where wastes are deposited. The wastes are periodically covered with a layer of earth, and additional wastes may then be deposited on top of it. The process may be repeated, with another layer of earth laid down on top of the new wastes. When landfills of this design have been used for some time, they may eventually take the form of a very large hill consisting of alternate layers of waste and earth.

This type of landfill solves some of the problems posed by open dumps. For example, odors are less readily released into the air, and fires are less likely to break out. Infestation by rodents, insects, and other animals is usually reduced also. But the most important problem posed by open dumps—pollution of surface and groundwater—remains. It is still possible for rainwater to seep through layers of dirt and waste, leaching out noxious and toxic materials into nearby bodies of water.

A *sanitary landfill* represents a modest improvement on a simple landfill. In a sanitary landfill, wastes are usually compacted and covered with a thin layer of dirt *each day.* Compaction helps reduce the amount of material washed away by rainfall. After the landfill has reached some given depth, it is covered with a thick layer of dirt, usually about two feet thick.

The most desirable type of landfill, environmentally, is a *secure landfill.* Secure landfills contain an underliner made of some impervious (impermeable) material that prevents leachate from draining out into the groundwater or adjoining lakes and rivers. The underliner can sometimes be some type of hard rock, such as granite. It can also be made of a synthetic material, usually an impervious, flexible plastic.

Secure landfills often have relatively elaborate designs, like the one shown in the diagram on page 141. In this design, wastes are trapped between a double lining at the bottom and a single lining at the top, covered by a thick layer of earth and grass. Outlet pipes are provided at the bottom to carry away any fluids that do seep through the lining and at the top to allow the escape of gases produced during decomposition of the wastes. Secure landfills can be constructed for any type of solid waste disposal. But the expense of their construction and maintenance means that they are often built only for locations where hazardous wastes are going to be dumped.

It is very difficult to estimate the number of landfills and dumps that have been closed in the United States. No specific method has been devised for counting such sites and, given the number of indi-

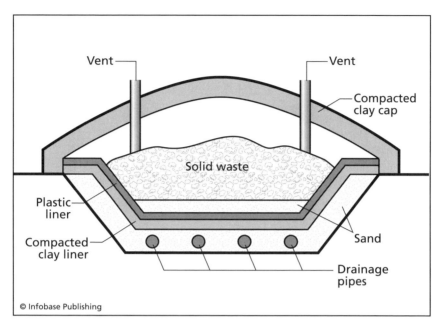

Vent

Vent

Compacted
clay cap

Solid waste

Plastic
liner

Compacted
clay liner

Sand

Drainage
pipes

© Infobase Publishing

Structure of a sanitary landfill

vidual communities in the nation, that number could be very large indeed. In 2005, the National Solid Wastes Management Association estimated that slightly more than 1,700 municipal solid waste landfills were still being used of the more than 20,000 such facilities operating in 1970.

By contrast, the U.S. Environmental Protection Agency from time to time reports on the number of active landfills in the United States. As shown in the graph on page 142, that number has continued to decline for many years. In 2001, the EPA reported the existence of 1,858 landfills in the United States. Still, the total volume of solid wastes in such landfills remains about constant because the size of individual landfills continues to grow.

While landfills pose a number of environmental problems, as already described, the most serious problems many urban areas face is not environmental but geographical: They are simply running out of space on which to dump their wastes. Many urban areas are having to look far afield for locations to send their garbage and trash. One example is Philadelphia, whose wastes traveled the world in search

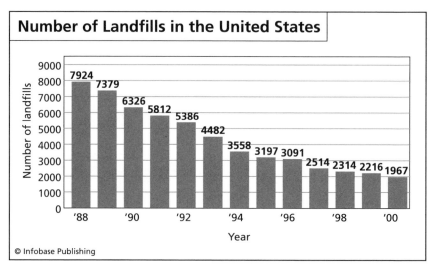

Number of landfills in the United States, 1988–2000

of a dump, as described at the beginning of this chapter. Another example is New York City.

For decades, the Fresh Kills Landfill, located on Staten Island, served as New York City's largest municipal landfill. Opened in 1948, by 2001 it had become the largest landfill in the world. Indeed, some observers have called Fresh Kills the largest man-made object in the world, a 2,000-acre (800-hectare) phenomenon that can easily be seen from space. Each day, about 27,000 short tons (24,500 metric tons) of the city's solid wastes were delivered to Fresh Kills.

Fresh Kills had many of the same problem as other landfills, however. At one point, authorities reported that it was leaking up to 2 million gallons (7.6 million liters) of liquid wastes into the ground each day. Finally, in 2001, Fresh Kills had reached capacity; there was no more room for wastes, and New York City's last landfill closed down on March 22 of that year. The city was forced to find another site to dump its solid wastes.

The two first choices were locations in Pennsylvania and Virginia, states with large rural areas that had long demonstrated a willingness to take MSW from other cities and states. But having to ship the city's wastes a few hundred miles each day promised to be an economic nightmare. By one estimate, the new waste disposal plan would cost the city an additional $370 million per year, with costs continuing to rise in future years. But the city had few choices. With no landfills of its own at that point, it could only depend on the kindness (and willingness to make a profit) of other states.

And New York City is hardly unique in this respect. Many large cities throughout the nation are now shipping their garbage and trash to other states or to more distant points in their own state with more open land and a willingness to accept their solid wastes. Seattle, for example, now ships out 100 percent of its solid wastes, and Chicago exports more than 60 percent of its wastes.

Each year, the Congressional Research Service prepares a *Report for Congress* that summarizes the shipment of solid wastes between states. In its 2002 report, it reported that the five largest exporters of solid wastes were New York, New Jersey, Illinois, Maryland, and Missouri. The largest exporter, New York, shipped 7,493,130 short tons (6,811,936 metric tons) of solid wastes to other states, while New Jersey transferred out 5,431,121 short tons (4,937,383 metric tons). By contrast, the largest importers of solid wastes were Pennsylvania, Virginia, Michigan, Ohio, and Indiana. Pennsylvania received by far the largest amount, 10,666,090 short tons (9,696,445 metric tons), compared with 4,098,684 short tons (3,726,076 metric tons) for Virginia. Both of these states rank high because they have relatively large rural areas capable of accepting waste materials and they are geographically close to urban areas (such as New York City and Philadelphia) with few or no disposal sites of their own.

Communities have traditionally had relatively few alternatives to dumping their solid wastes on land. The three most common alternatives have been dumping into large bodies of water, such as the Great Lakes or the oceans; incineration of solid wastes; and recycling. Of these three options, dumping into bodies of water is now large prohibited, so incineration and recycling are the only options available to most communities.

Municipal Solid Waste Disposal: Incineration

The incineration of solid wastes has a relatively short history. The first waste incineration plant was built in Nottingham, in Great Britain, in the late 1870s. Interestingly enough, the plant was designed to use the heat produced from burning solid wastes to heat a housing development in nearby St. Annes. The use of heat generated by waste incineration is frequently recommended in modern incineration programs, although it is not actually put to use in very many instances.

Interest in waste incineration grew relatively quickly in Great Britain, and more than 200 such plants were in use by 1910. A number of objections to the practice developed, however, and by 1996 only six incinerators remained in the whole nation.

Interest in waste incineration in the United States kept pace with that in Great Britain. The Boston Health Department declared in 1890, for example, that waste incineration was the "best and safest" means of trash disposal. But the cost of building municipal incinerators was so great that it recommended that individual families burn their own solid wastes in their kitchens! Still, by 1914, there were more than 300 incinerators (often called *cremators*) throughout the country. Incineration soon became even more popular than land disposal as a way of getting rid of solid wastes. A national survey conducted in 1924 showed that the single most common method of solid waste disposal was use as animal feed and fertilizer (a reflection of the nation's largely rural population), accounting for 38 percent of all such wastes, while incineration was the second most popular method (29 percent), and land disposal the third most popular (17 percent).

At first glance, incineration would appear to be a very desirable method of disposing of solid wastes. It certainly solves the single most important problem in most communities: lack of space for waste disposal. But a host of environmental problems associated with incineration limit its usefulness in many settings. First, incinerators tend to be very expensive to build. Although they are likely to pay for themselves many times over during their lifetimes, many communities are still unwilling or unable to pay the initial construction and start-up costs needed to start an incineration program.

Also, incinerators tend to release toxic substances into the environment. Some escape into the air when synthetic products are burned, while others are left behind in the ash that remains after incineration. Since these toxic products are easily ignored, a community may not be aware of the full environmental impact of incineration. In addition, environmentalists have observed that incineration plants are often sited in communities with large racial or ethnic minorities, creating an unfair burden on a portion of the society that is among the least able to fight for its own environmental rights.

The costs of incinerators and their pollution potential have made them far less popular in the United States than in many other parts of the world. (A form of incineration known as *high temperature combustion* remains a major method of waste disposal in Japan and some parts of Europe, however.) After World War II, construction of new incinerators decreased until the total number of plants in the United States fell to an all-time low of about 15 in 1960. Then the number rose for two decades before declining once more to the current level of about 112 incinerators, as shown in the graph. A major factor in the latest shift away from incineration as a method of waste disposal was the 1970 Clean Air Act, which strictly limited the amount and

Number of municipal solid waste incinerators in the United States (to 2002)

types of pollutants that could be released to the atmosphere by such plants.

Of the 112 U.S. incinerators reported in 2002, 102, or 91 percent, were *waste-to-energy facilities,* also known as *refuse-derived fuel* (RDF) facilities. These incinerators burn municipal solid wastes and use the heat produced to generate electricity. In 2003, these 102 incinerators burned about 15 percent of the nation's MSW, generating about 2,800 megawatts of power. This output accounted for about one-quarter of all the electricity generated from biomass (organic materials that can be burned to produce energy or converted into fuel), and about 1.4 percent of all the electricity generated in the United States.

Proponents of waste-to-energy facilities argue that they solve a number of environmental problems. For example, they prevent the release of greenhouse gases, such as methane, carbon dioxide, and oxides of nitrogen, that would further increase global warming. Incinerators also contribute to the conservation of valuable fossil-fuel resources, they say. And, of course, they essentially solve two problems at once by providing a method for dealing with problems of solid waste disposal while offering a new source of energy.

Critics of waste incineration argue that these plants often create more environmental problems than they solve. They point out, for example, that incinerators are a major source of dioxin, mercury, and halogenated hydrocarbon release into the atmosphere. In addition, incinerators are very expensive to build and to maintain, and they provide fewer jobs to members of the surrounding community than other methods of solid waste disposal. Also, companies have a dismal record of siting incinerators in disadvantaged communities, where residents suffer the worst consequences of incinerator use. Finally, waste-to-energy incinerators are of little value in tropical and subtropical countries, where the cost of plants and the availability of additional energy sources make them impractical.

Reducing Municipal Solid Wastes: Recycling

The idea of reusing materials is hardly a new one. Archaeologists know that most civilizations have reused building materials over and over again. The bricks and stones used to build a temple, a monument, or some other structure were often used in the construction of a later building. One of the great architectural traditions in Thailand, for example, was to use the dishes broken each day after they had been used to serve meals in the royal dining room to decorate the Wat Arun, one of the king's royal temples. In another example, the Roman Colosseum "served for centuries essentially as a quarry" from which stones were taken to build other structures in the city, as William Rathje and Cullen Murphy pointed out in *Rubbish! The Archaeology of Garbage.*

Still, recycling as we know it today—the intentional collection, (sometimes) reformulation and redesign, and reuse of materials, primarily to reduce the volume of solid wastes—is a relatively modern concept. Some historians point to the construction of the first paper mill in the United States, built on the shores of Wissachichon Creek near Philadelphia in 1690, as the earliest example of recycling in this country. But that assessment ignores the primary motivation of William Rittenhouse, the builder. Rittenhouse used old papers and rags in his mill not as a way of reducing solid wastes, but as an alternative method for producing paper.

Perhaps the earliest true example of systematic, large-scale recycling as a method of reducing the volume of solid wastes in the United States took place in 1897 under a new commissioner of street cleaning in New York City, Col. George E. Waring. Waring's stated goal for keeping New York's streets clean was twofold. First, he wanted not just to hide the garbage that was discarded in the city every day, but actually to get rid of it. Second, Waring wanted to transform the chore of waste removal from an additional expense for the city into an activity by which the city could actually make money.

To accomplish these goals, Waring established the country's first system for waste recycling. He appointed one group of workers to collect ashes and transport them to landfills, where they could be used to construct new land for profitable use. He selected another group of workers to collect animal wastes, which were then rendered for use as fertilizer. A third team of workers was assigned the task of collecting rages, paper, and other products that could be reused in their original form or to produce new materials (such as paper from rags and wastepaper). Waring's system applied to just about any material that might have some valuable future use, such as paper, metals, burlap bags, carpeting, twine, rubber, glass, and horsehair. Anything that could not be recycled profitably was sent to an incinerator, where it was burned to produce electricity that could be sold to residents.

Unfortunately, Waring remained in office only three months. When a new mayor was elected in December 1897, Waring resigned and his system for recycling wastes was abandoned. The city returned to its traditional methods of waste disposal, one of which was ocean dumping. By the 1890s, the city no longer dumped its wastes from specially built platforms above the East River, but from barges that traveled out into the Atlantic Ocean before disposing of their cargoes.

New York City's waste-disposal problems in the 1890s were not typical of those of the country at large. In 1900, the United States was still a predominantly rural nation, with 65 percent of the population living on farms and in other rural areas. Recycling programs in most of the country were relatively simple. Urban areas arranged to have their wastes transported to the countryside, where they were used for fertilizer, and food products and materials that could be used for fuel were returned to the cities from rural areas. Recycling was a routine part of most people's lives at the time. Worn-out clothing was not discarded, but cut up to be used for quilts, rags, paper, and other products. Milk bottles were returned to dairies, where they were washed, sterilized, and reused. In general, most of the materials used in cities and on farms were not really discarded but were simply recycled for other uses.

This pattern began to change around the 1920s in response to three important developments. First, the United States became more urbanized. By 1920, for the first time in the nation's history, more people lived in urban areas (about 55 million) than in rural areas (about 50 million). The volume of solid wastes produced in cities and towns increased proportionally, and simple recycling systems of two decades earlier were more difficult to sustain.

Second, economic growth during the same period brought about a corresponding increase in Americans' per capita income. That increase amounted to about 38 percent between 1900, when the per capita income was $757 (in 1960 dollars), and 1920, when it had reached $1,050. That trend continued throughout the century: Per capita income jumped by 30 percent between 1920 and 1940, by 56 percent between 1940 and 1960, by 347 percent between 1960 and 1980, and by 196 percent between 1980 and 2000. During the 20th century, the United States largely became a country that did not need to "pinch pennies" but could afford to throw out products and materials before they were used up, without thought of recycling.

The third factor affecting recycling patterns was the explosion of new materials and new products, most as the result of chemical research. The products we consume today are made largely of nonrenewable materials, such as plastics, that cannot be obtained from the Earth itself but are the products of scientific research. In 1900, about 40 percent of all the products consumed in the United States were made of renewable materials, such as wood, fibers, and agricultural products. The remaining 60 percent of materials were made of nonrenewable materials, such as metals, minerals, and synthetic organic compounds. By 2000, the ratio had changed dramatically, with only 8 percent of products consumed in the United States made of renewable materials, and the remaining 92 percent made of nonrenewable materials.

The joint result of these three factors was that, by the 1960s, Americans had adopted an attitude about solid wastes quite different from that of their 1900 forebears. They were consuming a much larger volume of materials, most of which were not naturally biodegradable, that were simply being dumped in the most convenient locations: in open dumps, landfills, large lakes, or the oceans.

The modern recycling movement had its origins in the late 1960s, along with the growth of the modern environmental movements. Books such as *The Waste Makers* (by Vance Packard, whose career is profiled in the sidebar on pages 150–151) and *The Affluent Society* (by John Kenneth Galbraith) called upon Americans to consider how their consumerist philosophy was affecting the environment. One of the campaigns that grew out of the new environmentalism aimed to find new ways of reducing the volume of wastes produced in the country and to develop environmentally friendly ways of disposing of those

◄ VANCE PACKARD (1914–1996) ►

Americans are often awakened to new environmental problems as a result of articles written or speeches given by prominent scientists or politicians who have become interested in the problem. Such was the case when Rachel Carson wrote about the dangers of pesticide pollution in her now-famous book *Silent Spring* (1962).

Sometimes, however, an environmental warning has an unexpected source, a fiction or nonfiction writer who, for reasons of his or her own, chooses to produce a work about a new threat to the environment. This was the situation when Vance Packard wrote his 1959 best-seller *The Waste Makers*. Packard's book took as its subject planned obsolescence, the policy adopted by many manufacturers to build the products they made to be out of date in a predictable period.

Vance Packard was born in Granville Summit, Pennsylvania, on May 22, 1914. He earned a B.S. from Pennsylvania State University in 1936 and an M.A. in the following year from Columbia University. His first job was as a reporter for the *Centre Daily Times,* the local newspaper for State College, Pennsylvania. He later worked as a reporter, editor, columnist, and feature writer at the *Boston Record* (1937–38), Associated Press Feature Service (1938–42), *American* magazine (1942–56), and *Collier's* magazine (1956). He lectured on reporting and magazine writing at Columbia University from 1941 to 1944 and at New York University from 1945 to 1957.

His first two books were *How to Pick a Mate* (with Clifford Rose Adams; 1946) and *Animal IQ: The Human Side of Animals* (1950), neither a particular success. His first triumph was the publication in 1957 of *The Hidden Persuaders,* a book about the techniques used by advertisers to sell their products. The book went on to become a *New York Times* best-seller, with sales of more than a million copies. The success of *The Hidden Persuaders* was repeated with other books on what was then known as "pop sociology," that is, analyses of popular social issues from a nonacademic perspective.

wastes that were being produced. Two methods of recycling are now in wide use in the United States. The first, called *resource recovery,* involves the construction of large plants to which a community's sol-

Unlike nearly all preceding generations of humans, 20th-century Americans had begun to accept the fact that many of the products they bought were not made very well. They were not surprised when items broke down or wore out in a relatively short period. When that happened, they could simply throw the product away and buy a new (and sometimes "improved") product. This policy of "planned obsolescence" made consumers happy because they were constantly presented with the opportunity of shopping for new items, and it made manufacturers happy because it kept plants operating at maximal capacity in the production of new products. The theme of Packard's book was a simple and powerful one: "Wastefulness has become a part of the American way of life."

The problem for the environment, of course, is that planned obsolescence virtually guarantees an ever-accumulating collection of trash, the first stage in the waste-management problem that the nation faces in such large volumes today. In *The Waste Makers,* Packard pointed out the social, economic, ethical, and environmental problems arising out of the "throw-away" mentality existing in the United States in the 1950s.

In addition to *The Hidden Persuaders* and *The Waste Makers,* Packard released *The Status Seekers* (1959), an exploration of class behavior in the United States; *The Pyramid Climbers* (1962), about men and women trying to climb the "corporate ladder" to success; *The Naked Society* (1964), dealing with the methods by which corporations intruded on individual privacy; *The Sexual Wilderness* (1968), a discussion of changing social mores in the United States; *A Nation of Strangers* (1972), an analysis of the ways in which increasing mobility of American workers was likely to have unforeseen and dangerous effects on society; and *The People Shapers* (1977), a somewhat terrifying study of the potential of medical and psychological research to change the very nature of human life.

By the end of the 1970s, Packard appeared to have exhausted the topics on which he could or wanted to write and he spent the last two decades of his life largely in retirement. He died in Martha's Vineyard, Massachusetts, on December 12, 1996.

id wastes are delivered. The plant then separates those wastes into various components, such as metals, plastics, and garbage. Ferrous metals, for example, can be extracted by passing the wastes under large magnets. These metals can then be sold to scrap metal dealers for recycling.

Combustible portions of the wastes that cannot be recycled are then burned to produce energy. In this respect, a resource recovery plant is similar to a waste-to-energy incinerator. In fact, the terms *resource recovery plant* and *waste-to-energy incinerator* are sometimes used interchangeably. Noncombustible materials in waste are then shredded and buried in a sanitary landfill. Since they are treated before dumping, they tend to take up less space and are more suitable for landfill disposal.

The second method of recycling is called *source separation.* In this system individual householders separate their own wastes into recyclable and nonrecyclable parts. For example, they may put empty glass bottles, aluminum cans, and wastepapers into one container and garbage and yard trimmings into a second container. Some cities require an even more refined separation process, requiring residents to place glass in one container, plastic in a second container, metals in a third container, paper in a fourth container, and so on. Sanitation workers then pick up trash at private homes, keeping each type separate and storing types in separate bins at a recycling center. From that point, the recyclable materials can be sold directly to scrap dealers and nonrecyclable materials can be incinerated or buried.

Recycling programs have been remarkably successful in the United States since the 1960s. In 2000, there were curbside "source separation" recycling programs in 9,250 communities. In addition, there were 3,800 separate programs for the collection of yard trimmings. As already noted, resource recovery plants had become somewhat less popular, with just over 100 such plants in operation in 2000. These plants had a total daily capacity of 95,700 short tons (87,000 metric tons) of wastes.

The accompanying graph shows the trends in U.S. recycling between 1960 and 2005 (the last year for which data are available). So little attention was paid to recycling prior to 1960 that the U.S. government has no long-term statistics on this topic. As the graph indicates, the percentage of municipal solid wastes being recycled increased from just over 6 percent in 1960 to about 30 percent in

2005. An additional 7 percent of biodegradable wastes were recycled in 2005 for composting. That number increased from 0 percent in 1960, 1970, and 1980, and from 2 percent in 1990, the first year in which measurable amounts of biodegradable materials were recycled in the country.

Overall trends in the management of solid wastes in the United States to 2000, the last year for which data are available, are also shown in the graph below. Notice that while the great majority of wastes are still sent to landfills or incinerated, increasing amounts are now recycled in one way or another.

For some environmentalists, finding better methods to get rid of municipal solid wastes is not a satisfactory goal. They argue that the real objective should be to reduce the amount of solid wastes produced. This philosophy has come to be known as *source reduction*. The EPA defines source reduction as "the practice of designing, manufacturing, purchasing, or using materials (such as products and packaging) in ways that reduce the amount or toxicity of trash created." The EPA also points out that "reusing items is another way to stop waste at the source because it delays or avoids that item's entry in the waste collection and disposal system."

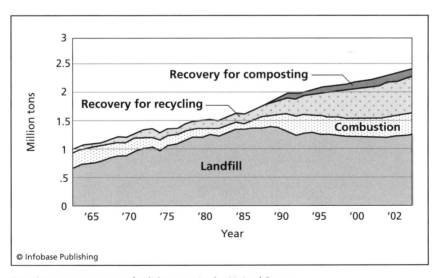

Trends in management of solid wastes in the United States

One major focus of source reduction are packaging materials. Many objects are sold or shipped today with multiple layers of packaging. According to some estimates, packaging materials constitute between a quarter and a third of all municipal solid wastes. These materials are used in some cases for only a few minutes or hours and then thrown away. A frequently quoted statistic about the packaging problem is that the total amount of plastic used for packaging increased five times as fast between 1990 and 1997 as did the rate of plastic recycling. If so, it is obvious that recycling is not going to make a major impact on the solid waste disposal problem in the long run.

Another area of possible savings are glass and plastic bottles. Again, containers of this kind have traditionally been made for a single use, after which they tend to end up in a landfill. But pressures have been building on manufacturers to encourage consumers to return used bottles, which can then be cleaned and reused. For example, in 1971 Oregon became the first state to enact a bottle deposit law. That law requires that consumers pay a deposit on all beers and carbonated drinks purchased in the state. The deposit for most containers if five cents. When the container is returned, the consumer receives a refund equal to the amount of the deposit. As of 2006, 11 states had passed some form of bottle deposit law: California, Connecticut, Delaware, Hawaii, Iowa, Maine, Massachusetts, Michigan, New York, Oregon, and Vermont.

A variety of other efforts are being made to prevent consumer products from ending up in waste-disposal systems, whether they be landfills, incinerators, or recycling centers. Many manufacturers have developed or are developing plans to have consumers return to them all or some portion of the products they sell. For example, in 2001 the Sony Corporation began to retrieve and recycle its consumer electronics, including televisions and computer monitors, in six states.

Many nations around the world have already made legal commitments to source reduction. For example, the European Union requires manufacturers to take back all automobiles made in Europe when consumers are ready to dispose of them, and 85 percent of those cars must be reusable or recyclable. Norway has passed a law requiring manufacturers of electrical and electronic products to collect and reuse or recycle the materials from which they were produced. And under its National Solid Waste Policy, Brazil requires corporations to obtain a special type of license that obligates them to take back all or part of the products they manufacture and sell.

Even modest efforts in manufacturing processes can produce significant gains. For example, the Environmental Protection Agency has reported that the average weight of a plastic soft drink bottle was reduced from 2.4 ounces to 1.8 ounces (68 grams to 51 grams) between 1977 and 1999. That change resulted in a savings of about 250 million pounds (113 million kilograms) of plastic per year. Similarly, the McDonald's Corporation made a number of seemingly minor changes that also contribute to source reduction. For example, they (1) reduced the size of their napkins by one inch, saving about 12 million pounds (5.4 million kilograms) of paper each year; (2) reduced the weight of paper used to wrap sandwiches from 20-pound test to 15-pound test, saving about 3 million pounds (1.4 million kilograms) of paper per year; (3) reduced the number of corrugated dividers in their cup packages, saving 2 million pounds (900,000 kilograms) of paper per year; and (4) replaced the heavy paper and foam used in their hot cups with a lighter material, saving more that 9 million pounds (4 million kilograms) of paper and plastic annually.

Overall, as a result of many seemingly minor changes such as these, more than 50 million short tons (45 million metric tons) of municipal solid wastes were saved in 1999 alone, according to the EPA.

Industrial Wastes

The solid wastes produced by industrial operations pose a problem similar to that of municipal solid wastes: simply the volume of waste produced annually. The volume of industrial solid wastes generated in the United States is roughly twice that of MSW, about 570 million short tons (518 million metric tons) in 2000. But industrial solid wastes also pose a very different kind of problem in that they also contain a number of chemical elements and compounds that are hazardous to the health of humans, other animals, and plants. These elements and compounds are classified as *hazardous wastes.* Hazardous wastes pose a variety of technological, economic, and

◄ ROBERT BULLARD (1946–   ) ►

Suppose your community has decided to build a new hazardous waste incinerator. Two sites are available. One is located at the edge of a golf course, near a development consisting of homes that cost $1 million or more. The other is located on the edge of the river in a "rundown" part of town. Property in this area is relatively inexpensive, and most of the people who live here are poor and members of minorities who do not own their own homes. Which site will you select for the new incinerator?

Questions like this one are very complex, and no simple answer is possible. However, a good deal of research has been done to find out what the answer most commonly given to such questions is. And the answer is that the poor, minority neighborhood is much more likely to become the home of the new incinerator, or the new waste dump, or any other disposal site at which hazardous wastes are likely to be deposited. Over the past two decades, a movement has developed in the United States known as *environmental justice*. It is based on the argument that environmental hazards in the United States (and most other parts of the world) are not distributed equally among people of all races and classes. Instead, poor people and people of color are far more likely to be burdened with a disproportionate share of those hazards, largely because they lack the educational, social, and political skills to fight effectively against the practice. One of the leaders of the environmental justice movement has been Robert Bullard.

Robert Bullard was born in Elba, Alabama, in 1946. He attended Alabama A&M University, from which he received his B.S. degree in government

social problems, some of which are described in the sidebar about the life and work of Robert Bullard.

The Environmental Protection Agency maintains a list of hundreds of elements and compounds classified as "hazardous" and classifies hazardous wastes into four categories, as shown in the table on pages 158–159. Any company that produces solid wastes must determine on its own whether those wastes contain any hazardous waste under the EPA's definition. If it does, it is required to treat, store, and/or dispose of those wastes by some method that has been approved by the EPA.

in 1968. He then earned his master's degree in sociology from Atlanta University in 1972 and his Ph.D. in the same field from Iowa State University in 1976. While still a student at Iowa State, he worked as an urban planner in Des Moines, as administrative assistant at the Office of Minority Affairs at Iowa State, and research coordinator for Polk County, Iowa.

Bullard's first academic assignment was as director of research at the Urban Research Center of Texas Southern University, from 1976 to 1978. In 1979, Bullard and his wife filed a lawsuit against the city of Houston, charging that Browning Ferris Industries, one of the largest national waste companies, practiced "environmental racism" in the siting of their landfills for hazardous wastes. That is, the Bullards said, Browning Ferris chose locations for their waste disposal sites to a significant extent on the basis of the skin color and income level of residents, rather than on strictly economic bases. Four years later, Bullard published one of the seminal scholarly papers on this issue, "Solid Waste Sites and the Black Houston Community" (*Sociological Inquiry* 53 [spring 1983]).

After 1978, Bullard held academic appointments at a number of universities, including Rice (1980), the University of Tennessee (1987–88), the University of California at Berkeley (1988–89), the University of California at Riverside (1989–93), and the University of California at Los Angeles (1993–94). In 1994, Bullard was appointed to his current position as Ware Professor of Sociology and director of the Environmental Justice Resource Center at Clark Atlanta University.

Bullard has authored a number of books that have become standards in the field of environmental justice. (See Further Reading.)

Under the conditions of the 1976 Resource Conservation and Recovery Act (RCRA), the Environmental Protection Agency focuses its efforts in dealing with hazardous wastes on 30 hazardous chemicals of special importance. Those chemicals are called *waste minimization priority chemicals* (WMPC). The list of WMPC, shown in the chart on page 160, changes over time, reflecting success in reducing the amount of one or another chemical in the environment, the ability to remove that chemical from the list, and the replacement of that chemical by another of environmental importance.

◀ CATEGORIES OF HAZARDOUS WASTES (AS DEFINED BY THE U.S. ENVIRONMENTAL PROTECTION AGENCY) ▷

CATEGORY	DEFINITION	EXAMPLE
F listed wastes	Commonly found wastes from non-specific sources	Spent cyanide plating bath solutions from electroplating operations, waste halogenated solvents used in degreasing, residues from the incineration or thermal treatment of contaminated soil, sludge from petroleum refining
K listed wastes	Wastes from specific manufacturing operations (usually chemical or pesticide manufacture)	Wastes from wood preserving operations, manufacture of paints, and manufacture of organic chemicals
P listed wastes	Highly toxic chemicals that are rarely used, are banned, or are permitted for limited uses	Acrolein, arsenic trioxide, dieldrin, heptachlor, methiocarb, osmium tetroxide, 2-propenal

CATEGORY	DEFINITION	EXAMPLE
U listed wastes	Less toxic chemicals that are usually intermediaries in some production process and not final commercial products	Acetaldehyde, 1,2-dichlorobenzene, calcium chromate, chloroform, DDT, mercury, paraldehyde, phthalic anhydride

The EPA prepares a biennial report on its list of waste minimization priority chemicals. This report summarizes the quantities of each chemical produced and the states in which the largest quantities of each chemical are produced, the major sources, the methods of disposal used, and other important data about the listed substances. The most recent biennial report, which covers the years from 1991 to 2001, was published in February 2004.

The five WMPCs produced in the largest volume in 2001 (the last year for which data are available), for example, were lead, naphthalene, hexachloro-1,3-butadiene, hexachlorobenzene, and hexachloroethane. Lead, naphthalene, and hexachloro-1,3-butadiene alone accounted for almost 80 percent of all WMPCs generated in 2001. Lead itself was the largest single WMPC produced during the year, accounting for nearly 37 million pounds (16 million kilograms), or 53 percent of all WMPCs produced during the year.

The industry responsible for the largest amount of WMPCs produced in 2001 was the alkalies and chlorine industry (SIC code 2812). (The Standard Industrial Classification [SIC] code is a system for categorizing all types of industries that operate in the United States.) The next four industries, in terms of WMPCs produced in 2001, were blast furnaces and steel mills (SIC code 3312), primary nonferrous metals (SIC code 3339), industrial inorganic chemicals (SIC code 2819), and storage batteries (SIC code 3691). Lead is an important by-product in all of these operations, accounting for the very large

◁ **WASTE MINIMIZATION PRIORITY CHEMICALS (WMPC) AS OF 2003, AS DEFINED BY THE EPA** ▷

ORGANIC CHEMICALS AND CHEMICAL COMPOUNDS

1,2,4-trichloro-benzene	Dioxins and furans	Naphthalene
1,2,4,5-tetrachloro-benzene	α and β-Endosulfan	PAH group
2,4,5-trichlorophenol	Fluorene	Pendimethalin
4-bromophenyl phenyl ether	Heptachlor	Pentachloro-benzene
Acenaphthene	Hexachlorobenzene	Pentachloro-nitrobenzene
Acenaphthylene	Hexachloro-1,3-butadiene	Pentachloro-phenol
Anthracene	δ-Hexachloro-cyclohexane	Phenanthrene
Benzo(g,h,i)perylene	Hexachloroethane	Pyrene
Dibenzofuran	Methoxychlor	Trifluralin

METALS AND METAL COMPOUNDS

Cadmium	Lead	Mercury

◁ TRENDS IN GENERATION FOR CERTAIN WMPCS, 1991–2001 ▷

CHEMICAL GROUP	CHEMICAL	1991 QUANTITY (LB)	2001 QUANTITY (LB)	CHANGE (%)
Metals	Lead and lead compounds	78,385,105	36,742,444	−53.1
	Cadmium and cadmium compounds	2,583,408	3,636,610	+43.2
PAHs	Naphthalene	26,872,979	9,918,049	−63.1
	Anthracene	10,821,191	370,586	−96.6
Chlorinated aliphatics	Hexachloro1,3-butadiene	11,490,810	6,482,741	−43.6
	1,2,4-Trichlorobenzene	1,137,181	2,126,359	+87.0

(continues)

▽ TRENDS IN GENERATION FOR CERTAIN WMPCS, 1991–2001 *(continued)* ▷

CHEMICAL GROUP	CHEMICAL	1991 QUANTITY (LB)	2001 QUANTITY (LB)	CHANGE (%)
Pesticides	Heptachlor	4	0	–100
	Methoxychlor	161	0	–100
Dibenzofuran	Dibenzofuran	5,104,604	91,620	–98.2
Mercury	Mercury and mer-cury compounds	186,718	105,769	–43.3

amount of the element and its compounds present in industrial wastes.

The 2001 report on WMPCs contained good news for the battle to contain hazardous wastes. The quantity of WMPCs generated in 2001 was 53 percent less than that of 1991, exceeding the EPA's goal of reducing such wastes by 50 percent by the year 2005.

The table on pages 161–162 lists some of the WMPCs for which progress was especially significant. Notice that the reduction of some chemicals on the list approached nearly 100 percent, indicating that the elimination of these chemicals as environmental risks had nearly been achieved.

The 2001 news was not all good, as the table suggests. The amounts of some WMPCs discarded increased—in some cases, as with cadmium and its compounds and 1,2,4-trichlorobenzene—quite significantly. Overall, the disposal of some of the most important hazardous chemicals was being put under control.

An interesting revelation of the 2001 report was the unequal distribution of hazardous waste disposal in the United States. Indeed, nearly 40 percent of the hazardous wastes disposed of in 2001 were from just one of the EPA's 10 regions, Region 6, consisting of Arkansas, Louisiana, New Mexico, Oklahoma, and Texas. And, as the table on page 164 shows, a dozen states accounted for just over 86 percent of all hazardous wastes generated in the whole nation.

A question of some importance, of course, is the method of disposal of these hazardous wastes. At one time, the two most popular methods of disposal were landfill and impoundment in surface bodies of water especially built to hold such wastes. Both of these methods pose serious problems, however, as hazardous wastes can sometimes evaporate into the air or soak into the ground and contaminate both surface water and groundwater. Some of the most deplorable cases of environmental pollution in the last century have been associated with one or the other of these two methods of hazardous waste disposal.

Today, trends in waste disposal have changed markedly, as shown in the table on page 165. The single most common method of disposal is deepwell or underground injection, in which wastes are buried in abandoned mines, caves, or other underground structures, where, the assumption is, they will remain for very long periods.

◁ QUANTITY OF HAZARDOUS WASTE GENERATED IN LARGEST WASTE-PRODUCING STATES, 2003 ▷

STATE	HAZARDOUS WASTE GENERATED (IN SHORT TONS)	PERCENTAGE OF U.S. TOTAL	RANK
Texas	6,585,102	21.8	1
Louisiana	4,559,668	15.1	2
Kentucky	2,441,400	8.1	3
Mississippi	2,004,551	6.6	4
Ohio	1,800,170	6.0	5
Alabama	1,252,012	4.1	6
New Jersey	1,236,150	4.1	7
New York	1,130,623	3.7	8
Illinois	1,125,485	3.7	9
Indiana	988,323	3.3	10

A variety of treatment methods are also available to convert hazardous materials to nonhazardous materials, after which they are disposed of in landfills, by *stabilization,* or by some other method. The term *stabilization* in this table refers to any chemical or physical

◁ **METHODS OF HAZARDOUS WASTE
DISPOSAL IN THE UNITED STATES, 2003** ▷

DISPOSAL METHOD	TONS OF WASTE MANAGED	PERCENTAGE OF ALL WASTE
Deepwell/under-ground injection	14,479,172	34.4
Aqueous organic treatment	5,584,326	13.3
Aqueous inorganic treatment	2,127,196	5.1
Landfill	1,675,669	4.0
Energy recovery	1,467,938	3.5
Incineration	1,273,040	3.0
Stabilization	748,077	1.1
Other treatments	7,745,624	18.4
Other disposal	3,349,082	8.0
All other methods	3,872,791	9.2

method used to prevent hazardous chemicals from escaping into the surrounding environment. In many cases, wastes are simply sealed up inside leak-proof containers, or materials are added to and blended with them to prevent their migration into the earth or groundwater.

Some of the most common stabilizing agents used in hazardous waste disposal are Portland cement, lime, fly ash, and cement kiln dust. Small quantities of hazardous wastes are disposed of by incineration, energy conversion, manufacture of fuels, or other practical applications.

Each of the methods of hazardous waste disposal listed poses potential risks to the environment. For example, every effort is made in injecting wastes into underground holes or deep wells, but there is always some risk of a break in the injection system, allowing wastes to seep into the surrounding earth and groundwater. Incineration is generally regarded as a relatively safe method of disposing of hazardous wastes, but there is always some risk that toxic gases will escape into the air. The disposal of contaminated ash resulting from incineration is an additional problem to be solved.

Nuclear Wastes

Nuclear wastes are wastes produced by a variety of processes and operations in which radioactive materials are used. The five most important generators of nuclear wastes are nuclear power plants, industrial plants, medical institutions, research universities and institutions, and government facilities. Research and development on nuclear weapons, such as fission and fusion bombs, are among the most important generators of nuclear wastes, although the volume of waste produced changes as the nation's military policy changes. Data on weapons production and waste generation from this source are difficult to obtain. As a result, most of the reliable statistics available on nuclear wastes report data from the five nonmilitary sources listed.

The volume of nuclear wastes produced is relatively small compared with the volume of municipal solid wastes and industrial wastes and is very much less than that of agricultural and mining wastes. Each year, for example, the 104 nuclear power plants now operating in the United States generate a total of about 30,000 short tons (27,000 metric tons) of nuclear waste. That volume is about 0.001 percent the amount of hazardous wastes produced every year. In the five decades that nuclear power plants have been operating in the United States, a total of about 9,000 short tons (8,200 metric tons) of nuclear wastes have been produced. Much larger volumes of wastes have also been generated by the use of radioactive *isotopes* in medicine, industry, and research.

The problem is that nuclear wastes contain radioactive isotopes that release life-threatening ionizing radiation that may pose a threat to humans and the environment for hundreds, thousands, or even millions of years. This radiation can cause carcinogenic, teratogenic, and mutagenic effects in small amounts and can result in radiation sickness and death in larger amounts.

Nuclear wastes are sometimes divided into two categories: *low-level wastes* and *high-level wastes.* The difference in these two categories is the intensity of radiation produced. Low-level wastes tend to produce relatively small amounts of radioactivity and pose moderate health problems compared with high-level wastes. About 99 percent of all low-level waste originates in nuclear power plants. Such wastes consist of protective clothing, trash, contaminated water, and contaminated equipment, such as filters, X-ray equipment, and smoke alarms. Worldwide, low-level wastes make up about 90 percent by volume of all nuclear wastes, but they account for only about 1 percent of the total radioactivity emitted by those wastes.

High-level wastes consist of spent nuclear fuel and reprocessed wastes. Isotopes of uranium make up by far the majority of high-level wastes, accounting for about 94 percent of the mass of all such wastes. An additional 1 percent consists of plutonium isotopes, and the remaining 5 percent, of isotopes of other elements.

For a variety of technical purposes, other classes of nuclear waste have also been defined:

➢ *Intermediary-level waste* is, as the name suggests, waste that contains more radioactivity than low-level waste and less radioactivity than high-level waste. It is often obtained from nuclear processes in which both low- and high-level wastes are mixed before collection and disposal.

➢ *Transuranic wastes* are so called because they contain isotopes of elements heavier than uranium, primarily plutonium, americium, and neptunium. Since these isotopes emit alpha particles, they present certain kinds of disposal problems not encountered with other kinds of nuclear wastes.

➤ *Mill tailings* are wastes produced when uranium ore is mined and then processed. In 2003, there were 26 sites licensed to handle mill tailings in the United States. Most of the sites were no longer processing uranium ore. In addition, another 24 sites have been abandoned. The licensed sites contain about 220 million short tons (200 million metric tons) of mill tailings and the 24 abandoned sites, about 29 million short tons (26 million metric tons) of tailings.

➤ *Spent-fuel wastes* is a term sometimes used to describe wastes from nuclear power plants consisting of spent *fuel rods*.

➤ *Defense high-level wastes* are those produced as a result of military research during the recovery of the uranium and plutonium used in making fission and fusion bombs.

Low- and high-level wastes pose very different kinds of disposal and storage problems. These problems are a result of the half-life of the isotopes present in each kind of waste. The *half-life* of an isotope is the time required for one-half of a given sample of the isotope to decay. The half-lives of most isotopes present in low-level wastes range from a few hours to a few years. Disposal systems need to isolate low-level wastes, therefore, for no more than a hundred years. By contrast, high-level wastes must be confined essentially forever, that is, for hundreds of thousands of years or more.

The technology of low-level waste disposal has evolved significantly over the past half-century. In the 1950s and 1960s, it was not unusual for such wastes to be dumped directly into a landfill, a settling pond, or some other open-air area. In most but not all cases wastes were first placed into metallic drums or concrete containers like those shown in the photograph on page 169 before being dumped into a landfill or pond. Various degrees of caution were used in sealing these containers. The result was that low-level wastes frequently leaked out of their containers, contaminating the surrounding soil and groundwater. One of the worst legacies of the use of nuclear ma-

Because no effective, long-term method for storing high-level nuclear wastes has yet been developed, such wastes are still stored underground, under water, in steel drums (as shown here), or in some other way that is not designed to provide safe storage for the very long periods required for such wastes. (U.S. Department of Energy/Photo Researchers, Inc.)

terials over the past 50 years has been the vast area of land seriously contaminated by leaks from low-level waste repositories.

The U.S. Department of Energy's Savannah River nuclear site is one such example. Environmental studies conducted in the last few years of the 20th century found 515 sites at which low-level wastes had been buried on the site's 310-square-mile area during its 35-year history as a nuclear weapons processing venue from 1953 to 1988. These sites ranged in size from a few square yards to a 195-acre burial ground. Leakage from these sites had contaminated about 5 percent of the groundwater beneath the site.

Similar findings have been reported at a number of other abandoned nuclear waste disposal sites. In most cases, radioactivity from leaking tanks, drums, and other containers can be detected as wide-spreading "plumes" that spread out underground in all directions or in one predominant direction from the buried wastes.

Today, burial of low-level wastes is a much more sophisticated process. Those wastes are usually first compacted or incinerated to reduce their volume and then deposited in heavily lined drums encased in concrete. Wastes may first be immobilized, by mixing with concrete or cement, before being deposited in tanks or other containers.

In contrast to historical waste-disposal practices, in which generators of wastes were responsible for its disposal, the U.S. Nuclear Regulatory Commission (NRC) now operates all licensed facilities for disposal of low-level wastes. The three licensed facilities are located at Barnwell, South Carolina; Hanford, Washington; and Clive, Utah. Three sites previously operated by the NRC—at Maxey Flats, Kentucky; West Valley, New York; and Sheffield, Illinois—have been closed as a result of environmental problems at each location. There is some evidence that leakage taking place at Barnwell and Hanford may also be impacting the environment and that they, too, will eventually have to be closed to protect soil and groundwater in surrounding regions.

The disposal of high-level nuclear wastes is arguably the most troublesome unresolved problem facing the nuclear industry and the U.S. government today. Quite astonishingly, more than 50 years after the nuclear industry had its beginning in the United States, no permanent system has been developed for the long-term storage of high-level nuclear wastes. As of 2007, all of these highly radioactive, long-lived wastes are being stored in "temporary" facilities, sometimes at the site where they were generated and sometimes at more remote locations operated by the U.S. government.

These "temporary" storage facilities were constructed with the understanding that the federal government would eventually devise a comprehensive plan for the collection, transport, and disposal of these most dangerous of all radioactive wastes. The most common system devised for "temporary" storage were *spent fuel pools*. Spent fuel pools are structures like swimming pools, with dimensions of about 40 feet by 60 feet (15 meters by 20 meters). Spent fuel from a reactor is transported through water-filled canals beneath the floor of the reactor into the pool, where it is covered with at least 20 feet (six meters) of water. This water is deep enough to absorb radiation produced by the spent fuel, thereby protecting workers in the plant.

By the late 1970s, existing spent fuel pools were beginning to fill with radioactive wastes from power plants, and alternative disposal systems had to be developed. The most common system adopted was some variation of *dry cask storage.* In the dry cask method, wastes that have been deposited in a pool for about a year are removed, dried, and inserted into a steel cylinder called a *cask.* The wastes are surrounded by an inert gas, and the cylinder is sealed. The cylinder is then placed inside a second, and sometimes a third, outer container, all of which are also sealed. The steel cylinders may also be surrounded by a concrete block. Whatever specific design is used, the purpose of the entombment process is to prevent radiation from escaping from the spent fuel and damaging the health of workers or the surrounding environment in general.

As of March 2003, there were 26 spent fuel storage facilities in the United States located in 21 states. A total of about 160,000 spent fuel units containing about 45,000 short tons (41,000 metric tons) of radioactive waste were stored on-site at nuclear power plants and off-site at special storage areas. More than 97 percent of the wastes were still being held at on-site facilities; the rest had been transported to off-site locations.

The U.S. government realized early in the history of nuclear power that some method would need to be devised for the long-term storage of high-level wastes. In 1957, a special study committee of the National Academy of Sciences recommended that these wastes be stored deep underground in an abandoned mine or some comparable engineered facility. Not much was done about the academy report for about 25 years. Then in 1982 the U.S. Congress passed the Nuclear Waste Policy Act, which outlined the government's general plant for long-term storage of high-level wastes.

Under the conditions of that plan, the Department of Energy (DOE) was instructed to locate suitable sites in the United States where high-level wastes could be buried. The first list of nine possible sites developed in 1983 had, by 1986, been whittled down to three possibilities: Hanford, Washington; Deaf Smith County, Texas; and Yucca Mountain, Nevada. A year later, the Congress selected Yucca Mountain from this list and directed the DOE to begin feasibility studies for the construction of an underground storage area buried deep under the mountain.

The plan for the storage of high-level wastes at Yucca calls for the construction of about 35 miles (55 km) of tunnels, 1,000 feet (300 meters) beneath the mountain's surface. The tunnels are designed to lie within a huge cigar-shaped artificial cavern at least 1,000 feet (300 m) above the water table, which lies at the base of the mountain. This design, along with other safety provisions adopted for the site, is intended to prevent the escape of radioactive wastes from the tunnels into the groundwater.

The tunnels, or "drifts," are to be accessed through two entrances in the side of the mountain. Railroad trains will carry nuclear wastes along tracks from one entrance into the bowels of the mountain, where the wastes will be deposited within one of the many drifts. Wastes will be delivered to the mountain in one of three formats, each of which involves a triple-sealing of wastes within specially designed and built steel tubes, about three feet (five meters) long and five feet (1.5 meters) in diameter. The tubes will be handled by giant gantries because they are so large, heavy (each between 46 and 79 short tons; 42 and 72 metric tons), and "hot," in terms of both temperature and radioactivity. Once in place, the tubes will be covered with titanium-steel "drip tubes" designed to prevent underground water from falling on the tubes and causing them to rust. The drifts will be monitored by remote methods for about 100 years, after which, if all goes well, the entrances to the mountain will be sealed. Plans are to deliver about 90 percent of all existing high-level wastes (about 69,000 short tons; 63,000 metric tons) to Yucca, beginning in 2010.

The goal may or may not be achieved. The state of Nevada and a number of environmental groups have been battling the Yucca Mountain plan since the day it was first announced in 1987. Some of the major concerns are that, in spite of all precautions, wastes may leak out of their containers and contaminate the water table;

that changes in climate may result in increased rainfall in the area, increasing the likelihood of waste containers' corroding and releasing wastes into the drifts; that earthquakes, ground movements, or volcanoes may cause waste cylinders to break open, releasing their content into the ground; that transportation of wastes to the mountain poses an unacceptable risk to communities along the shipping route. In addition, the state of Nevada has long argued that it simply is not fair to ask just one state out of 50 to accept *all* of the nation's nuclear high-level wastes. And as long as legal remedies are available to the state and to concerned environmental groups, the planned opening of Yucca Mountain as the nation's high-level waste repository continues to be in question.

In the meantime, nuclear power plants continue to produce an additional 2,000 short tons (1,800 metric tons) of high-level nuclear wastes every year.

A number of factors have contributed to the growth of solid waste disposal as a problem in modern society. One of these factors has been the success of the chemical industry in producing stronger, more durable products for the manufacture of commercial, industrial, and household products. These products have given Americans an impressive standard of living admired by other people around the world. But they have also created new and challenging problems of waste disposal: products that do not decay or that release harmful by-products as they do break down. As one source of the nation's solid waste disposal problem, the chemical industry may also be the nation's best hope for solving this problem. Research chemists today are challenged to find new methods for disposing of products released to the environment after they useful lives have ended. Alternatively, chemists are beginning to think of ways of making products designed to produce fewer solid wastes and less environmental impact in their disposal. The next chapter describes efforts in this direction.

6

GREEN CHEMISTRY

Times Beach, Missouri, was a sleepy town 17 miles west of St. Louis with a population of about 1,200 residents in the early 1970s. The town had been built on a flood plain on the banks of the Meramec River in the 1920s. Most of the homes in Times Beach were fairly simple, many of them constructed on stilts to protect them from the periodic flooding of the Meramec.

One of the few predictable problems the town's leaders faced was the dusty condition of the area's roads. Each year, the town budget had to include a charge for oiling of the roads, to help residents in their ongoing battle against dust. In the summer of 1972 and 1973, the town hired Russell Bliss, a waste oil hauler, to spray its roads. The deal was a bargain, residents thought, at the price of six cents per gallon of oil.

The deal soon proved to be less of a bargain than anyone expected. Bliss had decided to mix with his oil some wastes obtained from a chemical plant in nearby Verona, where the defoliant Agent Orange, used during the Vietnam War, was produced. Residents began to wonder about the oil treatment when the treated roads developed an eerie purple sheen and animals in the area began to die. Town officials soon decided to call in the newly created (1970) U.S. Environmental Protection Agency (EPA) to determine the effects (if any) Bliss's oil treatment had had on the community.

They soon discovered that the Verona wastes used by Bliss were contaminated with dioxins, a group of chemical compounds believed to pose a health threat to humans and other animals. EPA studies showed that the level of dioxins in the town's soil and water were so high that residents were at risk for development of cancer and perhaps other diseases. In one of the most dramatic actions ever taken by the agency, it decided (in cooperation with the state of Missouri and the Federal Emergency Management Agency) to buy the town and pay residents the cost of their relocation to other communities.

According to EPA's initial plans, cleanup of the Times Beach area was to begin in 1984. However, a number of lawsuits delayed that process until 1990, when the EPA hired the Syntex Corporation to remove and incinerate contaminated soil and restore Times Beach to a safe area. That process was finally completed in July 1997, when the area was reopened as the 409-acre Route 66 State Park.

The Problem: Releasing Hazardous Chemicals into the Environment

The chemical industry, in all of its many forms, is responsible for the release of very large quantities of hazardous wastes into the atmosphere, hydrosphere, and lithosphere. These wastes are released in a number of different ways, such as the following:

➤ When hazardous chemicals are used as raw materials in a process; for example, chlorine, a very toxic gas, is an important raw material in the manufacture of plastics, pesticides and herbicides, medical products, fabrics, and many other products.

➤ When they are used as catalysts, such as sulfuric and hydrofluoric acid and mercuric sulfate and mercuric chloride.

➤ When they are used as solvents in reactions; for example, most organic reactants are not soluble in water but are soluble in a variety of organic liquids, many of which are toxic or hazardous in other ways. Some of the most common hazardous solvents are

carbon tetrachloride, chloroform, tetrachloroethylene, trichloroethylene, 1,1,1-trichloroethane, benzene, toluene, and xylene.

➤ When they are the intentional and primary product of an operation; for example, all pesticides are toxic to one type or organism
or another, including humans.

➤ When they are released as secondary by-products. One of the
most notorious examples is dioxin.

➤ When they are set free or formed during the use and/or eventual
disposal of a product; for example, most plastics, when incinerated, produce hydrogen chloride as one product and, in some
cases, other hazardous gases, such as hydrogen cyanide and
phosgene.

Dioxins are a classic example of the way hazardous chemicals
are produced and released to the environment inadvertently. The
term *dioxin* refers to a class of organic compounds more precisely
known as the polychlorinateddibenzo-*p*-dioxins. The parent compound of this family is dibenzo-*p*-dioxin, whose structural formula
is shown on page 177. This compound has 73 possible polychlorinated derivatives, in which two or more of the eight hydrogen atoms
in the molecule are replaced by chlorine atoms. (There are also
two monochlorodibenzo-*p*-dioxins, for a total of 75 congeners of the
molecule.) The most thoroughly studied and one of the most toxic
of these derivatives is 2,3,7,8-tetrachloro-*p*-dioxin, whose structural
formula is shown. 2,3,7,8-tetrachloro-*p*-dioxin (2,3,7,8-TCDD) is a
colorless, odorless crystalline solid that was classified in 1997 by the
World Health Organization (WHO) as a class 1 carcinogen, that is, a
"known human carcinogen."

Dioxins are sometimes—but rarely—produced in nature, most
commonly during volcanic eruptions and forest fires. Their most
common source in the environment are industrial reactions in
which they occur as by-products of other chemical changes or during the incineration of certain synthetic organic compounds. For
example, trace amounts of 2,3,7,8-TCDD occur as an impurity in the
herbicide Agent Orange (a mixture of 2,4,5-trichlorophenoxyacetic
acid [2,4,5-T] and 2,4-dichlorophenoxyacetic acid [2,4-D]), which was

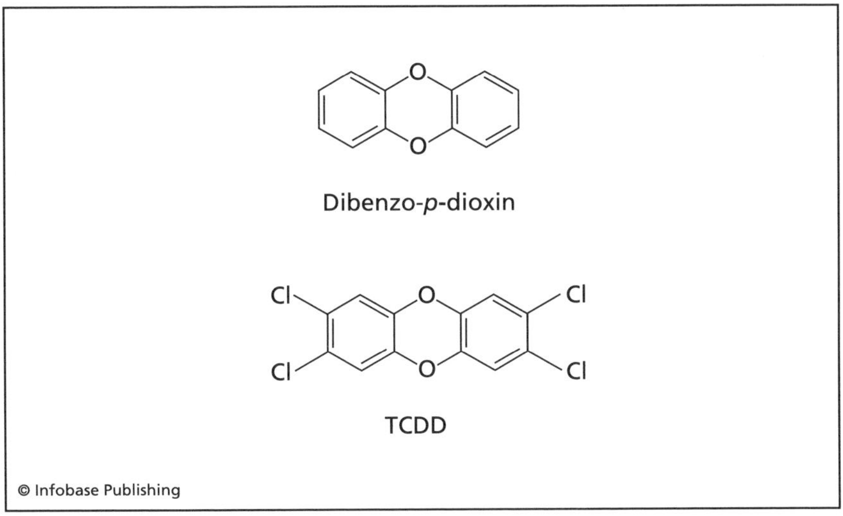

Dibenzo-*p*-dioxin

TCDD

© Infobase Publishing

Formulas for dibenzo-*p*-dioxin and 2,3,7,8 ± TCDD

used in very large amounts during the Vietnam War. It is also produced during the incineration of certain pesticides and herbicides, such as 2,4,5-T and 2,4-D.

There have been occasions in which relatively large quantities of dioxins were released as the result of chemical or industrial accidents. Explosions at chemical plants in Seveso, Italy, in 1976 and at Bhopal, India, in 1984 are examples of such incidents. High levels of dioxin have also been found in animal feed on a few occasions; the source and mechanism of this contamination have not always been clear.

Perhaps the most important point about dioxin pollution is that it has become a normal (although certainly not desirable) consequence of many chemical manufacturing processes used in many countries today. A 1999 report on dioxins from the WHO concluded: "Dioxins are found throughout the world in practically all media, including air, soil, water, sediment, and food, especially dairy products, meat, fish and shellfish. The highest levels of these compounds are found in some soils, sediments and animals. Very low levels are found in water and air." In other words, people around the world are regularly being exposed to some level—albeit small—of a very hazardous class of compounds.

And dioxins are by no means unique in regard to the risks that humans and other animals face as a result of chemical manufacturing operations. Indeed, one only need to look again at chart of Waste Minimization Priority Chemicals (WMPC) in chapter 5 to be reminded of the very large number of hazardous chemicals that have become a normal part of the environment today.

A Solution: Green Chemistry

Until recently, most people and nearly all corporations accepted the release of at least some level of hazardous wastes into the environment as an unpleasant, but necessary, consequence of the huge success of modern chemical technology. Certainly no one is happy about the presence of dioxins (and PCBs and PAHs and other hazardous chemicals) in the environment. They undoubtedly result in some number of health problems and deaths around the world each year. But that is a small price to pay, some would argue, for having such a diverse and rich supply of pesticides, drugs, perfumes, synthetic foods, medicines, and other chemical products.

Beginning in the 1980s, however, a small number of chemists began to question that assumption. Is the release of hazardous materials into the environment *really* inevitable? Must we invariably pay for chemical progress with disease and death?

For some brave souls, the answer to that question was a resounding "No!" We accept the production and release of hazardous chemicals, they said, only because chemists have lacked imagination and motivation to find alternative methods for the commercial production of chemical products. Chemists need to set for themselves a new goal for the 21st century, a goal of finding new processes for the manufacture of chemicals that will (1) make better use of existing raw materials and (2) reduce the amount of hazardous materials released to the environment.

An important force in the development of this new approach to chemistry was the "sustainable development" movement that arose in the early 1980s. The goal of this movement was to find ways for nations to improve the well-being of humans around the world without threatening local and global environments, thus the term *sustainable development.* In 1983, the United Nations appointed an international commission to suggest strategies for reaching this objective. That commission issued its report, entitled "Our Common Future," in 1987. The report is also widely known as the Brundtland Report, after the chair of the commission, Prime Minister Gro Harlem Brundtland of Norway.

One of the major themes in the Brundtland Report was a concept now known in green chemistry as *atom economy* (also sometimes known as *atom utilization*), the notion that chemical manufacturing should attempt to conserve as much of the raw materials (and, hence, atoms) with which it begins as possible and to prevent losing materials (and, hence, atoms) to the environment during manufacturing processes.

Perhaps the single most important event in the creation of a formal, clearly defined, and well-organized green chemistry movement, however, was the adoption in 1990 by the U.S. Congress of the Pollution Prevention Act (now Chapter 133 of Title 42 of the U.S. Code). The purpose of this act was to encourage manufacturers to think about pollution problems from a perspective different from that they had taken in the past. Rather than focusing on ways to *clean up* pollution once it is produced, legislators said, why not look for ways to *prevent* pollution? In the "Findings and Policy" part of the act, Congress pointed out that the United States produces millions of tons of pollutants each year and spends billions of dollars attempting to control that pollution. It further noted that a number of methods already exist for changing production operations that will result in less waste of raw materials, release of fewer pollutants, and reduced risks to worker health and safety.

Congress then went on to assign the Environmental Protection Agency responsibility for the development of green chemistry policies and practices. It charged the EPA with a number of tasks, including the establishment of standard methods for determining source reduction in manufacturing processes, coordinating efforts throughout the federal government to achieve source reduction, to encourage and facilitate source reduction by private business and industry, to establish an advisory council on source reduction technology, to provide training programs in green chemistry, to make recommendations to the Congress for eliminating barriers to source reduction activities, and to create an annual award program to recognize companies that had developed outstanding or innovative source reduction programs.

Within a year of the act's adoption, the EPA had assigned responsibility for its implementation to the Office of Pollution Prevention and Toxics, formed in 1977 to administer the Toxic Substances Control Act, and had begun the first federally funded green chemistry programs. By 1992, the National Science Foundation had also begun funding research on "environmentally benign [chemical] syntheses and processes."

The green chemistry movement also spread to other nations, including the United Kingdom, Australia, Italy, and Japan. In Italy, the green chemistry effort was given the name of INCA, for Interuniversity Consortium "Chemistry for the Environment," a group of 30 universities working to develop environmentally benign methods of chemical manufacture. In the United Kingdom, green chemistry programs were administered largely under the sponsorship of the Royal Society of Chemistry's Green Chemistry Network. One important accomplishment of the network was the creation of the journal *Green Chemistry* in 1999. The journal carries reports of recent research, editorials and news reports on developments in green chemistry, and books. In Japan, a group of chemical organizations formed the Green & Sustainable Chemistry Network, Japan, in 1998. The Japan Chemical Innovation Institute serves as the institutional home for the network.

The Structure of Green Chemistry in the United States

Since it began its formal existence in 1990, the green chemistry philosophy has already resulted in the formation of a variety of programs and agencies. For example, in 1995, the EPA announced the establishment of the Presidential Green Chemistry Challenge Awards. These awards are designed to recognize and promote advances in three general areas:

➤ The development of alternative pathways for chemical reactions, such as new kinds of catalysts; the use of natural processes, such as photochemical reactions; and the use of less harmful and ecologically benign feedstocks (raw materials)

➤ The development of alternative reaction conditions, including the use of more benign solvents and greater attention to the kinds of wastes released to the environment

➤ The use of safer chemicals that are less hazardous than existing materials and that pose less of a threat to workers in the industry and the general public

The first winners of the Green Chemistry Challenge Awards were four chemical corporations, Pharmacia (formerly the Monsanto Company), the Dow Chemical Company, the Rohm and Haas Company, and the Donlar Corporation, and one individual, Professor Mark Holtzapple of the Department of Chemical Engineering at Texas A&M University.

In 1997, a virtual, Internet-based nonprofit organization called the Green Chemistry Institute (GCI) was established, largely through the efforts of Joseph J. Breen, whose career is described in the sidebar on page 182. Members of the institute consisted of representatives of academia, the chemical industry, national laboratories, and other organizations. The institute's primary objective originally was "to facilitate industry-government partnerships with universities and national laboratories to develop economically sustainable clean-production technologies." In 2001, GCI began a discussion with the American Chemical Society (ACS) about developing a cooperative relationship that was realized two years later when the ACS provided the institute office space and funding. The EPA has also worked with academic institutions, industries, and other agencies to encourage research on new technologies for pollution prevention.

Finally, a coherent theoretical framework for the green chemistry movement has been developed by two of its pioneers, Paul T. Anastas (whose career is described in the sidebar on page 185) and John C. Warner, professor of chemistry at the University of

◁ JOE BREEN (1942–1999) ▷

Green chemistry is a movement that has been inspired to a very significant extent by the wholehearted and lifelong efforts of two individuals, Joe Breen and Paul Anastas.

Joseph J. Breen was born in Waterbury, Connecticut, on July 22, 1942. He earned his bachelor's degree from Fairfield University in 1964 and his doctorate in chemistry from Duke University in 1972. He served in the U.S. Marine Corps during the Vietnam War and for two years in the Peace Corps before accepting an appointment at the EPA in 1979. During his tenure at the EPA, Breen was also an adjunct professor in environmental chemistry at Hood College, in Frederick, Maryland, and at Trinity College and American University in Washington, D.C.

Breen spent most of his working life at the U.S. Environmental Protection Agency, in the Office of Pollution Prevention and Toxics (OPPT). At the OPPT, he was involved with the Asbestos in Schools and Public Buildings Program, the National Human Adipose Tissue Survey, the Childhood Lead Poisoning Prevention Program, and a joint study with the Veterans Administration on toxins in the adipose (fatty) tissue of Vietnam veterans. He was awarded the EPA's highest honor, the Gold Medal, largely for his development of the "Check Our Kids for Lead" program.

In 1995, Breen organized one of the first large-scale symposia on green chemistry, a "Design for the Environment" session at the Washington, D.C., meeting of the American Chemical Society. More than 140 speakers pre-

Massachusetts at Boston. In their book *Green Chemistry: Theory and Practice,* Anastas and Warner list a set of guidelines known as the "12 Principles of Green Chemistry." The book has been widely praised for presenting together a wide array of ideas about the goals and practices of green chemistry and the way those ideas can be put into practice by practicing chemists in industrial and research settings. The principles are as follows:

1. Prevention: It is better to prevent waste than to treat or clean up waste after it has been created.

sented papers on various aspects of green chemistry and related topics. In 1997, Breen founded the Green Chemistry Institute, a nonprofit organization designed to encourage research on environmentally benign chemical processes. The institute was later provided a physical and intellectual home by the American Chemical Society.

Breen was also cofounder of the ACS's Kids in Chemistry program, which encourages the development of connections between youngsters and professional scientists. Under the program, scientists visit schools on a regular basis and meet with students in small groups to talk about chemistry and its role in society. Breen was also involved in the creation of the Science-by-Mail Program. In this program, individuals or groups of children are matched with professional scientists who oversee their work on three different "challenge packets" sent out each year; the packets are designed to encourage hands-on activities by children in grades four through nine. Breen was also an editor of the experimental high school chemistry program known as Chemistry in the Community.

Breen died of pancreatic cancer on July 19, 1999. He has been honored and remembered in the Green Chemistry Institute's Joseph Breen Leadership in Green Chemistry Program, which provides funding to promote green chemistry activities in research, education, and outreach, and in the Joseph Breen Memorial Fellowship, which sponsors the participation of a young chemist in a green chemistry technical meeting, conference, or training program.

2. Atom economy: Synthetic methods should be designed to maximize the incorporation of all materials used in the process into the final product.

3. Less hazardous chemical syntheses: Wherever practicable, synthetic methods should be designed to use and generate substances that possess little or no toxicity to human health and the environment.

4. Design safer chemicals: Chemical products should be designed to effect their desired function while minimizing their toxicity.

5. Safer solvents and auxiliaries: Auxiliary substances—solvents, separation agents, and others—should be made unnecessary wherever possible and innocuous when used.

6. Design for energy efficiency: Energy requirements of chemical processes should be recognized for their environmental and economic impacts and should be minimized. If possible, synthetic methods should be conducted at ambient temperature and pressure.

7. Use renewable feedstocks: A raw material should be renewable rather than depleting whenever technically and economically practicable.

8. Reduce derivatives: Unnecessary derivatization (use of blocking groups, protection/deprotection, and temporary modification of physical/chemical processes) should be minimized or avoided if possible, because such steps require additional reagents and can generate waste.

9. Catalysis: Catalytic reagents (as selective as possible) are superior to stoichiometric reagents.

10. Design for degradation: Chemical products should be designed so that at the end of their function they break down into innocuous degradation products and do not persist in the environment.

11. Real-time analysis for pollution prevention: Analytical methodologies need to be further developed to allow for real-time, in-process monitoring and control prior to the formation of hazardous substances.

12. Inherently safer chemistry for accident prevention: Substances and the form of a substance used in a chemical process should be chosen to minimize the potential for chemical accidents, including releases, explosions, and fires.

The Twelve Principles of Green Chemistry can be further distilled into two major ideas. The first is sustainability: That is, reac-

◄ PAUL ANASTAS (1962–   ) ►

Paul Anastas has been called "The Father of green chemistry" for a variety of reasons, one of which is his coining of the term green chemistry in 1991. Anastas served as chief of the Industrial Chemistry Branch of the U.S. Environmental Protection Agency from 1989 to 1999. He then left the EPA to become assistant director for environment at the White House Office of Science and Technology Policy. In that position, he has responsibility for a variety of environmental issues, including climate change, green chemistry, air and water quality, sustainability, mercury pollution, the oceans, and environmental indicators.

Paul Anastas was born in Quincy, Massachusetts, on May 16, 1962. He attended the University of Massachusetts at Boston, from which he earned his B.S. degree in chemistry in 1984. He then studied at Brandeis University, outside Boston, where he earned his M.A. in 1987 and his Ph.D. in organic chemistry in 1989. His first job was as a consultant to chemical industries on the development of new analytical and synthetic chemical processes.

At the EPA, Anastas was responsible for the regulatory review of industrial chemicals under the Toxic Substances Control Act and for the development of rules, policy, and guidance dealing with hazardous chemicals. He was also very active in the development of the underlying principles and practices that now make up the field of green chemistry. He established the U.S. Green Chemistry Program at the EPA, designed and implemented the Presidential Green Chemistry Challenge Award, cofounded with Joe Breen the Green Chemistry Institute, introduced the subject of green chemistry into the Gordon Conferences, and was cofounder of the Annual Green Chemistry and Engineering Conference.

In 1998, Anastas and John C. Warner collaborated in the writing of *Green Chemistry: Theory and Practice,* the "Bible" of early green chemistry thought. In this book Anastas and Warner first enunciated the Twelve Principles of Green Chemistry that motivate much of the research going on in the field today. *Green Chemistry* was reissued in 2000 and has been translated into five languages. Anastas has also authored and edited many other scientific and technical books. (See Further Reading.)

tions should be carried out with the least possible amount of waste. The second is waste reduction: That is, reactions should result in the formation of as little toxic, hazardous, and other waste products as possible. The following sections of this chapter present examples of the kinds of progress being made in the achievement of these goals.

Atom Economy

Every student of chemistry is familiar with one method for measuring the efficiency of a chemical reaction: percentage yield. That is, it is possible to calculate the amount of reactant to be expected in a reaction, given the amounts of reactants with which one begins. The percentage yield can range from nearly 100 percent for some reactions, to less than 10 percent for many others. A number of important organic reactions in which commercially significant products are made sometimes have percentage yields of less than 25 percent, making them economically undesirable from at least one perspective.

Another method for determining the efficiency of a chemical reaction is atom economy. Atom economy is a method of determining the efficiency with which raw materials (reactants or feedstocks) are used *regardless of* the percentage yield obtained in the reaction.

Consider the reaction in which ethyl chloride (CH_3CH_2Cl) is to be produced in the reaction among ethyl alcohol (CH_3CH_2OH), sodium chloride (NaCl), and sulfuric acid (H_2SO_4):

$$\textbf{CH}_3\textbf{CH}_2OH + Na\textbf{Cl} + H_2SO_4 \rightarrow \textbf{CH}_3\textbf{CH}_2\textbf{Cl} + NaHSO_4 + H_2O$$

(In the equation, the atoms that are actually needed to form the desired product are shown in **boldface.**) The atoms that are *not* directly involved in the formation of the product and are, therefore, "wasted" atoms are shown in regular print. These atoms are regarded as "wasted" because, once the desired product is formed, they must be disposed of in some way. In this particular example, the final by-products, sodium bisulfate and water, are relatively harmless and cause no threat to the environment. But many chemical reactions result in hazardous chemicals that do pose a threat to the health of plants and animals and that do, therefore, become factors in air and water pollution and waste management issues.

▲ CALCULATING ATOM ECONOMY IN A REACTION ▶

REAGENT	FORMULA WEIGHT	ATOMS UTILIZED	WEIGHT OF ATOMS UTILIZED	ATOMS NOT UTILIZED	WEIGHT OF ATOMS NOT UTILIZED
CH_3CH_2OH	46	CH_3CH_2	29	OH	17
NaCl	58	Cl	35	Na	23
H_2SO_4	98	—	—	H_2SO_4	98
TOTAL:					
2C, 8H, 5O, 1Na, 1Cl, 1S	202	2C, 5H, 1Cl	64	3H, 5O, 1Na,1S	138

One can easily calculate the efficiency with which atoms are used in a given reaction by constructing a simple table, like the one shown on page 187. Notice in this chart that only eight of the original 18 atoms in the reactants are actually utilized in the final product. The remaining 10 atoms are "lost," in the sense that they are not used in making the final product.

An even more precise measure of the atom economy of the reaction is the mass percentage of reactants used in the final product. By dividing that number by the total mass of reactants, a numerical measure of atom economy can be obtained. That is:

$$\text{atom economy} = \frac{\text{formula weight of all reactants utilize}}{\text{formula weight of all reactants}} \times 100\%$$

For the example:

$$\text{atom economomatom economy} = \frac{64}{202} = 32\%$$

That is, no matter how large the percentage yield of the reaction might be, no more than about a third of the atoms used in the reaction will be present in the final product; the remaining two-thirds become part of the reaction's waste.

One goal of the green chemist, then, is to find a way of making the same product with the waste of fewer reactant atoms. One well-known option is to chlorinate ethane (CH_3CH_3) directly with chlorine gas, as shown in the following equation:

$$CH_3CH_3 + Cl_2 \rightarrow CH_3CH_2Cl + HCl$$

The chart on page 189 provides a summary of the utilized and unutilized atoms in this reaction. Notice in this case that the atom economy of the reaction is about double that of the first reaction:

$$\text{atom economy} = \frac{64}{101} = 63\%$$

◄ CALCULATING ATOM ECONOMY IN AN ALTERNATIVE REACTION ►

REAGENT	FORMULA WEIGHT	ATOMS UTILIZED	WEIGHT OF ATOMS UTILIZED	ATOMS NOT UTILIZED	WEIGHT OF ATOMS NOT UTILIZED
CH_3CH_3	30	CH_3CH_2	29	H	1
Cl_2	71	Cl	35	Cl	35
TOTAL:					
2C, 6H, 2Cl	101	2C, 5H, 1Cl	64	1H, 1Cl	36

One of the best-known examples of atom economy to have been developed commercially thus far is used in the preparation of ibuprofen (Advil, Medipren, Motrin). The original method for preparing ibuprofen was developed in the 1960s by a English pharmaceutical corporation, the Boots Company. The method involved six steps in

Boots synthesis of ibuprofen

which a number of reactant and catalyst atoms were "lost," that is, not present in the final product. The diagram on page 190 shows the steps involved in the Boots process for making ibuprofen. The chart on pages 192–193 shows the atoms and their mass that are utilized and not utilized in the Boots process. Notice that the overall atom economy of the reaction is about 40 percent.

$$\text{atom economy} = \frac{206}{514} = 40\%$$

In the late 1980s, the BHC Company began work on an alternative method of producing ibuprofen that was designed to be more atom-efficient. That method was awarded a U.S. patent in 1991. The alternative pathway to the production of ibuprofen, illustrated by the equations on page 194 and in the accompanying chart on page 195, shows the increase in atom economy provided by this alternative method of making ibuprofen. The atom economy for this series of reactions is:

$$\text{atom economy} = \frac{206}{266} = 77\%$$

nearly double that of the original Boots process. The efficiency of the reaction increases even more if the acetic acid produced as a by-product of step 1 in the BHC process is recovered. Under those circumstances, the atom economy reaches 99 percent. The BHC Company received a Presidential Green Chemistry Challenge Award in 1997 for its development of this synthesis.

Alternative Raw Materials

Among the most troublesome problems of many chemical manufacturing processes are raw materials that are in and of themselves toxic or hazardous. One might hope that all such reactants were actually used up in such processes, but that is probably never the case. After the process has been completed and the desired product

▽ ATOM ECONOMY OF THE BOOTS SYNTHESIS OF IBUPROFEN △

COMPOUND	FORMULA WEIGHT	ATOMS UTILIZED	WEIGHT OF ATOMS UTILIZED	ATOMS NOT UTILIZED	WEIGHT OF ATOMS NOT UTILIZED
1: $C_{10}H_{14}$	134	$C_{10}H_{13}$	133	H	1
2: $C_4H_6O_3$	102	C_2H_3	27	$C_2H_3O_3$	75
3: $C_4H_7ClO_2$	122	CH	13	$C_3H_6ClO_2$	109
4: C_2H_5ONa	68	—	0	C_2H_5ONa	68
5: H_3O	19	—	0	H_3O	19
6: NH_3O	33	—	0	NH_3O	33
7: $2(H_2O)$	36	HO_2	33	H_3	3

COMPOUND	FORMULA WEIGHT	ATOMS UTILIZED	WEIGHT OF ATOMS UTILIZED	ATOMS NOT UTILIZED	WEIGHT OF ATOMS NOT UTILIZED
0C, 42H, 1N, 10O, 1Cl, 1Na	514	13C, 18H, 2O	206	7C, 24H, 1N, 8O, 1Cl, 1Na	308
TOTAL:					

BHC synthesis of ibuprofen

(hazardous or not, as may be) has been recovered, some amount of the original reactant will remain in the product as an impurity or as part of the wastes from the manufacturing process.

The green chemistry solution to this problem is to avoid hazardous feedstocks to begin with, replacing them with benign substances that will cause no harm to humans or the environment whether they appear as impurities in a product or as wastes. One example of this solution is the modification that has been suggested for the traditional method of making adipic acid (hexanedioic acid; $COOH(CH_2)_3COOH$). Adipic acid is traditionally one of the 50 top chemicals produced in the United States each year. It is used primarily for the production of nylon and urethane foams. The traditional method for making adipic acid begins with benzene, a chemical

▼ ATOM ECONOMY OF THE BHC SYNTHESIS OF IBUPROFEN ▲

COMPOUND	FORMULA WEIGHT	ATOMS UTILIZED	WEIGHT OF ATOMS UTILIZED	ATOMS NOT UTILIZED	WEIGHT OF ATOMS NOT UTILIZED
1: $C_{10}H_{14}$	134	$C_{10}H_{13}$	133	H	1
2: $C_4H_6O_3$	102	C_2H_3	27	$C_2H_3O_3$	75
3: H_2	2	H_2	2	—	0
4: CO	28	CO	28	—	0
TOTAL:					
15C, 22H, 4O	266	13C, 18H, 2O	206	2C, 4H, 2O	60

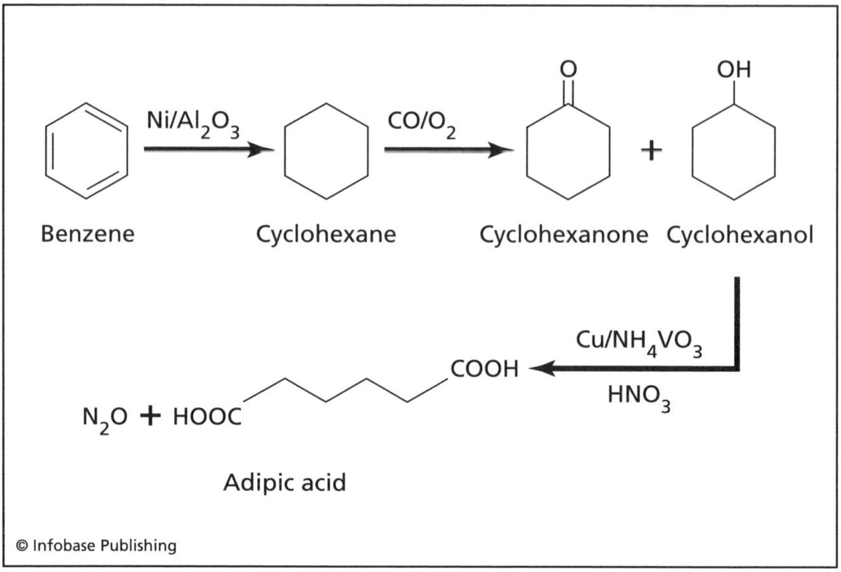

Traditional synthesis of adipic acid

that has been implicated in a number of health problems and has been classified by the EPA as a class A carcinogen, a known human carcinogen. That process is outlined in the diagram above. Notice in this reaction not only that a hazardous chemical is used in the production of adipic acid, but also that an environmentally harmful by-product, nitrous oxide (N_2O), is formed. Given the large amount of adipic acid formed throughout the world each year, the traditional process is believed to be an important source of this undesirable greenhouse gas.

An alternative approach to the production of adipic acid has been proposed by Karen M. Draths and John W. Frost at Michigan State University. Draths and Frost won a Presidential Green Chemistry Challenge Award in 1998 for the development of this technique. Their approach, shown in the diagram on page 197, begins with an environmentally safe feedstock, ordinary glucose. The catalyst used in the reaction is also less hazardous than that traditionally employed in the synthesis of adipic acid, a mixture of nickel and aluminum oxide. Finally, no nitrous oxide is released during the Draths-Frost process. The alternative method proposed by Draths and Frost is environmentally desirable for three reasons: First, a safer reactant (glucose rather than benzene) is used. Second, a safer catalyst (a microorganism rather than a metallic mixture) is used. And third, no environmentally harmful by-product (nitrous oxide) is released during the reaction.

A second example of the use of alternative feedstocks was reported in 1996 by Kyosuke Komiya and his colleagues at Japan's Asahi Chemical. The process shown in the diagram on page 198 is one traditionally used for the manufacture of polycarbonate, a thermoplastic resin used in making a variety of molded products, structural parts, piping, tubes, household appliances, and nonbreakable windows. Nearly 3 million short tons (2.7 metric tons) of polycarbonate is produced annually worldwide, the third-largest quantity of engineering plastic produced in the world.

The traditional method of making polycarbonate is environmentally dubious, however, for two reasons. First, one of the starting materials, phosgene, is a highly toxic compound. Second, the catalyst used in

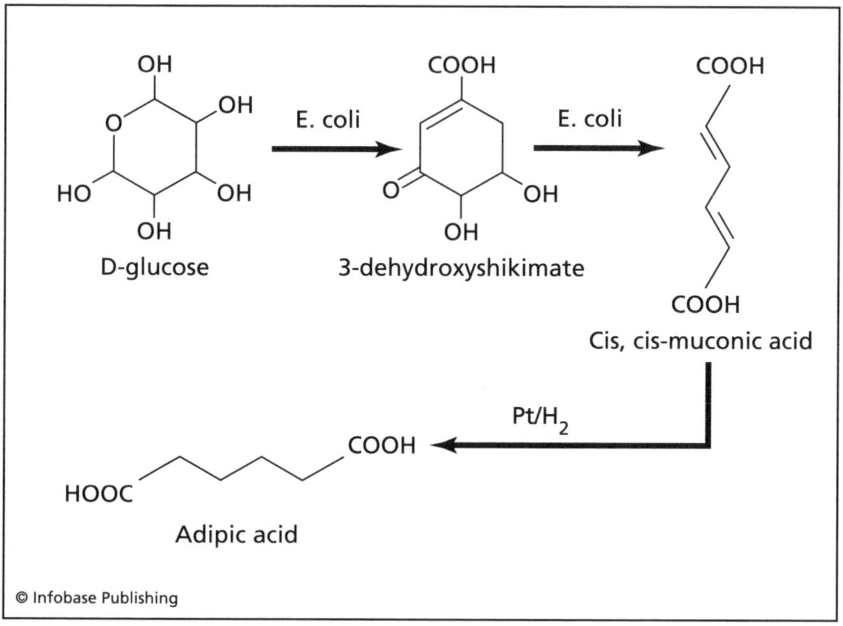

© Infobase Publishing

Green synthesis of adipic acid

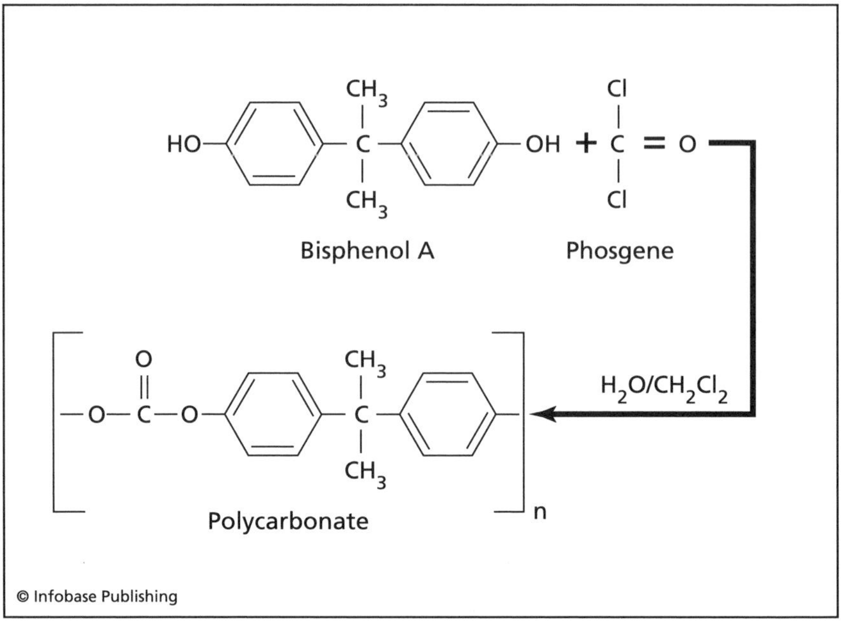

Traditional synthesis of polycarbonate

the reaction, methylene chloride (CH_2Cl_2), has been designated by the National Institute for Occupational Safety and Health (NIOSH) as "a potential human carcinogen in the workplace." The catalyst poses special problems because it must be used in very large quantities, roughly 10 times the weight of the product obtained from the reaction.

The Asahi alternative has the advantage of omitting both phosgene and methylene chloride entirely from the reaction. Instead, as shown in the diagram on page 199, bisphenol A is mixed with diphenylcarbonate and a catalyst of lithium hydroxide, and the mixture melted. At temperatures of 400°F–600°F (200°C–300°C), a viscous mass of polycarbonate polymer begins to form. Since the reaction is reversible, the by-product, phenol (C_6H_5OH), is removed by applying a high vacuum to the reaction. In the presence of the vacuum, the phenol evaporates from the reaction and can be recaptured and reused. Removal of the phenol also drives the reaction to the right, resulting in the formation of polycarbonate, until reactants are exhausted. In the Asahi variation, two potentially hazardous chemicals, phosgene and methylene chloride, are avoided, producing a reaction that is, overall, much more environmentally desirable.

Catalysis

The Draths-Frost method for making adipic acid illustrates a common goal in much green chemistry research, the ability to include more than one green chemistry principle at a time in new processes. Not only did Draths and Frost find a way of substituting a safer feedstock in their reaction, but they also found a safer catalyst, the simple bacterium *Escherichia coli.* The use of the bacterium eliminated the necessity of using hazardous metals as catalysts in the traditional reaction.

Researchers have explored a number of other ways in which improved catalysis can reduce the release of hazardous substances into the environment. For example, Tomoko Matsudo and his colleagues at Ryukoku University in Japan have found a way to carboxylate organic compounds, an important early step in many synthetic

© Infobase Publishing

Green synthesis of polycarbonate

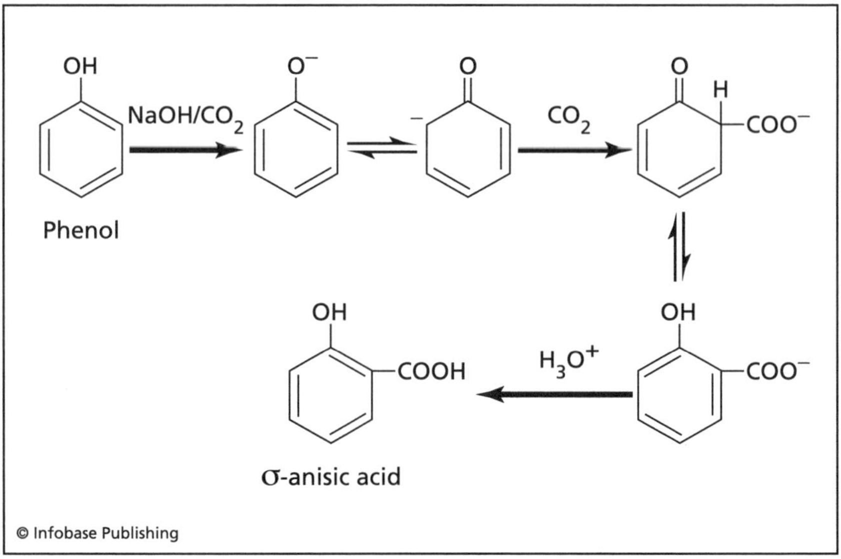

Traditional Kolbe-Schmidt synthesis

processes. Carboxylation is the process by which carbon dioxide is added to a compound. The diagram above shows a historically important example of carboxylation, the addition of carbon dioxide to the phenolate ion (the Kolbe-Schmidt reaction).

Matsudo's team uses the bacterium *Bacillus megaterium* in supercritical carbon dioxide at temperatures of about 100°F (40°C) and 100 atmospheres of pressure to bring about carboxylation. The process illustrates yet one more way of using more than one green chemistry principle in a process: the use of a safer catalyst as well as a safer solvent. (The role of supercriticial carbon dioxide as a solvent will be discussed in the next section.)

Another approach to the "greening" of catalysts has been the use of rare-earth compounds known as *triflates*. The term *triflate* is an abbreviation for the trifluoromethanesulfonate (SO_3CF_3) cation. Some typical triflates that have been used in research include the lanthanides, scandium, and hafnium. These triflates act as Lewis acids (electron acceptors) and can, therefore, be substituted for stronger mineral acids (such as sulfuric acid) with undesirable environmental consequences. The chemical structure of a typical triflate, lithium trifluoromethane sulfonate, is shown below.

Anthony G. M. Barret, at London's Imperial College of Science, Technology, and Medicine, and his colleagues have used triflates to catalyze a number of commercially important chemical reactions, such as the nitration of aromatic compounds and the acetylation of alcohols (esterification). The nitration of aromatic compounds is a very important early step in the synthesis of dyes, plastics, and pharmaceuticals. Esterification also has many important commercial applications, including its use in the manufacture of synthetic detergents, emulsifiers, cosmetics and perfumes, and artificial flavorings. The diagram on page 202 illustrates both the nitration of aromatic compounds and an esterification reaction.

The green chemistry advantages of using triflates are not only that it helps avoid the use of hazardous catalysts, but also that the triflates themselves can be recovered and reused rather easily. In one series of reactions involving the reaction between phenethyl alcohol and acetic acid, for example, Barrett's team found that yields of 95–98 percent were possible, with catalyst recovery amounting to no less than 98 percent and, in most cases, nearly 100 percent. The team concluded one of their reports on the use of triflate catalysts by suggesting that the catalysts they used were "readily recyclable and we believe this to be a major step forward in the area of clean technology for aromatic nitration" (Francis J. Waller, et al., "Lanthanide(III)

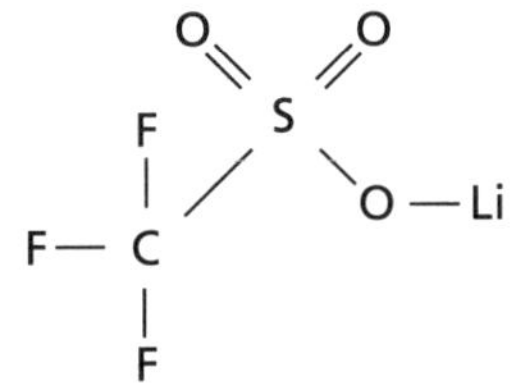

© Infobase Publishing

Chemical formula for lithium triflate

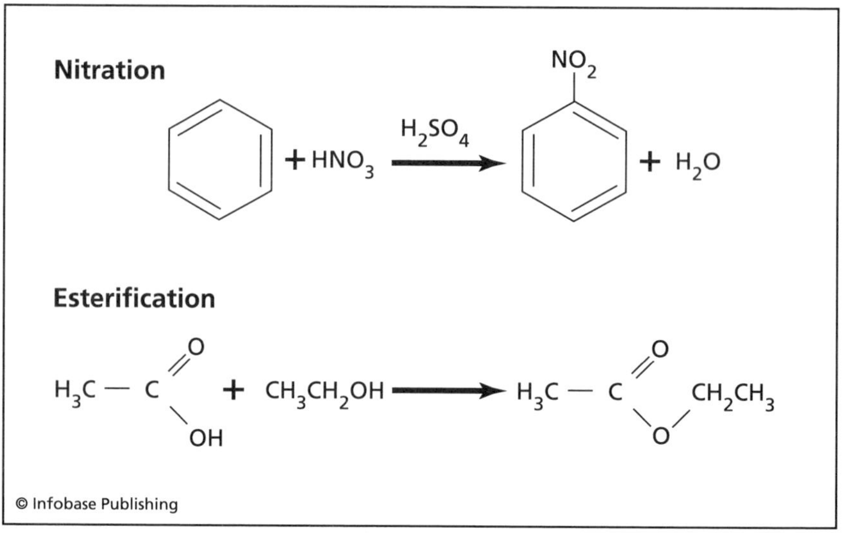

Examples of nitration and esterification reactions

Triflates as Recyclable Catalysts for Atom Economic Aromatic Nitration," *Chemical Communications* [1997]: 613).

Another promising group of environmentally benign catalysts are the tetra amido macrocyclic ligand (TAML®) iron(III) activators, developed by Terrence J. Collins of the Institute for Green Oxidation Chemistry at Carnegie Mellon University. Collins won a 1999 Presidential Green Chemistry Challenge Award for his work on these catalysts. TAML® catalysts, like those shown in the diagram on page 203 are designed to mimic some of the oxidizing enzymes that occur naturally. In nature, for example, these enzymes bring about the separation of lignin from cellulose and hemicellulose, a process that is also fundamental to the process of papermaking. The papermaking industry, however, has traditionally used chlorine to produce this separation, a practice that has resulted in the release of millions of tons of chlorine wastes into the environment each year. A combination of TAML® and hydrogen peroxide can cause the same separation at temperatures of about 120°F (50°C), making it both economical and environmentally safe.

TAML® catalysts show promise in a number of other fields. For example, they can be used as additives in synthetic detergents, where they do not affect dyes attached to fabric but do attack dye molecules that have been released from those fabrics. This set of properties makes it possible for TAML® catalysts to prevent the transfer of a dye from one material to another during cleaning. Research is also being conducted on the use of TAML® catalysts to disinfect water, as substitutes for the toxic chlorine and bromine now widely used for that purpose.

Solvents

Manufacturing processes in which organic products are made are of special interest to green chemists for a variety of reasons, largely because so many of the raw materials used to make such products, the by-products formed in the reactions, and the final products themselves are likely to be toxic or hazardous in other ways. Historically, the problem with such manufacturing processes is that they have required the use of organic solvents, such as carbon tetrachloride, chloroform, tetrachloroethylene, trichloroethylene, 1,1,1-trichloroethane, benzene, toluene, and xylene. A major thrust, then, has been to find satisfactory substitutes for these organic solvents.

© Infobase Publishing

Chemical structure of a tetra amido macrocyclic ligand

The most desirable choice, of course, would be water, since it has essentially no harmful effects on humans or the environment. The problem is that most organic substances do not dissolve in water. One of the most exciting alternatives with promise for use in organic syntheses, however, is another widely available and environmentally benign compound, carbon dioxide. The carbon dioxide used in organic reactions exists in a phase not generally familiar to most people, the *supercritical phase.*

Carbon dioxide, as can most other substances, can exist in any one of three phases—solid, liquid, or gas—depending on temperature and pressure. At low temperatures, carbon dioxide exists as a solid ("dry ice") at almost any pressure. At temperatures greater than about $-76°F$ ($-60°C$), however, carbon dioxide may exist as a gas or as a liquid, depending on the pressure. At some combination of temperature and pressure, however, carbon dioxide (and other substances) enters a fourth phase, known as the *supercritical phase,* whose properties are a combination of gas and liquid properties. For example, supercritical carbon dioxide (often represented as *SCCO2, SC-CO2, SC-CO$_2$,* or a similar acronym) diffuses readily and has a low viscosity, properties associated with gases, but is also a good solvent, a property one often associates with liquids. The critical temperature and pressure at which carbon dioxide becomes a supercritical fluid are $31.1°C$ ($88.0°F$) and 73.8 atm (1,070 pounds per square inch).

One of the most obvious applications of SCCO2 is in the laundering and dry cleaning industry, where cleaning fluids have long presented serious environmental problems. As any consumer today knows, many fabrics now carry a "Dry Clean Only" label that precludes the use of soap and water for cleaning purposes. In addition, cleaning agents are needed in a host of industrial operations, in which dirty machinery cannot be cleaned by soap and water either.

At one time, the dry cleaning industry relied on petroleum products for their cleaning agents. Currently, the single most popular solvent used by dry cleaners is a compound called perchloroethylene, widely known by the nickname of *perc.* About 30,000 dry cleaners in the United States alone use perc for their cleaning operations, accounting for about 80 percent of all such cleaning done in the country.

But perc has its health and environmental disadvantages. Short-term exposure may cause dizziness; fatigue; headaches; sweating; loss of coordination; irritation of the skin, eyes, nose, and throat; and, in rare cases, unconsciousness. These symptoms are unlikely among consumers, provided that their dry-cleaned clothes have been adequately aired, but they may pose such threats to workers in a dry-cleaning plants. Tests with experimental animals suggest that the compound may cause kidney and liver damage, and there is some concern that it may be a possible human carcinogen. Because of these potential health risks, dry cleaning establishments must follow strict procedures in preventing the release of perc to the atmosphere, to groundwater, or to other parts of the environment.

In the 1990s, Joseph DeSimone, professor of chemistry at the University of North Carolina at Chapel Hill, suggested using SCCO2 as an alternative cleaning fluid. SCCO2 by itself could not serve as the cleaning fluid since, as with water, it does not have polarity (or lack of polarity) sufficient to remove grease and oil molecules from fabrics. However, DeSimone discovered another group of compounds that *do* have detergentlike properties and that can be dissolved in SCCO2. These compounds are made by combining the common plastic polystyrene with fluorinated polyacrylates. In this hybrid molecule, the polystyrene end of the molecule is hydrophobic (water-avoiding), with a tendency to attach to grease and oil molecules, while the fluorinated polyacrylate end is hydrophilic (attracted to water), with a tendency to attach to carbon dioxide molecules. The grease–polystyrene–fluorinated polyacrylate–carbon dioxide micelles formed in this way act much as the grease-detergent-water micelles (groups of molecules that contain both polar and nonpolar molecules) formed by traditional methods of washing with soap and water do.

SCCO2 has many environmental advantages as a cleaning fluid. If it does escape into the environment, for example, it poses no threat to human health or to the rest of the environment (with the possible exception of climate change effects). Also, pretreating certain kinds of stains, as is now necessary in most dry cleaning operations, is no longer necessary with SCCO2 systems. Finally, some materials that cannot be cleaned by perc or most other current cleaners, such as leather and suede, can be cleaned by SCCO2 procedures. In recognition of his work in the development of SCCO2 cleaning operations, DeSimone was awarded a 1997 Presidential Green Chemistry Challenge Award.

A worthy goal for almost any green chemist would be the development of some process in which all 12 principles of green chemistry were realized. In 2002, the EPA recognized the Cargill Dow Chemical Company for doing just that. Cargill Dow had earlier announced the development of a system for preparing a product known as NatureWorks® polyactic acid (PLA), a family of polymers with a host of potential practical uses, including synthetic fabrics that mimic natural materials as well as anything ever produced and packaging materials for a variety of different uses.

The Cargill Dow process begins with corn because of its ready availability as a source of starch in the United States, although the company points out that other raw materials, such as grass, wheat, and straw, might be more abundant feedstocks in other parts of the world. The starch obtained from corn is hydrolyzed and then fermented, as shown in the diagram below, to produce lactic acid. The process is highly efficient, with a yield approaching 100 percent. It

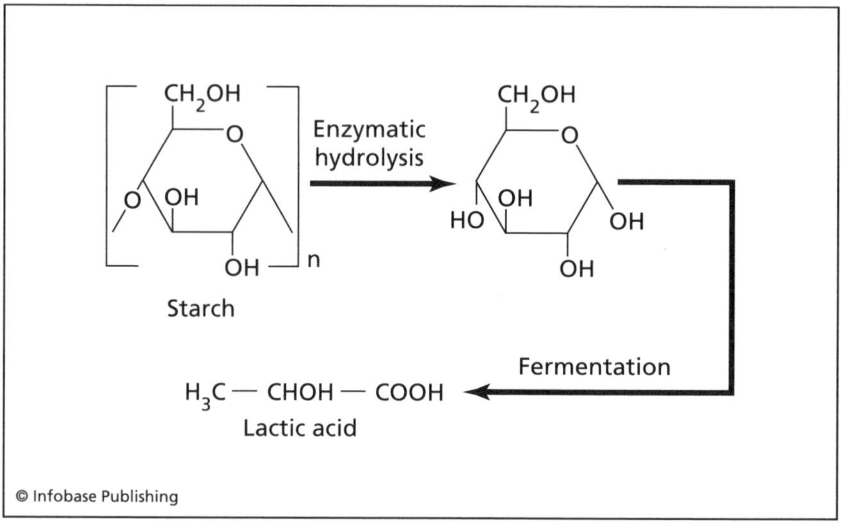

Green synthesis of lactic acid

requires only natural enzymes and water with the addition of only very small amounts (in the parts-per-million range) of other catalysts.

The lactic acid formed in the first set of reactions is then converted into a prepolymer by the removal of water in a traditional condensation reaction. That prepolymer is then depolymerized (broken apart) to form a molecule known as a lactide, which is itself polymerized to form a high-molecular-weight polymer, polylactide (PLA). The PLA can then be processed to make any number of different types of materials. Applications suggested by Cargill Dow for its new material include cold drink cups, electronics packaging, trays and lids, shrink wrap, envelope and carton windows, milk and oil packaging, fashion apparel, sport and active wear fabrics, shoe liners, hygiene products, bedding and drapery materials, upholstery, pillows and comforters, structural protective foams, and raw materials for certain chemical syntheses.

The company has been very proud of the way it has incorporated the 12 principles of green chemistry in its PLA synthetic scheme. Not only does it use readily available natural materials, but the production process uses considerably less energy than methods for the synthesis of comparable materials, and the final product of the process is essentially 100 percent biodegradable. One can hardly ask for much more from research in green chemistry. It is hardly surprising, therefore, that Cargill Dow was awarded one of the 2002 Presidential Green Chemistry Challenge Awards.

Conclusion

The modern environmental movement is relatively young. Prior to Earth Day 1970, comparatively few people in the United States and many other parts of the world were concerned about the quality of the air and water on which they depended for their survival. A number of reasons can be offered for this fact. First, life in the 1930s and 1940s was still fairly simple in technological terms, especially compared with daily life in the 1990s and 2000s, at least in developed countries. Also, while population growth in most developing nations was fairly high, it had not yet begun to "take off" in most developed countries, as it would in the 1950s and 1960s. Also, many societies had developed and were using somewhat effective methods for the control of their wastes. In most cases, the volume of wastes was quite limited, or systems were used for their removal and recycling, or the wastes that were produced were comparatively harmless.

As noted earlier in this book, these conditions began to change fairly dramatically in the 1950s and 1960s. An abundance of synthetic new products became available to a rapidly growing population of Americans (and Europeans and Japanese) who quickly developed a philosophy of "use it up; throw it out." And that philosophy quickly led to serious new problems of air and water pollution and of waste management. This revolution in waste disposal practices soon led to a renewed appreciation for the value of a clean and safe environment and the rise of the modern environmental movement.

So how effective has that movement been in the three decades of its existence? Certainly, there are some encouraging signs. The troublesome problem of ozone depletion appears well on its way to being solved. The 2002 report of the Scientific Assessment Panel of the Montreal Protocol on Substances That Deplete the Ozone Layer indicated that the size of the Arctic and Antarctic ozone holes has stayed about the same over the past decade, in spite of efforts to control this problem. But the concentration of chlorine in the troposphere, a key clue to the development of the ozone holes, has apparently peaked and seems now to be decreasing. By contrast, the concentration of bromine (from halons), is still increasing, although its rate of increase has begun to slow since international agreement on the manufacture of bromine-containing compounds has been reached.

Progress in tropospheric air pollutants, such as carbon monoxide, sulfur dioxide, and oxides of nitrogen, has been mixed. In the years since the U.S. Environmental Protection Agency has been monitoring these substances, observers have noted improvements for all pollutants except oxides of nitrogen. But by mid-2003, people were questioning how much progress was really being made. By the end of July 2003, Los Angeles County had reported 40 days of unhealthy air quality, more than double the number of such days in the preceding decade. For the first time in more than five years, the county also declared a stage 1 smog alert—the most dangerous smog concentration warning. Unusually warm temperatures were one reason for this increase. But another reason was the additional 4 million vehicles on California's roadways during that period, a majority of which were large and fuel-inefficient.

Progress similar to that for most air pollutants cannot be reported for water pollutants. As discussed in chapter 4, the percentage of lakes, rivers, estuaries, and other bodies of water in the United States that can be classified as "good" (versus to "threatened" or "impaired") has changed hardly at all in nearly a decade.

So, are the United States and the rest of the world making progress in solving our individual and joint environmental problems, or not? The relative shortage of hard data on the subject makes it difficult to say. Probably the most important single study to attempt to answer that question was conducted by the National Center for Economic and Security Alternatives in 1995. In it the center analyzed 21 generally accepted environmental trend indicators for air, land, and water quality; chemical and waste generation; and automobile and energy use. The study then calculated the improvement or decline in each category for nine developed nations: Canada, Denmark, France, Germany, Japan, the Netherlands, Sweden, the United Kingdom, and the United States.

The results of the study were not encouraging. While there was some level of progress in some areas in all nations, the overall trend in environmental quality from 1970 to 1995 was in a negative direction. Denmark and the Netherlands earned the best scores, showing declines in environmental quality of 10.6 percent and 11.4 percent, respectively. The two nations with the most disappointing results were Canada and France, with a decrease in environmental quality of 38.1 percent and 41.2 percent, respectively. The United States occupied a middle point in the range, with a decrease in environmental quality of 22.1 percent.

The task of protecting and preserving the natural environment in the 21st century is a daunting one. Even three decades into the modern environmental movement, Western culture still encourages people to buy more new, sophisticated, made-to-wear-out products and not to worry about the cost of producing and disposing of those products. One of the great hopes for a change in this philosophy is the young science of Green Chemistry. This discipline is effectively disproving the assumption that consumer products have to be short-lived and wasteful to be profitable. Green Chemistry–type products can make better use of raw materials, produce less hazardous waste and less waste overall, *and* be economically sound both to manufacturers and to consumers. By promoting human stewardship and protection of the world around us, Green Chemistry may provide our greatest hope for preserving and enhancing the natural environment.

GLOSSARY

acid deposition   Any form of atmospheric deposition whose pH is significantly less than that of normal rainwater. Acid deposition may occur with water (wet deposition) or without water (dry deposition).

acid precipitation   Any form of precipitation (rain, snow, hail, dew, and the like) whose pH is significantly less than that of normal rainwater (about 7.0).

acid rain   *See* ACID PRECIPITATION.

air pollutant   Any material released into the atmosphere, either directly or indirectly, at a level that poses risk to humans, other animals, plants, or the physical environment.

atom economy   A concept from green chemistry that stresses the need for conserving as much of a raw material as possible during a chemical manufacturing process; also known as atom utilization.

atom utilization   *See* ATOM ECONOMY.

beneficiation   Any method of treating a fuel or an ore to remove impurities and reduce the amount of pollution produced when the fuel is burned or the ore is processed.

biodegradation   The breakdown of organic materials into simpler components by microorganisms.

biological (or biochemical) oxygen demand (BOD)   The amount of oxygen consumed by bacteria as they decompose organic wastes in water; a test used to measure water quality.

catalyst   Any substance that changes the rate of a chemical reaction without actually undergoing any change itself.

catalytic converter   A device installed in a motor vehicle's exhaust system that is designed to reduce the amount of pollutant gases released by that vehicle to the atmosphere.

chemical oxygen demand (COD) A test used to measure water quality, based on the quantity of organic matter present in a sample of water.

chlorosis An abnormal yellowing of the leaves of a plant, usually caused by a deficiency of iron and/or manganese in the soil.

climate The average weather conditions over an extended period, usually at least 30 years.

climate change A phenomenon in which climatic patterns around the world undergo significant changes as the result of increases or decreases in the Earth's annual average temperature.

coliform bacteria Common microorganisms found in the intestinal tract of warm-blooded animals and in the soil and plants. *Also see* FECAL COLIFORM BACTERIA.

cooling pond An artificial body of water constructed to hold water used in some industrial process for a period, during which its temperature drops to some satisfactory level.

cremator A term sometimes used for a waste incinerator.

criteria pollutant One of a group of six air pollutants for which the U.S. Environmental Protection Agency has established air quality standards. The six criteria pollutants are carbon monoxide, nitrogen dioxide, ozone, lead, particulate matter, and sulfur dioxide.

defense high-level wastes Nuclear wastes produced as a result of military research during the recovery of the uranium and plutonium used in making fission and fusion bombs.

dioxins A class of organic compounds that occur as the by-product of various chemical manufacturing operations. More precisely, they are known as polychlorinateddibenzo-p-dioxins.

dobson A unit used to measure ozone concentration in the atmosphere defined as a layer of ozone 0.01 mm thick at standard temperature and pressure (0°C and 1 atm).

dry cask storage A method for storing high-level nuclear wastes by sealing them inside protective containers.

dry deposition *See* ACID DEPOSITION.

dump *See* OPEN DUMP.

ecotoxicology   The study of the adverse effects of chemicals on natural species and populations.

environmental justice   A social movement based on the assumption that hazardous waste sites and other facilities that release pollutants into the environment are located in or near communities whose primary inhabitants are people of color or of lower economic class.

eutrophication   The process by which lakes and ponds become enriched with dissolved nutrients, resulting in increased growth of algae and other microscopic plants.

fecal coliform bacteria   Common microorganisms found in the intestinal tract of warm-blooded animals.

flue gas   The mixture of gases and fly ash leaving the furnace in a coal-fired boiler.

free radical   A very reactive chemical species (atom, ion, or molecule) that contains an unpaired electron. The unpaired electron is responsible for its activity. Free radicals are usually represented with the chemical symbol of the element with which the unpaired electron is associated and a small dot: $R^{\bullet}$.

fuel rod   A long slender metallic tube that holds the fuel needed to operate a nuclear reactor.

gasohol   A mixture of gasoline and alcohol that burns with fewer pollutants than does pure gasoline itself.

global warming   A phenomenon in which the Earth's average annual temperature increases significantly over an extended period.

green chemistry   The utilization of a set of principles that reduce or eliminate the use or generation of hazardous substances in the design, manufacture, and application of chemical products.

greenhouse gas   Any gas with the ability to absorb infrared radiation emitted from Earth's surface, thereby increasing the atmosphere's average annual temperature.

green revolution   A term used to describe the dramatic increase in agricultural output during the period from 1950 to 1975 as a result of greater use of fertilizers, pesticides, and other modern technology on farms in developing nations.

half-life   The time required for one-half of a given sample of a radioactive isotope to break down into a simpler isotope.

hazardous wastes   Waste products that pose a threat to the health of plants, humans, or other animals.

heavy metal   *See* TOXIC METAL.

high-level (nuclear) wastes   Nuclear wastes that emit relatively large amounts of radiation.

hydrodenitrogenation   The removal of nitrogen from organic compounds to reduce the amount of nitrogen oxides produced during combustion.

isotope   A form of a chemical element that has the same number of protons in its nucleus as other atoms of the same element but a different number of neutrons and thus a different atomic weight.

landfill   Any site for the disposal of wastes in which some effort is made to prevent those wastes from escaping into the environment, for example, by covering over the wastes with layers of dirt. *Also see* SANITARY LANDFILL; SECURE LANDFILL.

limiting factor   The single element or compound in an aquatic system that determines the rate at which eutrophication of that system can proceed.

London smog   A type of air pollution produced when smoke from vehicle exhausts, industrial processes, or other sources is trapped by and mixes with fog. *Also see* PHOTOCHEMICAL SMOG.

low-excess-air firing   A method for burning fuels that makes use of just enough oxygen to allow combustion of the fuel, while reducing the amount of nitrogen oxides produced in the process.

low-level (nuclear) wastes   Nuclear wastes that emit relatively modest amounts of radiation.

macronutrient   Any element or compound required in relatively large amounts for plant growth.

micronutrient   Any element or compound required in relatively small amounts for plant growth.

mine tailings   Wastes that are produced during the mining of an ore.

municipal solid wastes (MSWs)   Discarded materials produced by individual, family, and community activities.

nutrient   Any substance necessary for plant growth. *Also see* MACRONUTRIENT; MICRONUTRIENT.

open dump   Any facility or site for solid waste disposal that is not a sanitary landfill.

oxygenated gasoline   Any type of gasoline that has been specifically designed to burn more efficiently and produce less of carbon monoxide and other pollutants.

ozone   An allotrope (form) of oxygen that contains three atoms per molecule (O_3) rather than the two atoms per molecule (O_2) found in ordinary oxygen.

ozone-depleting potential   A measure of the ability of any given chemical species to destroy ozone molecules in the stratosphere.

ozone hole   A vertical column in the Earth's atmosphere in which the concentration of ozone is significantly less than normal.

ozone layer   A thin layer in the Earth's stratosphere that contains a relatively high concentration of ozone, compared with other portions of the atmosphere.

particulate   Any type of solid particle or liquid droplet that occurs in the atmosphere.

Patrick principle   The principle that the quality of a body of water and the changes caused by human activities on that water can be determined by the type and number of organisms found there. The principle is named after microbiologist Ruth Patrick.

perc   An abbreviation for a commonly used dry cleaning fluid, perchloroethylene.

peroxyl radical   A chemical species that contains an organic group attached to two oxygen atoms, whose general formula can be given as ROO•.

persistent organic pollutants (POPs)   Organic compounds that are not easily biodegraded and that tend to remain in the environment for extended periods.

pH   A quantitative measure of the acidity of a solution. pH values range from about 1.0 (very acidic) to about 14.0 (very alkaline; not acidic at all).

photochemical smog   A pale-yellow to brownish haze produced when sunlight promotes reactions between oxides of nitrogen and hydrocarbons to produce poisonous products. *Also see* LONDON SMOG.

primary particulate   Any particulate released directly to the atmosphere as a solid particle or liquid droplet.

reformulated gasoline   *See* OXYGENATED GASOLINE.

refuse-derived fuel facility *See* WASTE-TO-ENERGY FACILITY.

resource recovery The process of attempting to recapture and reuse substances in solid wastes.

sanitary landfill A landfill in which wastes are covered over on a regular basis, usually daily.

scrubber A device added to the exhaust system of an industrial plant to remove pollutants from the flue gases leaving the plant.

secondary particulate A particulate that is formed in the atmosphere as the result of a chemical or physical reaction between other particles.

secure landfill A landfill that has protective linings above, below, and around the wastes stored within.

sedimentation The process by which fine particles settle out of water onto a lake, river, or ocean bottom. The process is also sometimes referred to as siltation.

siltation *See* SEDIMENTATION.

smog *See* LONDON SMOG; PHOTOCHEMICAL SMOG.

source reduction A method of dealing with solid waste disposal problems by reducing the amount of wastes produced.

source separation A recycling method in which consumers are expected to divide their wastes into two or more categories, such as waste paper, glass, metal, and plastic.

spent-fuel pool An artificial body of water used for the temporary storage of spent fuel rods from a nuclear reactor.

spent-fuel wastes Wastes from nuclear power plants, consisting of spent fuel rods.

stabilization Any chemical or physical method used to prevent hazardous chemicals from escaping into the surrounding environment.

supercritical phase A state of matter that has characteristics of both a liquid and a gas.

Superfund A program created by the Comprehensive Environmental Response, Compensation, and Liability Act of 1980, designed to find and remediate toxic waste sites in the United States.

syndet An abbreviation for the term *synthetic detergent.*

synthetic detergent A cleaning product made of synthetic materials rather than natural soaps.

thermal pollution A significant increase in the temperature of a body of water, such as a river or lake, as the result of industrial, energy-producing, or other human activities in the vicinity of the water.

total organic carbon (TOC) A test used to measure water quality based on the amount of organic carbon present in a water sample.

toxic organic chemicals (or compounds; TOCs) Any toxic synthetic compound that contains the element carbon.

toxic metal Any chemical element that is hazardous to the health of humans and other animals. The term usually refers to elements with high atomic number but may also refer to lighter elements (such as beryllium and aluminum) and to semimetals (such as arsenic and antimony). Such elements are also referred to as heavy metals.

transuranic wastes Nuclear wastes that contain isotopes of elements heavier than those of uranium.

triflates A group of catalysts especially popular for use in green chemistry reactions, more precisely known as trifluoromethanesulfonates.

volatile organic compound (VOC) Any carbon-containing compound that exists as a gas or that vaporizes easily.

waste minimization priority chemicals (WMPCs) A group of about 30 hazardous chemicals whose presence in the environment is tracked by the U.S. Environmental Protection Agency for the purpose of reducing hazardous wastes released by industry into the environment.

waste-to-energy facility A plant in which solid wastes are incinerated and the heat produced used for some productive purpose, such as the generation of electricity; also known as refuse-derived fuel facilities.

waterborne disease Any infectious disease that is transmitted primarily or exclusively by means of moist environments.

wet deposition *See* ACID DEPOSITION.

FURTHER READING

PRINT RESOURCES

Anastas, Paul, Lauren G. Heine, and Tracy C. Williamson, eds. *Green Engineering*. Washington, D.C.: American Chemical Society, 2000.

Anastas, Paul, Paul H. Bickart, and Mary M. Kirchhoff. *Designing Safer Polymers*. New York: Wiley, 2000.

Anastas, Paul, and Tracy C. Williamson. *Green Chemistry: Frontiers in Benign Chemical Synthesis and Processes*. New York: Oxford University Press, 1998.

Anastas, Paul, and Carol A. Farris. *Benign by Design: Alternative Synthetic Design for Pollution Prevention*. Washington, D.C.: American Chemical Society, 1994.

Bullard, Robert D. *Dumping in Dixie: Race, Class and Environmental Quality*. 3rd ed. Boulder, Colo.: Westview Press, 2000.

——. *People of Color Environmental Groups Directory 2000*. Flint, Mich.: Charles Stewart Mott Foundation, 2000.

——. *Sprawl City: Race, Politics, and Planning in Atlanta*. Washington, D.C.: Island Press, 2000.

——. *Just Transportation: Removing Race and Class Barriers to Mobility*. Gabriola Island, Canada: New Society Publishers, 1997.

——. *Residential Apartheid: The American Legacy*. Los Angeles: UCLA Center for African American Studies Publications, 1994.

——. *Unequal Protection: Environmental Justice and Communities of Color*. San Francisco: Sierra Club Books, 1994.

——. *Confronting Environmental Racism: Voices from the Grassroots*. Cambridge, Mass.: South End Press, 1993.

Cothran, Helen. *Garbage and Recycling*. Opposing Viewpoints Series. Farmington Hills, Mich.: Greenhaven Press, 2002.

DeVilliers, Marq. *Water: The Fate of Our Most Precious Resource*. New York: Houghton Mifflin, 2000.

Edelstein, Michael R. *Poisoned Places: Seeking Environmental Justice in a Contaminated World*. Boulder, Colo.: Westview Press, 2004.

Godish, Thad. *Air Quality*. 4th ed. Boca Raton, Fla.: Lewis, 2003.

Guha, Ramachandra. *Environmentalism: A Global History.* Reading, Mass.: Addison-Wesley, 1999.

Haley, James, ed. *Pollution.* Current Controversies Series. Farmington Hills, Mich.: Greenhaven Press, 2002.

Jacobson, Mark Z. *Atmospheric Pollution.* Cambridge: Cambridge University Press, 2002.

Lankey, Rebecca L., and Paul Anastas. *Advancing Sustainability through Green Chemistry and Engineering.* New York: Oxford University Press, 2002.

Laws, Edward A. *Aquatic Pollution: An Introductory Text.* 3rd ed. New York: Wiley, 2000.

Manahan, Stanley E. *Environmental Chemistry,* Boca Raton, Fla.: Lewis, 1999.

Neimark, Peninah, and Peter Rhoades Mott. *The Environmental Debate: A Documentary History.* Westport, Conn.: Greenwood Press, 1999.

Rahm, Dianne, ed. *Toxic Waste and Environmental Policy in the 21st Century United States.* Jefferson, N.C.: McFarland, 2002.

Spiro, Thomas G., and William M. Stigliani. *Chemistry of the Environment.* 2nd ed. Upper Saddle River, N.J.: Prentice Hall, 2003.

Tangri, Neil. *Waste Incineration: A Dying Technology.* Berkeley, Calif.: Global Anti-Incinerator Alliance, Global Alliance for Incinerator Alternatives, July 2003. Available online. http://www.no-burn.org/resources/library/wiadt.pdf. Accessed on August 31, 2006.

Tundo, Pietro, and Paul Anastas. *Green Chemistry: Challenging Perspectives.* New York: Oxford University Press, 2000.

Wright, John. *Environmental Chemistry.* London: Routledge, 2003.

INTERNET RESOURCES

Air Now. The U.S. Environmental Protection Agency's introductory Web site on air pollution and related topics. http://www.epa.gov/airnow/. Accessed on September 1, 2006.

Air Pollution. Sponsored by the U.S. National Library of Medicine and the National Institutes of Health, this page focuses on health issues related to air pollution. http://www.nlm.nih.gov/medlineplus/airpollution. html. Accessed on September 1, 2006.

Clean Water & Oceans: Water Pollution: In Depth. A collection of reports and articles about water quality from the Natural Resources Defense Council. http://www.nrdc.org/water/pollution/depth.asp. Accessed on September 1, 2006.

EnvironmentalChemistry.com. Contains more than 300 pages of information on a host of chemical and environmental issues. http://environmentalchemistry.com/. Accessed on September 1, 2006.

Green Chemistry. A good beginning point for more extended searches on the subject of green chemistry. http://www.epa.gov/oppt/greenchemistry/. Accessed on September 1, 2006.

Indoor & Outdoor Air Pollution. An excellent general introduction to many aspects of air pollution, sponsored by the Lawrence Berkeley National Laboratory. http://www.lbl.gov/Education/ELSI/pollution-main.html. Accessed on September 1, 2006.

Intergovernmental Panel on Climate Change. IPCC was established by the World Mctcrological Organization and thc Unitcd Nations Environmcnt Programme to study and report on climate change and has the most extensive collection of information on the subject generally available. http://www.ipcc.ch/. Accessed on September 1, 2006.

Municipal Solid Waste in the United States: 2000 Facts and Figures. The EPA's annual report on municipal solid waste generation and disposal in the United States. A hard copy of this report can be obtained by calling the EPA's National Service Center for Environmental Publications at 1-800-490-9198 and asking for publication EPA530-R-02-001. http://www.epa.gov/epaoswer/non-hw/muncpl/report-00/report-00.pdf. Accessed on September 1, 2006.

National Water Quality Inventory, 2002 Report. Latest biennial report on water quality in the United States. Also available in print form by calling the EPA's National Service Center for Environmental Publications at 1-800-490-9198 and asking for publication EPA-841-R-02-001. http://www.epa.gov/305b/2000report/. Accessed on September 1, 2006.

U.S. Environmental Protection Agency. A detailed listing of the many topics to be found on this site is located at http://www.epa.gov/epahome/topics.html. http://www.epa.gov/. Accessed on September 1, 2006.

Wetlands, Oceans, and Watersheds. EPA's introductory page on water resources and pollutions, with leads to many other useful Web sites within and outside EPA. http://www.epa.gov/owow/. Accessed on September 1, 2006.

Zero Waste Alliance. The primary Web site for a coalition of universities, government, businesses, and other organizations working to develop and promote more efficient methods of dealing with wastes. http://www.zerowaste.org/. Accessed on September 1, 2006.

INDEX

Italic page numbers indicate illustrations.

A

acid deposition 40, 61. *See also* acid rain
acidity, and water pollution 124–125. *See also* pH
acid mine drainage (AMD) 125
acid rain (acid precipitation) 27, 34, 55, 57–67, *64, 65*
ACS. *See* American Chemical Society
adipic acid 194, 196–197
Adirondack Lakes 66
adsorption systems 45–46
Aerobacter aerogenes 114
aerobic bacteria 102
Affluent Society, The (Galbraith) 149
Agent Orange 13, 174–177
agriculture 109, 111, 134
air pollutants 18–54, *20, 37*
　air quality standards 51–54

carbon monoxide 18–24
Clean Air Act and 9
definitions 18
early examples of 2–6
lead 48, 50–51
oxides of nitrogen 24–33
ozone 46–50
particulate matter 38–42
sulfur dioxide 33–38
treatment of 209
VOCs 42–46
Air Pollution Control Act (1955) 8
air quality control regions (AQCRs) 9
air quality standards 51–54
algae, thermal pollution and 128
aluminum 58
AMD. *See* acid mine drainage
American Chemical Society (ACS) 181
amines 38
ammonia 33
anaerobic bacteria 102
Anastas, Paul T. 181–182, 185

Antarctica, ozone levels over 68, 69, 77–78
AQCRs. *See* air quality control regions
aquatic life. *See also* fish
　acidity's effect on 124, 125
　acid rain's effect on 62
　and oxygen depletion of water 102
　oxygen requirements of 100–101
　sedimentation and 110
　thermal pollution and 126–128
　TOCs and 117
Arrhenius, Svante 84–85
Asahi Chemical 197–199
asbestos 40
atmosphere 55–94
　acid rain 57–67
　changes in 55–94
　global climate change 79–94
　ozone layer depletion 67–80
atom economy 179, 183, 186–195

automobile exhaust. *See* internal combustion engine exhaust

B

Bacillus megaterium 200
bacteria 102, 109–110. *See also* pathogens, as water pollutants
baghouse 41–42
barium carbonate 30–31
Barrett, Anthony G. M. 201
BAS. *See* British Antarctic Survey
beneficiation 35–36
berylliosis 40, 123
BHC Company 191, 194
biodegradation 101–102
biofiltration 46
biological oxygen demand (BOD) 102–105
bisphenol A 198
Bliss, Russell 174–175
BOD. *See* biological oxygen demand
Boots Company 190–191
Breen, Joseph J. 181–183
British Antarctic Survey (BAS) 68, 78
bronchiolitis fibrosa obliterans 26
Brundtland Report 179
Buisson, Henri 67
Bullard, Robert 156–157
bullets, lead 51
Bush, George W., and administration 93–94

C

Cairns, John, Jr. 100–101
calcium carbonate 109
Callendar, Guy Stewart 85

Canada 66
cancer/carcinogens
dioxin 176
MBTE 23
methylene chloride 198
nuclear wastes 167
ozone layer depletion 46
perc dry cleaning fluid 205
VOCs 43
carbonaceous fuels 19
carbon dioxide
and acid rain 57
in catalytic converter 29
and climate change 84–93
as green solvent 204–206
and infrared radiation 84
carbonic acid 57
carbon monoxide 18–24, 29, 31–32
carboxylation 199–200
Cargill Dow 206–207
Carson, Rachel 8, 10–11
Carter, Jimmy, and administration 14, 87
catalysis
for green chemistry 199–203
Eugene Houdry's studies 30, 31
and ozone layer destruction 74, 75
catalytic converter 22, 28–32, *29, 32*, 45
catalytic incineration 45
CFCs. *See* chlorofluorocarbons
Chadwick, Edwin 4–5
Charles II (king of England) 3

chemical oxygen demand (COD) 104
chlorine, for water treatment 115
chlorine free radicals 73, 74
chlorofluorocarbons (CFCs) 69–80, 87–89
chlorosis 63
cholera 6
Cicerone, Ralph 88
Clean Air Act (1963) 9
Clean Air Act (1970) 15, 145–146
Clean Air Act Amendments (1977) 41
Clean Air Act Amendments (1990) 23, 48, 65
Clean Water Act (1948) 7–9
Clean Water Act Amendments (1990) 129
Cleveland, Ohio 1–2
climate change, global warming v. 81
Clinton, Bill 13, 91
coal, sulfur dioxide and 34
coal mines 125
coarse particulates 38
COD. *See* chemical oxygen demand
coliform bacteria 114
Collins, Terrence J. 202
combustion 22, 25–26
combustion systems 27–28
Comprehensive Environmental Response, Compensation, and Liability Act (1980) 17
Congressional Research Service 143